Sources Of
American Spirituality

Marie of the Incarnation

SELECTED WRITINGS

Edited by Irene Mahoney, O.S.U.

PAULIST PRESS
New York ◊ Mahwah

Library of Congress Cataloging-in-Publication Data

Marie de l'Incarnation, mère, 1599–1672.
   [Selections. English. 1989]
   Marie of the Incarnation: selected writings/[edited] by Irene Mahoney.
      p.   cm.—(Sources of American spirituality)
   Translated from French.
   Bibliography: p.
   Includes index.
   ISBN 0-8091-0428-8·
      1. Marie de l'Incarnation, mère, 1599–1672—Diaries.   2. Nuns-Québec (Province)—Diaries.   3. Spiritual life—Catholic authors.   4. Québec (Province)—Biography.   I. Mahoney, Irene.   II. Title.   III. Series.
BX4705.M36A3   1989
271'.974'02—dc20
   [B]   89-34078
                                                                        CIP

Published by Paulist Press
997 Macarthur Boulevard
Mahwah, N.J. 07430

Printed and bound in the United States of America

CONTENTS

For Sister Justin McKiernan, O.S.U.
Whose initial work inspired my own
and whose encouragement sustained me

GENERAL INTRODUCTION

In the history of North American spirituality, there are few figures who have produced a corpus of writings that closely resemble the writings of the mainstream Catholic mystical tradition. To be sure, many works like Bishop Neumann's *Mon Journal* reflect its influence, but very few are able to produce an original expression of that tradition with its characteristically exhaustive analysis of the spiritual development of the soul toward union with its beloved. Marie Guyart Martin, Marie of the Incarnation (1599–1672) is a significant exception, and as such deserves a place in this series.

As the superior of the first Ursuline community in the New World, she brought to the icy environs of Quebec the fiery passion of a spirituality formed by the teachings of Pierre de Bérulle. She followed the master in his devotion to the Incarnation of Christ. Throughout her writings we see the devotion to the Sacred Humanity of Christ, to his Precious Blood, to his Sacred Heart that were popular in mid-seventeenth-century France. Her emphasis on self-denial and humility is blended with a confidence in the guidance of the inner light of the Holy Spirit and in the practice of mental prayer. Her severe acts of asceticism, her longing for martyrdom, her indifference to suffering all were classic elements of the French school that she transplanted, and to a remarkable degree preserved intact, in the new environment. One searches in vain for signs of how "the American experience," whether it be the presence of the frontier or some other combination of factors, shaped her spirituality in any profound way. That, doubtless, was a function of the fact that she lived not in a lively British colony but in a cloister in Quebec.

There are parts of that Bérullian tradition, to be sure, that we, some three centuries later, find strange. Throughout the *Relations* of 1633 and 1654 she recounts the guilt that she felt when she left her eleven-year-old son to join the convent. She had borne the child when

1

she was nineteen to a husband who had died and left her without resources. For years she had lived with her sister and brother-in-law, into whose care she entrusted her son when she entered the convent. Her son, Claude Martin, went on to become a Benedictine and collected and published her papers. It is curious indeed to read their correspondence. "You have been abandoned by your mother and your relatives," Marie writes, "yet hasn't this abandonment been to your advantage? I had to obey his divine will." Strange will, indeed. Equally odd to the modern reader is Claude Martin's response. He wishes that his mother may become a martyr! One is tempted to see beneath the pietistic language of self-abnegation the human realities of guilt and resentment. Religion, one could argue, provided Marie with a socially acceptable escape from a life of drudgery as a virtual servant in her brother-in-law's home where she was constantly riddled by guilt over her inability to provide for her son.

But what an escape it was! It was an escape from a world of compromise to the carefully constructed environment of the cloister in which every effort was made to be joined with Christ. Nothing was held back in the quest to attain the ideal, pure love of God, to give over every trace of self-will to the will of God, to live a life in the way of perfection. The force of that effort comes through in the text of the *Relation of 1654,* which is included in its entirety, as well as in the excerpts of the *Relation of 1633,* the retreat notes, and letters contained in this volume. The relentlessness of such a quest, the thoroughness of its effort, the whole heartedness of its form are striking and must be dealt with, even by us bemused journeyers of the closing decades of the twentieth century. How shall we respond?

Some will instinctively see the value of such a spirituality. They will embrace its excesses as models, they will hold it as an ideal to be attained. Others will, just as instinctively, reject it as worse than harmless. They will see it as a pernicious tool of self-guilt and oppression. They will value not the words of Marie but their own abilities to detect the social structures out of which she spoke, not her announced intention, but the secrets of her unconscious.

Both responses are extreme. The ideal lies somewhere in between where one can see critically, yet penetrate beyond the hyperbole, the self-delusion, the social structures to a fresh glimpse of life in a remote colony, and to the mystery, of life, and of love.

John Farina

PREFACE

My interest in Marie Guyart began many years ago. I found it both regrettable and perplexing that this extraordinary woman who founded the first school for girls in North America should remain so unacknowledged. Her own writings, long unavailable, were at that time just becoming accessible through the work of Dom Albert Jamet, O.S.B. These, it is true, were in French, as were almost all of the worthwhile works about her. While this was not sufficient explanation, it was certainly a partial reason for her obscurity.

In time I was able to set to work on a biography of Marie of the Incarnation in English. It was during those happy years that I first made the acquaintance of Marie's spiritual daughters, the Ursulines of the Old Monastery in Quebec. Here I spent many happy months with Mother St. Joseph, then the archivist, hovering over me, heaping precious volumes on my desk, pouring into my ears quantities of fascinating information. She made all the treasures of the archives available to me with a graciousness and generosity I shall never forget.

When I began the work for this volume, it was to the Ursulines of Quebec that I turned. Once again I was warmly received by old friends and new. Special gratitude must go to Sister Fernand Bedard, O.S.U., whose generous assistance was without measure.

I must acknowledge also the work of Dom Guy Oury, O.S.B., without which this present work could not have been completed, as well as the encouragement and assistance of Robert Michel, O.M.I., whose work and enthusiasm has been a constant inspiration.

Most of all I wish to thank Dena Petersen, O.S.U., whose astute and unflagging assistance in the work of translation has made her my *sine qua non*.

Feast of St. Angela
January 27, 1987

INTRODUCTION

On the morning of August 1, 1639, Marie Guyart Martin, known in religion as Marie of the Incarnation, along with two Ursuline companions and their lay foundress, Madeleine de la Peltrie, were helped from the launch which had brought them up the St. Lawrence and were welcomed with a solemn salvo of cannon fire to the colony of Quebec.

They had been on the water since May 4. They were tired and dirty; their stomachs were sour from weeks of inadequate food and drink; they were nauseous from the rolling of the boat and the inescapable smell of fish. Yet when they knelt to kiss the ground, it was an act of pure gratitude. For Marie Guyart her dream was realized: she was here at last "to build a house for Jesus and Mary" and to win for the "kingdom of Jesus Christ" the souls of the Indian children "for whom he had shed his blood."

The scene is a perfect model of French seventeenth century missionary spirituality: the implacable determination for total consecration, the conviction that suffering is an essential element of a life of holiness, a devotion to the Precious Blood of Jesus Christ, and the unwavering belief that souls can be saved only within the sacramental life of the Church. We have only to read the *Jesuit Relations*[1] to see this spirituality set before us again and again both in the slow martyrdom imposed by missionary existence itself and in the more dramatic accounts of the actual martyrdoms of such figures as Jean de Brébeuf, Isaac Jogues, Noël Chabanel, etc. Nor need we limit this ideal to the

---

1. The *Jesuit Relations* were a series of accounts sent from Quebec to interest France in the work of evangelization in Canada. Begun by Paul Le Jeune, S.J., in 1639, they continued until 1673.

Jesuits. The Recollect Friars had already given similar witness as will the Sulpicians in the years to come.[2]

On this morning, however, the pattern had taken a somewhat different shape: these were women, the first of many who would come to give their lives, to shed their blood if God would so favor them, in order to win souls for Jesus Christ. Within a week they had set up a school for Indian children along the banks of the St. Lawrence. And with that act there was begun that vast and enduring system of schools, established and run by religious women, which would some day cover all of North America and become the dominant tool for conserving and developing the Christian faith within the Catholic Church.

Unlike the male missionaries whose work on the missions was often viewed as a temporary assignment, none of the women who arrived in Quebec that August were ever to return to France. Marie and her sisters considered their act to be a permanent commitment. For the next thirty-five or forty years they worked in Quebec, doing what they could for the conversion of the restless, capricious Indian children, enlarging their schools to include the children of the French settlers, learning the Indian languages, and sharing their food and lodging with the destitute among the savages.

We are fortunate in having a vast store of details about those first years through the writings of Marie Guyart, carefully conserved by her son. During Marie's lifetime she wrote two accounts of her spiritual life (the *Relation of 1633* and the *Relation of 1654*) at the command of her spiritual director.[3] She also jotted down notes from two retreats. Before coming to Canada she had put together a catechism for her work with the Ursuline novices as well as a small treatise on the Song of Songs. While in Canada she composed a catechism in Huron as well as dictionaries in both Huron and Algonquin. Above all, she was a conscientious and stimulating letter writer. It is estimated that she composed as many as three thousand letters, most of them substantial letters, providing accounts of daily life, of Indian customs, and of the activities of missionaries traveling into the interior. Unfortunately, not all of this material has come down to us. Only a small section of her first spiritual account remains; of the vast collection of letters less than three hundred are extant. And the Indian dictionaries and catechism

---

2. The Recollect Friars, a branch of Franciscans, were brought to Canada by Champlain in 1626. The Sulpicians, founded by Jean-Jacques Olier in 1642, came to Montreal in 1657.

3. "Relation," the French word for "account" or "report," has been the only title given to these works.

have been completely lost, either destroyed by fire or generously lent to a missionary.

What remains is largely the work of her son, Dom Claude Martin, a Benedictine of the Congregation of St. Maur, who during his mother's lifetime scrupulously collected what he could of her writing. Marie, fearing the use he might make of the private papers she had entrusted to him, wrote at one point: "I don't want anyone to share this communication . . . and I beg you to write on the cover, Con-science matter, so that no one will touch it or glance at it without scruple. . . . Should you fall ill and be in danger of death, have some-one throw this into the fire; or rather, so that I may be even more assured, send it to my niece who will take care of it for me if I should survive you. . . . This letter is short so that it will make more of an impression on you."[4]

Happily, however, Dom Claude paid scant attention to his mother's injunction and shortly after her death began the publication of her manuscripts. In 1677, just five years after her death, there appeared *Vie de la Vénérable Mère Marie de l'Incarnation.* Three years later, in 1681, appeared *Lettres de la Vénérable Mère Marie de l'Incarnation.* The texts presented in these two volumes provide the essential sources for any life of Marie Guyart. For the present study the texts have been chosen with the purpose of exploring both the mystic and the missionary aspects of Marie's life. Thus included here are *Notes from a Ten-Day Retreat* (1634); sections from the *Relation of 1633* (treating the events antedating her entrance into religious life); the *Relation of 1654* (a memoir of her life to the date of writing); and letters spanning the years 1639 to 1670 (dealing primarily with her life on the Canadian Mission).[5]

These texts, though replete with details in some aspects, are singu-larly spare in others, and are thus often frustrating for the modern reader. It must be kept in mind that nothing was written for a general readership; each document had in mind a specific reader as well as a specific purpose. The *Relation of 1633* was written at the command of her spiritual director, Georges de la Haye, S.J., who was attempting to find an explanation for her spiritual trials and to evaluate her spiritual life. The retreat notes were written for the same reader and with much the same purpose. The most complete of the documents, the *Relation of 1654,* was written to provide her son with an account of those graces

---

4. Letter of September 27, 1654. Dom Guy Oury, ed., *Marie de l'Incarnation, Ursuline, Correspondance* (Solesmes, 1971), p. 548.

5. For a more complete explanation of the texts, see the introduction, pp. 34–40.

which had led her along so many paths and which ultimately drew her to Canada. In none of these cases was she primarily concerned with external details, nor did she need to provide explanation for people and events with which her readers would be familiar. Only in her letters is she concerned with the external world, and as a consequence they provide us with a wealth of detail. Even here, however, her allusions are often baffling.

Her language, too, is often a source of confusion. We are inclined to be repelled by the flowery expression and exaggerated rhetoric so admired by her epoch and to which Marie all too frequently fell victim. This should not surprise us. It was, after all, the religious language most familiar to her. The miracle is, rather, that in an age when most girls of her economic condition hardly had the advantage of more than two or three years in the "petites écoles," Marie was capable of writing so clearly, so surely—and so much.[6]

It is hoped that this introduction, primarily biographical in nature, will provide a setting against which Marie Guyart's own narratives can be read more intelligently and more discriminatingly. That they are of enormous importance and interest for the theology of both mysticism and mission, for the history of Canada, as well as for women's studies cannot be denied.

PREPARATIONS

When at the age of fifty-six, after seventeen years on the Canadian Mission, Marie of the Incarnation, as she was now known, began to review the events of her life in preparation for the account she had promised to write for her son, it seemed to her that everything in her life had been a preparation for the Canadian Mission. Hindsight can sometimes lead to a false interpretation but this is not so in her case. With her clear-minded appraisal of her life, she shows no tendency to schematize, to regiment events or tendencies into neat patterns. She simply reflects with her clear, practical intelligence and finds that, in fact, everything had converged toward her missionary vocation.

As the middle child in a middle-class family (her father was a baker) in an average French city (she was born in Tours, a pretty and

---

6. The "petites écoles," teaching the rudiments of reading and writing, would have been the only schools available to a child of Marie's economic status.

prosperous city on the Loire), it would seem that she was destined for an unexceptional existence. Tours in 1599, the year of her birth, was, like most French cities, enjoying the peace brought by the Edict of Nantes, which had been proclaimed the previous year. It ended the overt combat between Catholics and Protestants that was known by the incongruous name of the Wars of Religion. Religion, so long a martial affair, was now enjoying a spiritual resurgence, with the result that monasteries were undergoing reformation and religious orders were expanding their membership and establishing new foundations. Henri Brémond can find no more appropriate phrase to describe the movement which now swept through France than "l'invasion mystique."[7] It was a century of high calling, and the names who heard the divine call and followed it form an impressive litany: Bérulle and Condren of the Oratory; François de Sales and his protégée Jeanne Françoise de Chantal; Jean Eudes with his cult of the Sacred Hearts of Jesus and Mary; Vincent de Paul and his spiritual daughter, Louise de Marillac; and Jean-Jacques Olier of St. Sulpice, whose missionary sons Marie would meet in Canada. Contemplation, as Brémond remarks, was à la mode; and dreams, visions, and revelations were an accepted element in the spirituality of the day.

It may not be surprising, then, that Marie Guyart at the age of seven experienced a dream which, throughout her life, she would invest with profound significance, interpreting it as the first step in that long pilgrimage which will bring her ultimately to Canada. At first reading the dream seems to be one that any child raised in Christian piety might have.

> During my sleep one night when I was about seven years old, it seemed to me that I was playing some childhood game with one of my companions in the yard of a country school. I was looking upward when I saw the heavens open and Our Lord Jesus Christ in human form emerge and come toward me. "Look!" I cried to my companion, "There's Our Lord and he is coming to me!" . . . As this most adorable Majesty approached me, my heart felt on fire with love for him and I started to open my arms to embrace him. Then he, the most beautiful of all the children of men, took me in his arms and

---

7. Henri Brémond, *Histoire littéraire du sentiment religieux en France* (Paris, 1930–38), VI, pp. i–vi.

with a look full of indescribable sweetness and charm, kissed
me with great love and asked me, "Will you be mine?" I
answered, "Yes!"[8]

All the elements of childhood piety are present: the schoolyard, the
companion, the conventional image of Jesus descending from a cloud,
the loving embrace, and the spontaneous response to affection. The
critical interpretations of the dream vary, but whatever her commentators indicate, for Marie herself the dream was of seminal importance, opening the door of her mystic vocation as a later dream will
open the door of her missionary vocation.

It was not until twelve years later that Marie experienced another
extraordinary grace. This time there can be no doubt of its supernatural character. In the intervening years she had briefly harbored the
thought of a religious vocation, a thought countered by her parents
who felt she lacked the requisite temperament for such a life and
instead arranged a good practical marriage with Claude Martin, a
reputable young silk merchant of the city. By the age of eighteen Marie
had borne her first child and less than a year later she was left a widow.
Not yet nineteen she found herself burdened not only with a baby but
with debts so large that she was advised that bankruptcy was her only
recourse. Now there came to the fore another side of Marie's nature, a
quality which at first glance seems to contradict her contemplative
gifts. This was her "talent pour négoce," as she later called it, that
remarkable business acumen which in her later life was to be of such
value in establishing the Ursuline monastery in Quebec. Contrary to
the advice she was given she determined to do what she could to
unravel and salvage something of her husband's business.

It was as she set out on the morning of March 24, 1620, on her
usual round of business that she was caught up in that profound
mystic experience which she would refer to throughout her life as her
"conversion." As she was repeating her usual prayer, "In Thee, O
Lord, have I put my trust; let me never be disappointed," she suddenly
lost contact with the world about her and was rapt into the world of the
spirit. This time it was not a consoling vision. "My inner eyes were
opened," she wrote, "and all the faults, sins, and imperfections that I
had committed since my birth were shown to me in the most vivid
detail. At the same moment I saw myself immersed in the blood of the

---

8. *Relation of 1654,* pp. 41–42. All references to the *Relation of 1654, Relation of
1633,* and to the *Letters* are to this present edition unless otherwise indicated.

Son of God, shed because of the sins which had been shown to me; and further, realizing that it was for my salvation that this Precious Blood had been shed."[9]

Her conversion was immediate—"transformed through the mercy of him who had wrought this wonderful grace," she wrote. She was a new creature, brought to a new level of both humility and love. The penetrating recognition that it is the blood of Jesus by which she has been saved is the first reference to that aspect of the redemption which will become a leitmotif of her spirituality. Submerged for a while beneath other graces, it will reappear with compelling urgency as her missionary vocation takes shape and her vision broadens to encompass the whole world, a world filled with souls for whom Jesus Christ had shed his blood but who have not yet been brought into his kingdom.

With this extraordinary grace Marie was led into the mystic life properly so called. While anterior to this she seems to have led the life of a virtuous woman—carrying out her duties as a wife, frequenting the sacraments, participating in the church services, the processions, the devotions which were a normal part of Christian life, even relinquishing the romances which she had once enjoyed reading for more spiritual reading—yet her life had not been extraordinary. Now she is drawn into a new way—a way that encompassed a deeper awareness of self and a profound and constant awareness of God.

In fact, the ten years following her "vision" of the Precious Blood were, in terms of mystical experience, the most extraordinary of her life. During that period she had the first experience leading to her devotion to the Sacred Heart, an abiding sense of the presence of Jesus Christ, a passionate devotion to the Eucharist, and her two first "visions" of the Trinity. It was during the second of these that she received the grace of spiritual marriage or transforming union, characterized by the most complete self-giving of God to the soul and the soul to God. This exalted gift, usually regarded as the culmination of the spiritual life, is generally given only at the end of a life of great holiness; but at the time of this union Marie was but twenty-seven years old. In attempting to provide an explanation for this divergence from the norm, her commentators have made various suggestions. Claude provides the most radical of these by maintaining that this is a "mystic marriage," a lesser union than the true "spiritual marriage" which will only take place at the end of Marie's life.

9. *Relation of 1654,* pp. 49–50.

It is clear from Marie's own testimony, however, that this is, indeed, the spiritual marriage:

> Then, engulfed in the presence of this adorable Majesty, Father, Son, and Holy Spirit, adoring him in the awareness and acknowledgement of my lowliness, the Sacred Person of the Divine Word revealed to me that he was in truth the spouse of the faithful soul. I understood this truth with absolute certainty and this very understanding became the imminent preparation for this grace to be effected in me. At that moment, this adorable Person seized my soul and embracing it with indescribable love united it to himself, taking it as his spouse.[10]

With this grace Marie's state is totally changed once again. As she puts it: "Hitherto it had been in continual longing and expectation. . . . Now the soul has no further longing because it possesses him whom it loves. The soul is all his."

It is Marie's own words which continue to tease us. "The soul has no further longing. . . ." It would appear that she has reached the apotheosis of her spiritual life. She possesses him whom she loves. What can remain but eternal beatitude? Yet, as we have seen, Marie is but twenty-seven years old and will live into her seventies. What remains? Has God lifted her to the pinnacle of the mystic life when two-thirds of her natural life still lie before her? And to what purpose?

At this stage we may come to a clearer understanding of the position of this culminating grace by shifting our perspective and looking at a concurrent aspect of Marie's life. Following her vision of the Precious Blood, in the first flush of her new spiritual discovery, her attraction to a life of solitude and poverty had asserted itself. She moved to the attic of her father's house, spending her time in prayer and in service to the poor and supporting herself by needlework, for which, we are told, she had a remarkable talent. Within a year, however, she was called from her solitude: her sister Claude, married to Paul Buisson and with a large household to administer, needed Marie's help. Despite her initial reluctance Marie went. At first she worked there only during the day (the houses were no more than a quarter of a mile apart), leaving her son to the care of his grand-

---

10. *Relation of 1654*, pp. 81–83.

mother.[11] Soon, however, acceding to her sister's wishes, she moved into the Buisson home, becoming part of the household and thus making herself more available for work.

Thus began an entirely new role in Marie's life, a role which, she later affirmed, was her "novitiate" for Canada. It may well have been so, for the work itself and the virtues it demanded matched perfectly the qualities she later would recommend for those inclined to the Canadian Mission. At first her tasks did not seem contradictory to her spiritual goal, especially to the virtues of poverty and humility which were becoming the keystone of her life. She supervised the domestic help, worked in the kitchen, tended the sick. The household was a large one, consisting not only of the immediate family but, as was the custom, the workmen who assisted Paul Buisson in his substantial carting business.

As Marie's efficiency manifested itself, her work expanded. Paul Buisson, with a shrewd eye for business, recognized that Marie's considerable ability could be better utilized, and he soon induced her into becoming the assistant in his business. The work could not have been further from her dream of solitude. Now she spent her days on the wharfs or in the storehouses; she spent them with tradesmen, carters, dock-workers, stablemen, stevedores. She supervised loading and unloading. She checked invoices, examined merchandise, and counted money. She was sometimes humiliated by men who vented their annoyance at a woman's jurisdiction. She often found the language unbearable. From one day to the next the only mention of God was made by those who took his name in vain.

Yet at the same time that she felt pushed to the limit of endurance in this hostile atmosphere, she was absorbed in a life of grace so powerful that had God not sustained her, she tells us, she would not have been able to live. Even while engulfed in God's presence she never lost her quick practical common sense. She will tell her son later that because she did things so well, people thought she loved her work and were astonished when she left it to enter religious life.

It is in assessing these years of activity—activity far outside the scope of a seventeenth century woman's province—that we may find an explanation for the early grace of spiritual marriage. For Marie the

---

11. Although it has been generally accepted that Jeanne Guyart had died some time before, Dom Oury's research indicates that she was still alive and that it was this grandmother who took care of Claude while Marie was at work. Dom Guy Oury, *Dom Claude Martin* (Solesmes, 1983), p. 16.

grace was not to be a culmination but formation. While with this union God elevated her to the peak of human capacity, the summit of contemplative grace, Marie's vocation was not to be solely contemplative; she was to be shaped for apostolic ministry as well. In some way the spiritual marriage was not an end but a preparation. She was not to live the enclosed life of the pure contemplative but the engaged life of the missionary—impelled always by the indwelling Spirit of God of whom she never loses sight and whose spouse she is.

In time these two movements will mesh perfectly, but during this initial period they were still not perfected. Although Marie felt that the work she was doing was God's will and although she acknowledged that she lived in union with God no matter how preoccupying her tasks, yet she longed to be free of them, to be taken "from the world," into that secluded space where her contemplative longings would have free reign. Her childhood desire for religious life reasserted itself, and she begged God to remove her from this atmosphere so inimical, she felt, to the graces she was receiving. Even the fact that she had a child still dependent on her was not enough to dampen her desires, and in time God gave her hope that he would grant her desire.

At this time she saw little value in the work she was doing beyond the fact that it was of service to her sister and brother-in-law and that it provided her with humility and mortification. Only many years later, having experienced the labors of the mission, did she see how well she had been prepared. She learned the practical aspects of business, she learned to be firm in the face of opposition, she learned patience and prudence, she learned to adjust to an environment which was often crude and irreverent; most of all, she learned to entrust herself to God's providence.

When in 1631 at the age of thirty-one she "left the world" to enter religious life, it was, to the surprise of many, a teaching order rather than a contemplative order that she chose. Through the Feuillant Fathers who had been her spiritual directors for more than ten years she had been offered a place with the Feuillantines, a rigorously reformed group of nuns whose prayer and penances seemed peculiarly appropriate for Marie. She was also well acquainted with the Carmelites, recently established at Tours, and was attracted to them through her reading of their foundress, Teresa of Avila. She had as well been offered a place with the Visitation, founded by François de Sales precisely for "unusual" vocations such as Marie's. But in the end it was the Ursulines she chose because they were engaged in the salvation of souls, something to which she felt herself singularly attracted. Later she recalled while writing to her son, "I remember that the first thought I had of being a religious after my conversion had been to be an Ursuline."[12]

Her choice which at first glance runs counter to her fervent longing for a life of prayer and penance (the Ursulines were not pure contemplatives nor did their work permit them the austerities practiced by such congregations as the Feuillantines), in fact, launched her forward on her ultimate vocation, that of an active/contemplative, a vocation which would come to perfection on the Canadian Mission. At the moment, however, Marie made the choice almost blindly, relying only on that sense of "fitness" by which the Spirit guided her.

The convent she chose had been established by the Ursulines of Saumur only ten years before. The original Company of St. Ursula, founded in Brescia in 1535 by Angela Merici, had neither vows nor cloister. They were bound only by a simple promise of chastity, lived in their own homes or in the homes where they were employed, gathered together periodically for support and encouragement, and had for their general purpose the instruction of young girls—usually those without other resources. Seventy-seven years later, however, when the Ursulines established themselves in Tours, little of this original design, so carefully devised by its foundress, still remained. Vows and cloister had become *de rigueur* in the Church, and when Marie Guyart entered the Ursulines in Tours she entered an autonomous monastery, strictly bound by cloister and by the religious vows of poverty, chastity, and obedience. The work for which the Company had been founded remained to some extent the same. But prohibited by cloister from seeking children in the streets or in their own homes, the nuns' apostolate was now restricted to instruction within the structure of the boarding school where pupils, as well as nuns, lived protected by the grille.[13]

The point is profoundly significant, for against such a background Marie's mission vocation takes on a more dramatic tone. Since each Ursuline monastery was not only cloistered but autonomous, one could have no legitimate expectation but to live and die within its walls. The point is further significant because it is not only the background from which Marie herself emerged but the one which shaped many European religious women coming to the New World, and

12. *Relation of 1654*, p. 93.

13. For the beginnings and development of the Ursuline Order, see Teresa Ledochowska, *Angela Merici and the Company of St. Ursula*, 2 vols., tr. Mary Teresa Neylan, O.S.U. (Rome, 1969); Marie de Chantal Gueudré, *Histoire de l'Ordre des Ursulines en France*, 3 vols. (Paris, 1957–60).

which would significantly determine their goals, their expectations—
and their problems—in the mission country.

Marie's high expectations of religious life were idyllically fulfilled
in her first few months, and shortly after receiving the religious habit
in March of 1631, she wrote: "All that I saw in religion seemed filled
with the Spirit of God." Shortly after her clothing, however, her happiness gave way to a period of unparalleled darkness. It is easy enough to
find reason for such a period of darkness. Marie at the age of thirty-one
had left a life of extreme action and responsibility, a life in which she
gave orders and discharged important duties. She had experienced
marriage, motherhood, widowhood. She had been gifted with extraordinary graces and lived a life of awesome physical austerity. Suddenly,
without intermission, all this was replaced by the small, exacting life of
a French novitiate where her companions were almost young enough
to be her daughters. To be "singular" was unacceptable and she was
faced with the formidable task of "conforming." Enough reason, certainly, for the descent of blackness. But there was more. The son she
had left in her sister's care was just eleven, and although she had
calmed his initial fear and anger, once she was gone the extent of his
loss dawned upon him and for the first weeks following his mother's
departure Claude did everything possible to win her back. It was not
until he was accepted in the Jesuit school at Rennes later that winter
that Marie's anxiety for him abated.

The depths of Marie's suffering during her year of novitiate was
extreme, so extreme that she wrote in the account she gave to her
director that she thought she was losing her mind. She distrusted
everything: her own graces, the advice of her superior, the consolations
of faith—most of all, her own judgment. Two important events, however, emerged from this period of darkness: she met Georges de la
Haye, S.J., who became her director and who would later be a strong
influence in deciding her Canadian vocation. And she wrote an account of her spiritual life from her earliest years to the present, an
invaluable account which Dom Claude uses to advantage in his
biography.

Were one to analyze Marie's first two years in the Ursuline monastery without benefit of future evidence, one would be tempted to
doubt her religious vocation. Her sureness, her quickness, her spontaneity, her passionate love of God—all seem paralyzed. She is plunged
into a darkness which nothing can alleviate. When from time to time
the cloud was lifted, this momentary relief only emphasized the recur-
ring blackness. To her contemporaries with their tendency toward a
vertical spirituality, this was interpreted as one of those trials sent by

God and designated as a "dark night." From the viewpoint of modern psychology it has all the evidence of a depression brought about by profound and painful loss. Although there was a part of Marie which longed to cast aside the noise, the activity, and the responsibility in which she had been plunged, yet it would seem that these very things were outlets needed by her nature, without which she could not maintain her spiritual balance. Cut suddenly free from her "bonds" and immersed in the life of the cloister, she found herself strangely adrift, the very things she had longed for now becoming the source of her suffering. She had not yet found the balance between her talent for business and her contemplative graces. It was Canada which would bring the two into harmony.

However we interpret this period of darkness, it was to come to an end in the winter of 1633. Shortly after Christmas of that year Marie had the second of her mysterious dreams. If we interpret her childhood dream as her entrance into a life of contemplation, this second dream can be interpreted as the explicit entrance into her missionary vocation. She dreamed, she later wrote, that in company with an unknown woman—a secular—she traveled through a strange and difficult land until they reached a place of great beauty. It was a place of quiet, a vast place, full of forests and mountains and shrouded in mist. Coming to a church, they found Jesus and Mary enthroned on its pinnacle. Overcome with joy Marie ran toward them with open arms. "I saw her bend and look at her blessed Child to whom, without speaking, she conveyed some important thought. In my heart I felt that she spoke to him of this country and of me and that she had some plan on this subject."[14]

When she awoke she found herself both joyful and bewildered— penetrated by the sweetness of the Virgin's kiss but confused as to the meaning of the dream. Although ignorant of its practical significance, Marie found that in an instant it had effectively changed her spiritual state. While the salvation of souls had always been dear to her, shaping her decision to enter the Ursulines, now this concern became the impelling force in her life.

> My body was in our monastery, but my spirit, united to that of Jesus, could not remain shut up there. This apostolic spirit carried me in thought to the Indies, to Japan, to America, to the East and the West, to the most inaccessible northern

---

14. *Relation of 1654*, p. 109.

countries—in short, to every part of the inhabited world where there were souls who belonged by right to Jesus Christ.[15]

Thus she is launched unreservedly on her apostolic journey. For the rest of her life she will be propelled by what she calls "apostolic spirit . . . none other than the spirit of Jesus Christ."

The chronology of the next few years is difficult to ascertain. We know, however, that her dream was confirmed by two further supernatural experiences; that three Jesuits in turn ratified her dream, identified the land as Canada, and provided her with further information about mission activities there; that through a strange concatenation of events the woman of her dream was identified as Madeleine de la Peltrie, a young widow inspired to give both life and fortune to the Canadian Mission.[16]

Marie later claimed that at the time of her dream she did not know that Canada existed—a statement hard to accept literally, since Jesuit missionary activity had begun as early as 1611 and had been well publicized throughout France. Paul Le Jeune, S.J., had already begun his promotional tracts known as the *Jesuit Relations,* which would keep France abreast of Jesuit missionary activity for half a century. Huron Indians had been brought across the Atlantic to be displayed at Court and paraded in the streets of Paris. Concern and support for the Indian missions was, in fact, fashionable and to submit that the monastery at Tours was ignorant of it tests credulity.

Nowhere does Marie manifest herself more as a child of her time than in the language she uses in describing her apostolic mission. Although she asserts again and again her love and concern for the Indian children—whom she has not yet seen!—yet their well-being is only her secondary consideration. In first place is God: God's rights, God's justice, God's grandeur, God's omnipotence. Everything must be judged from God's point of view, recognizing the All-ness of the Divine Being and the nothingness of the creature—its poverty, lowliness, sinfulness. In giving her life to the Indians Marie gives it primarily that the kingdom of God may be extended, that the rights of Jesus Christ may be vindicated, and that the world which is his by inheritance may become his in actuality. Her compassion for the Indians is itself the product of her theology. Unless they are brought to baptism

---

15. *Relation of 1654,* pp. 112–113.
16. See p. 117, n. 8.

they will remain under the power of the devil, enemies of God, destined for the eternal fires of hell. In their present state they are children of Satan, doomed for all eternity. Only baptism can draw them into the Church; and, outside the Church there was—in the seventeenth century—no salvation. It was a powerful spur and remained so throughout her life; for Marie, despite her profound experience of God's mercy, seems never to have widened her vision of salvation.

It may, perhaps, be noted here that Marie Guyart, despite her extraordinary vocation, does not seem to be a woman of unusual imagination. Although her sanctity certainly singularizes her, it is its degree rather than its shape which makes it unusual. Her devotion to the Eucharist, to the Incarnate Word, to the Precious Blood, her profound sense of sin and the consequent need for severe penance, her emphasis on the nothingness of the creature and the limitless grandeur of God—all this was present in the spirituality of her day.

It is at this point that we may profitably examine some salient aspects of Marie's spirituality against the backdrop of contemporary piety. In many ways this is a delicate task, a task to be approached by implication rather than by direct reference, for Marie rarely troubles to indicate the influences which shaped her.[17] As we have already mentioned, the spirituality of Pierre de Bérulle was of extreme importance in Marie's formation. Although he is never identified in her writings, his influence is undeniable.[18] It may be, as Dom J. Huijben suggests, that she came to know him through the Carmelite convent in Tours where he was the official visitor.[19] In any case, his most significant writings were available by 1621 and his doctrine was already pervasive. We know also that the works of the popular Jesuit writer, St. Jure, heavily Bérullian in his spirituality, were available to Marie and that his *L'Homme spirituel* was one of the cherished volumes in the small library of the Ursuline novitiate in Quebec.[20]

As Marie's name would suggest, the Incarnate Word was at the center of her spirituality as it was also at that of Bérulle, to whom

---

17. For a summary of the influences on Marie, see Joseph Klein, *L'Itinéraire mystique de la Vénérable Mère Marie de l'Incarnation* (Rome, 1937), pp. 216–40.

18. Pierre de Bérulle (1575–1629), founder of the Oratory of Jesus, contributed widely to the spirituality of his day. Christocentric in his emphasis, he preached the importance of living by and in the spirit of Jesus and participating in the mysteries of Christ. Sacrifice, immolation, reverence, worship, adoration were key words in his spirituality.

19. See Dom J. Huijben, "La Thérèse de la Nouvelle-France," in *La Vie spirituelle* v. 22 (March 1930): 97–128.

20. Dom Guy Oury, O.S.B., "Marie de l'Incarnation et la bibliothèque du noviciat des Ursulines de Québec," *Revue d'ascétique et de mystique* XLVI (1970): 397–410.

Urban VIII gave the title, "Apostle of the Incarnate Word." In Bérulle's popular and influential work, *Les Grandeurs de Jésus,* he wrote,
"Jesus is the true center of the world and the world must be constantly
moving toward him." It is a statement we shall find reiterated in
various forms throughout Marie's writings. Again, in Marie's explanation of her early gift of prayer, "a union with all the sacred mysteries of
Our Lord Jesus Christ from his birth until his death," she echoes a
popular Bérullian devotion. Like Bérulle, Marie is preoccupied less by
the physical elements and events of Jesus' life than by his inner state,
that mysterious consciousness rising out of his divine nature.

It will be no surprise to find in the wake of this single-minded
thrust toward Jesus Christ devotion both to the Precious Blood and the
Sacred Heart. For Bérulle, the Sacred Heart was the symbol of the
constant, unswerving love of Jesus and, as such, worthy of homage and
adoration. It remained for him, however, primarily symbol. It was left
to his disciple, Jean Eudes, to take the devotion one step further,
incarnating the symbol and focusing his devotion on the physical heart
of the Sacred Humanity of Christ.[21] Marie seems to stand somewhere
in the middle, speaking of a "union of hearts," describing how one
slips into the other and is lost, yet always warning us that in these
"visions" the senses played no part.

Although devotion to the Passion and the Precious Blood are both
recognizably Bérullian, yet several other sources must be acknowledged. These devotions had always been part of the Franciscan tradition, and since the Capuchins were the best-known preachers in Tours
during Marie's childhood, she had doubtlessly incorporated these
themes into her spirituality at an early age. In this area Marie is also
indebted to Catherine of Siena whose writings she knew and who is
one of the few saints she specifically mentions in her own writings.[22] It
would be foolish, however, to attempt to pinpoint influences too rigorously, for devotions such as these were in the very air, and she absorbed them with the same spontaneity with which she breathed.

One must take cognizance of those two spiritual masters, Teresa
of Avila and John of the Cross, although their influence on Marie is
difficult to determine. The works of Teresa were recommended to her
early in her spiritual journey while she was still under the direction of

---

21. See Dom Guy Oury, "Le coeur du fils de Dieu," *Ce que croyait Marie de
l'Incarnation* (Paris, 1972), pp. 128–37. See also, "Coeur (Sacré)" in *Dictionnaire de
spiritualité,* II, pt. 1, cols. 1023–1031.

22. For Catherine of Siena's influence on Marie, see Dom Guy Oury, "Le sang de
Jésus Christ," in *Ce que croyait,* pp. 107–16.

Dom Raymond. These included the *Autobiography* and *The Way of Perfection,* which had been translated into French by 1601. Marie's laconic response provides little help in assessing Teresa's influence. "Sometimes they consoled me," she wrote, adding that generally such reading was impossible because of her profound state of recollection. As for John of the Cross, there is no evidence that Marie read him, for even in those periods of frightening blackness she makes no mention of the Master of the Dark Nights. By way of explanation, Joseph Klein reminds us that John of the Cross was not well known in France during the first half of the seventeenth century and that even in his own country he continued to be misunderstood and unknown.[23]

One other classic treatise on the spiritual life should be mentioned here: *Introduction à la vie dévote* by François de Sales. Marie was given this to read shortly after her "conversion" and found it a great practical help. "It enlightened me about many aspects of the interior life," she wrote, "among others, what one should do to make a vow of chastity which Our Lord was urging me to make."[24] Yet as helpful as this treatise was, it did not quite fit her spirituality. While it was outlining a way of holiness for those continuing to live in the world, Marie felt herself increasingly drawn to religious life. Even the rule designed by François de Sales for the religious order he helped found did not quite satisfy Marie. When the bishop of Dol visited Marie at Tours to ask her to establish a Visitation convent in his diocese, she refused, saying she was not attracted to this way of life. On one point, however, Marie and de Sales were in complete accord. François de Sales was strong in his conviction that Holy Communion should be seen in its original intention: as nourishment for the soul, not as a reward for virtue. This thrust toward more frequent Communion was, as we shall see, of immense importance to Marie.[25]

The most direct spiritual influence in Marie's life came, however, through the schools of spirituality represented by her directors: the Feuillants and the Jesuits. The Feuillants, their Cistercian spirit honed and dramatized by their reforming father, Jean de la Barrière, lived an asceticism which often seems bizarre in its extremes. Prayer, penance, corporal austerity were watchwords—watchwords rigorously preached by Dom Raymond and ardently followed by his young penitent, Marie Martin.

---

23. See Klein, *L'Itinéraire,* pp. 221–23.
24. *Relation of 1654,* p. 55.
25. See "Eucharistie," in *Dictionnaire de spiritualité,* IV. See especially cols. 1611–12 which describe Marie as being "au premier rang des mystiques eucharistiques."

Marie's account of her vocation makes it clear that her Feuillant director at first strongly opposed her desire to enter the Ursulines, expecting her to join the Feuillantines, whose asceticism emulated that of their brother order. Apostolic spirituality was not part of Feuillant spirituality, and it was left to the Jesuits who succeeded the Feuillants as Marie's directors to strengthen and clarify this aspect of Marie's vocation. In one sense almost all of Marie's adult life was shaped by Ignatian spirituality. From the time of her novitiate until her death some forty years later, her directors were, without interruption, Jesuits. That her mission vocation was both influenced and determined by the Jesuit Missions of New France is incontestable. Her imperious desire to bring those pagan souls redeemed by the Precious Blood of Jesus into the kingdom of Jesus Christ is essentially an Ignatian thrust.

Yet in another sense Marie seems outside the pale of strict Ignatian spirituality as it was then preached. From the beginning, her prayer was at odds with the rigors of the *Exercises*. Although she did her best, she tells us, to prepare her meditation and to follow it through according to the outlines she was given, this simply did not work for her. Despite her valiant efforts, in a second, without further thought, she was absorbed in God. When she persisted with "the method" she was rewarded with a blinding headache which lasted for months.

It is perhaps in Marie's response to the Eucharist that she shows herself most unique. In the seventeenth century the reception of the Eucharist was considered less as nourishment for the weak and hungry than as an exclusive food for those who merited it by their virtue. Frequent Communion was, therefore, regarded with hesitation if not suspicion—for who could merit such a gift? Bérullian spirituality with its emphasis on God's grandeur and purity and man's sinfulness and infidelity was completely in accord with this aspect of his age. Yet even in an atmosphere such as this, Marie did not hesitate to ask her director for the privilege of daily Communion—a privilege she maintained until she entered the Ursulines and was obliged to follow their custom. Marie's rationale in this matter was clear: the Eucharist was not a reward for the good but nourishment for those in need.

Marie, then, for the most part, conformed to and absorbed the spiritual climate of her day. Her "originality"—if the word can be rightly used—is manifested in that keen practical imagination and active faith which translated with superb sureness the dreams and theories of her time into daily reality.

Just five years after her initial dream, Marie, accompanied by a twenty-two-year-old Ursuline, Ursule de la Troche, known in religion as Marie de St. Joseph, left Tours for Paris where their final preparations were negotiated. Two months later, having been joined by a third Ursuline, Cécile de Ste. Croix, they embarked at Dieppe on May 4, 1639, for their three-month voyage. We have only Marie's account of the transactions preceding their departure, and with characteristic reticence she records nothing controversial. If we follow her account we find only peace, joy, and holy emulation on the part of the Tourangelle community when Marie's vocation to Canada was revealed. Yet surely convincing her superiors and her community that the unprecedented act she contemplated was in conformity to the Ursuline Rule must have been a formidable task.

The fact that several important Jesuits sanctioned Marie's vocation undoubtedly influenced the decision, for the Ursulines were accustomed to accepting Jesuit guidance. Father Dinet, the Jesuit provincial, Father de la Haye, Marie's spiritual director, and Father Poncet, in charge of the affairs of the Canadian Mission all sanctioned her enterprise. Father Le Jeune, resident superior of the Canadian Mission, had already stirred interest by writing in the *Jesuit Relations,* "Is there not to be found some good virtuous woman who would wish to come to this country to gather up the blood of Jesus Christ by instructing these savage little girls?"[26] In addition, there was the "divine" quality of Marie's dream, showing her clearly a land she had never seen and directing her to go there to build "a house for Jesus and Mary." Finally, there was the revelation of the "miraculous" identity of the unknown woman of the dream as Madeleine de la Peltrie, who had quite independently vowed her life to the Mission of Canada.

Thus was established with the consent of the Ursuline community and the archbishop of Tours a new model of religious vocation—the missionary sister, a vocation which would in the following centuries shape the life of the Church in North America and provide a new pattern of life for religious women. The acknowledged goal of the three Ursulines who embarked in 1639 was very simple: they were giving their lives to win souls redeemed by the Precious Blood of Jesus, specifically through the education of Indian girls to the one true faith. What neither they nor their community could foresee were the difficulties they would confront: not simply the difficulties of mission life itself but the far more complex difficulties in government, in community life, in the ambiguous nature of their relationship with their parent communities with their consequent misunderstandings—

---

26. *Jesuit Relations and Allied Documents,* ed. Reuben Gold Thwaites (Cleveland, 1896–1901), VI, p. 261.

misunderstandings often far more painful than the physical austerities they gallantly endured.

Such difficulties were mercifully hidden from Marie and her companions when they embarked for New France. They were filled, instead, with that flush of joy that comes with the fulfillment of a cherished dream. Recalling those final hours in France, Marie wrote: "What can I say of the donation that I then made? Never have I done anything so gladly . . . and I felt that the Incarnate Word was pleased with what I gave him. . . ." As she stepped into the launch which was to take them to the waiting ship, all the fears and anguish which had plagued her as she made her final preparations were transformed into joys. "At that moment," she wrote, "I thought I entered paradise."[27]

MISSION

The paradise they entered was one reserved for hardy souls. Even after thirty years of colonization Quebec numbered less than three hundred inhabitants. Were it not for the practical administration of its late first governor, Samuel de Champlain, it might not have succeeded even this well, for the initial ventures to establish permanent habitations in Canada had resulted in failure and death. The vast, untamed country understandably daunted its first pioneers. Some families came, shook their heads, and after a season of mortal cold, returned to France. Only such hardy Bretons as the Héberts, the Couillards, and the Hubous remained.

In 1627, Richelieu, recognizing the potential value of the colony, created the Company of One Hundred Associates and put Quebec under its administration. The Company was given vast powers and vaster benefits, primarily the exclusive rights over the lucrative fur trade in perpetuity. This became their dominant interest. Colonization, cultivation of the land, and evangelization of the native population were of little concern to them except as ways of increasing their profits. Their policies, clearly determined by self-interest, were in time to become ruinous for the Quebec Colony.

None of this, however, was apparent to the nuns who were enthusiastically greeted at the wharf by Quebec's second governor, Charles de Montmagny, sent to replace Champlain three years earlier. Surrounded by a curious and eager crowd (the day had been declared a

---

27. *Relation of 1654*, p. 133.

holiday), they were led up the steep incline to the church of Notre Dame de Recouvrance, where they sang the Te Deum, the Church's official hymn of praise and gratitude, and assisted at Mass before going to the Fort for their first meal of the day. That afternoon they were shown around the colony, which still resembled a trading post rather than a town, and that evening joined in the festivities for the long-awaited birth of the dauphin, the future Louis XIV. That night they slept in temporary shelter, for their convent was not yet ready for occupancy.

In the following week they saw all that they would ever see of the Quebec Colony, for by August 7 their house was ready and they established their cloister—a cloister as rigorous as that which had governed them in France. Meanwhile, however, they were taken up the St. Lawrence to visit the Jesuit Mission at Sillery, just two miles from Quebec itself. Here the Jesuits had established a mission for the Algonquin Indians, convinced that conversion could be brought about only by drawing the Indians from their nomadic ways and organizing them into settlements where they would build permanent houses and develop at least minimal agriculture. Here at Sillery the nuns had their first (and last) experience of a native Christian settlement. Madeleine de la Peltrie, less restrained than the Ursulines, astonished the Indians by kissing every child she saw and before the day was over becoming the godmother of a little girl. Less demonstrative but equally moved the nuns were brought to tears, Marie wrote, at the faith and devotion manifested by the Indians.

Just a week after their arrival their own small house, consisting only of two rooms, a cellar, and an attic and situated precariously near the river in the lower town, was ready for permanent occupancy; and apparently without a second's hesitation, the nuns retired behind their cloister wall.

Two major interlocking concerns now faced the missionaries: the rule which would determine their way of life; and the scope and method of their apostolic labors. Although the second was the more immediate, it was to a large degree dependent on the former.

At this period Ursuline monasteries in France, while autonomous and under the jurisdiction of the ordinary of the diocese, belonged to one of several congregations, the two major ones being Paris and Bordeaux.[28] Although both congregations claimed Angela Merici as their foundress and were dedicated to the works of teaching, yet there

---

28. See Gueudré, I, pp. 101 et seq.

were notable differences in their rules. Significant among these was a radical difference in habit and the fact that the Congregation of Paris took a fourth vow, that of educating young girls, while the houses adhering to the rule of Bordeaux took only the three vows of religion, affirming that teaching was implicit in the vow of obedience. The Quebec Mission had from the start members of both congregations: Marie and Marie de St. Joseph were from Tours, which followed the rule of Bordeaux; Cécile de Ste. Croix belonged to the community of Dieppe, which followed that of Paris. The new community must come to terms with their differences if they were to form, in actuality, a single community.

From the beginning Marie had been warned—principally by the Jesuits—of the difficulties consequent upon choosing religious from different congregations; but she was adamant. The strength of the mission, she felt, lay precisely in its broad base. On fire with zeal for the conversion of the savages and impatient with the juridical problems, she was determined to accept religious of any congregation who indicated their readiness for mission life and who showed the requisite characteristics. Well aware of the difficulties, she was too high-minded to regard them as insuperable obstacles. In 1640, with the arrival of two more missionaries, both from the Congregation of Paris, work began on an Act of Union, a temporary measure which would guide them until such time as new constitutions could be drawn up.

Whether or not Marie had originally felt that the Quebec Mission should be autonomous is hard to determine, but the Act of Union clearly indicates its autonomous character. By this Act the sisters from the Congregation of Paris will adopt the dress of those of Bordeaux; the Bordeaux sisters will take the fourth vow for as long as they remain part of the Canadian community; the two congregations must be kept in numerical balance; the initiative for new members must come from Quebec and not from the French houses. The most interesting clause, perhaps, one clearly indicating the independent nature of the mission is that providing for the possible failure of the mission itself. The act reads:

> In the event of a return to France, the religious of the two Congregations will have the freedom to go back to the house of their origin . . . and in the case of such a return, they will have the right to choose . . . to live together in some town in France . . . remaining under regular observance while awaiting the opportunity to re-commit themselves in New France to help the natives. If it should be in the providence of

God to give them this grace, they will then make use of such revenues for the said establishment as they can retrieve from the foundation as well as the funds from the sisters' dowries.[29]

Clearly the Quebec Mission while recognizing its parent-bonds considered itself an independent entity.

Thus the first hurdle was successfully cleared: compromises had been made on both sides and a state of harmony reached. Such an act, however, was only provisional.

Marie was very firm that an autonomous monastery in a country with such unprecedented demands must have its own constitution. The task was a difficult one. By 1641 the community now numbered five religious: two from the Congregation of Paris; three from that of Bordeaux. Opinions and attitudes inevitably differed. Both groups felt the need to uphold the "honor" of its congregation, and Marie recognized that no constitution could be drawn up without some impartial arbiter. No such person was available, however, until the arrival in Quebec of Jérôme Lalemant in 1645. Engaged in the mission to the Hurons since 1639, Father Lalemant now replaced Father Vimont as superior of the mission and, consequently, became the ecclesiastical superior of the Ursulines. For the next three years he worked closely and patiently with the community, particularly with Marie who, relieved of her office as superior, now had more time to give to the important work of the constitutions.

The Act of Union had made it clear that the constitutions were to be drawn up in the mission country, by those whose experience could best determine the pattern of life. It was a clause of far-reaching wisdom, imbued with the recognition that while the nuns would always be rooted in the tradition from which they had come, yet this tradition could not be transplanted whole but must be permitted to adapt to new soil and new climate.

The constitutions and regulations drawn up by Father Lalemant, assisted by Marie, were meticulous to a fault, consisting of 158 handwritten pages. Every rule was amplified by an exhortatory essay. Every generality was divided into its component parts. It is clear that Father Lalemant was a man at ease with detail and Marie herself, although her graces had broadened her spirit, often indicates that by nature she tended to be exacting and painstaking. In addition, the

---

29. Dom Guy Oury, Marie de l'Incarnation (Solesmes, 1973), II, p. 357.

necessity of providing for so much that was still so new and so unknown in the life ahead must have brought to the fore their natural
precision.

In 1647 the constitutions were ratified, and as far as one can tell
the nuns lived under them in peace and harmony for the next twelve
years. In 1659, however, conflict arose, not between the two Ursuline
congregations but between the monastery and its newly-arrived ecclesiastical superior: the first instance in North America of nuns striving
to maintain their rights against the superior power of a bishop.

With the growth of the Quebec Colony, the question of ecclesiastical authority had come increasingly to prominence. The Jesuits who
as superiors of the mission were, in fact, the ecclesiastical superiors of
the country, recognized that this temporary measure was no longer
adequate. The growth of both Quebec and Montreal made the need for
a hierarchical structure more urgent. Marie had her own reasons for
strongly favoring such a step, for the Holy See had refused to send a
bull giving canonical approbation to the Ursuline convent until such
time as a bishop was there to receive it. Although this delay in no way
restricted the nuns' work, it did relegate them to a canonical limbo—
not a situation with which the seventeenth century religious spirit
could be at ease.

After months of diplomatic feints and sallies, François de Mont-
morency-Laval was named apostolic delegate to New France, and the
following month he was consecrated bishop of Petrea. The following
June he surprised Quebec by arriving unannounced—the letters which
were to have prepared the colony for his arrival having been delayed.
Marie summed him up shrewdly: a person of singular virtue, of extraordinary personal qualities, a person of integrity, no respecter of
persons, living the life of an apostle. What she does not mention is
his iron will—and it is precisely this which will lead to the storm between them.

Just a year after his arrival he made his first canonical visitation to
the Ursulines. By the time the visitation was over he had suggested
striking changes in their constitutions. Clearly, the initial suggestion
for some of the changes had come from members of the community
who, feeling that their regulations were spelled out with unnecessary
detail, had recommended that an "abridgement" might suit them better. Whether Marie represents the majority of the community or only
herself when she writes following the bishop's visit, "Our constitutions
have been effectively ruined," is hard to determine. Laval gave them a
specific period of time for reflection on the changes he had recommended. Even those who had originally suggested some revisions

found these changes dangerously inappropriate for their way of life, "more suitable for Carmelites or for the Sisters of Calvary than for Ursulines." The Community's decision was to reject Laval's proposal. Thus Laval retreated, saving face by ordering the sisters to make changes in five articles dealing largely with sacramental matters. Out of a manuscript of 158 pages, it was not a great victory.[30]

The Ursulines continued with their original constitutions until 1681, nine years after Marie's death, when Laval once again drew up his battle lines. This time he was triumphant: the constitutions drawn up on native soil were repudiated and the monastery adopted the constitutions of the Congregation of Paris. In the end ecclesiastical power had triumphed. It would be unfair, however, to interpret this only as a struggle for power. The fact is that Quebec had changed vastly in those thirty years, and many of the points spelled out so carefully by Lalemant and Marie were no longer relevant. The constitutions of Paris, more spacious in their outline, were perhaps more appropriate for the growth and development of the Canadian Ursulines.

When the Quebec Ursulines ratified a constitution which established them as an autonomous monastery, they took upon themselves two serious responsibilities: finance and personnel. Juridically, Quebec was never economically dependent on Tours. Although, along with several other Ursuline communities, they sent generous gifts to Quebec, the gifts were a matter of charity rather than obligation; nor were these alms sufficient for the needs of the mission. Such obligation devolved largely on their foundress, Madeleine de la Peltrie; but Madeleine's income was far smaller than they had originally expected, and Madeleine herself proved to be a capricious, if generous, woman. When, three years after their arrival, she announced her decision to follow the newly-arrived Jeanne Mance to Montreal, the Ursulines were left in a perilous state.[31]

Jean de Bernières, the layman in France who had official care of their finances, was blunt in his appraisal of their situation: unless some other means of support could be found, they would have to return to France. Even in the face of this approaching disaster Marie continued

---

30. *Letters,* pp. 261–62. The five points Laval changed dealt with singing during mass, times for exposition of the Blessed Sacrament, frequency of receiving Holy Communion, the voting privileges of the young professed. Oury, *Marie,* II, p. 532. See also the edition of the *Rule of 1647. Constitutions et règlements des premières Ursulines de Québec,* ed. Gabrielle Lapointe, O.S.U. (Quebec, 1974).

31. Marie does not mention this in the *Relation of 1654* but describes the event at some length in a letter of September 29, 1642. *Letters,* pp. 225–27.

to order supplies for the building of their boarding school and retained the workmen even though she could not imagine where she would get the money to pay them.

The country itself could not be expected to help in the sisters' support. Many of the necessities for both food and clothing still had to be imported from France at exorbitant prices. With no animals to help clear the forests or plow the fields, agriculture made a meager contribution. Although later, as the colony prospered, the French pupils would pay something toward their upkeep, generally in produce (a pig, dried peas, firewood), at the beginning the Ursulines' work was almost entirely with the Indians and from these, of course, nothing was expected.

For years they lived poised on the brink of bankruptcy; but although such economic independence made those first years very difficult, it saved them from a restrictive dependence on a parent house. They were free to make their own decisions about the use of funds, about building, about the size of their school, about new foundations —about all those matters which could best be decided in the mission country by the personnel of that country. They were spared the anguish of many later foundations where economic dependence reinforced ties which could ultimately be severed only with painful misunderstanding on both sides.

An equally daunting responsibility consequent upon the autonomy of the Ursuline Mission was that of personnel. Here again Tours had no obligation to maintain and increase the community at Quebec. Nor did they, except for two sisters who arrived in the summer of 1642. However, Marie's determination not to tie the mission to a single house or congregation but to open it to all Ursulines proved successful. In the first fifteen years of the mission's establishment, volunteers came from various parts of France: Paris, Ploermel, Bourges, Magny-en-Vexin. The fire had spread. By 1652, however, Canada had begun to provide its own vocations. At first these were young women born in France who had emigrated to Quebec; later it would be the daughters of colonists who had been educated in the Ursuline school. Between the years 1657 and 1671 no religious came from France, and the last recorded French missionaries arrived in September 1671. At Marie's death in 1672, of the twenty-three nuns in the community, nine had made their religious profession in France and fourteen in Quebec. Meanwhile, Marie's hope (as it had been that of the Jesuits) of training the Indians for religious life was short-lived. They could be devout, patient, courageous, she discovered, but they could not adjust to the daily discipline demanded by religious life.

Once again the pattern which emerged in Quebec became the customary pattern for other religious groups in North America. The initial European vocations gave way to native vocations, thus leading to a two-fold development: the growth of a more indigenous and apposite spirituality and a gradual distancing from the European model. As in the question of finance, the problem of personnel endured a hazardous period but in the end provided an atmosphere for healthy community.

When Marie and her sisters sailed for New France, their understanding of the life they were about to face was understandably vague. Even their perusal of the *Jesuit Relations* would have been of little help in preparing them for day-to-day realities; for Father Le Jeune was keenly aware that promotional tracts, if they were to be successful, must inspire and animate rather than frighten or repel. Yet whatever their ignorance, they were transparently clear on the fact that their mission was to young Indian girls and women. Their later constitution said it succinctly: "to employ themselves to the best of their ability in working for the salvation of their neighbor . . . especially in the instruction of girls and women, in particular the Indians."[32] This was at the heart of Marie's mission theology: to snatch souls from the power of the devil and win them for Jesus Christ. For this, she avowed again and again, she was willing to shed her blood.

This process of christianization was a complex one as, indeed, it has remained well into the twentieth century. To christianize meant to Europeanize. For the French, to plant the cross meant to plant the fleur-de-lys as well. The two were so closely allied that most missionaries saw no distinction. Naked bodies were unchristian and to christianize them meant clothing them in French breeches or pinafore. Cleanliness was next to godliness, and the nuns spent days scrubbing the bodies of little Indian girls, freeing them from the bear grease with which their parents had covered them as protection from the elements. The Indians were understandably confused, for they saw nothing clean in the long black robes of the men and women which trailed along the ground or in the heavy animal-like growth of hair with which many Frenchmen covered their faces.

The question of language was a deeper issue. To their credit both nuns and priests prepared themselves diligently for their ministry by studying the Indian languages. Marie describes in vivid detail the difficulties of learning Algonquin even with such a practiced teacher as

---

32. *Constitutions et règlements*, p. 1.

Father Le Jeune. She had the advantage of the dictionary he had compiled, but the language system bore no resemblance to French. Wearied from this unaccustomed labor she wrote, "learning all these words by heart, as well as memorizing all the verb-forms . . . was like having stones rolling around in my head. The whole thing seemed to me to be humanly impossible." "But," she continued later, "the desire to talk accomplishes a great deal. . . . I want my tongue to be able to express my heart so that I can tell these dear children about the love of God and of Jesus our Master."[33]

Though religious instruction was given in the native language, the basic contour of the system was decidedly French. The model followed was the only one they knew: the French boarding school, which, in turn, was shaped by the rule of cloister. No element of their rule was more determining in shaping the education they offered than that of cloister. One would have thought that after their brief encounter with the Indians at Tadoussac on their way up the St. Lawrence or during the day spent at the Jesuit Mission at Sillery, the nuns might have had some second thoughts concerning the limitations imposed by cloister. But it was not so. Even more amazing, their Jesuit advisors, experienced in the ways of the natives, raised no objections. Instead, they manifested a scrupulous exactitude in following this rule so precisely formulated by the Council of Trent. The mystique this rule had assumed can be seen in the Quebec constitutions in which Father Lalemant includes cloister in the chapter dealing with the vow of chastity, spelling out all its ramifications in meticulous detail.

Thus, from the beginning a European model was imposed not only on the nuns but upon their freedom-loving charges. Since nuns must never leave their cloister—not even for their work—their pupils must be brought into the cloister and live their lives within it. Boarders, the constitution stipulated (and all Indian children would be boarders), are not to be encouraged to leave the cloister even to visit with relatives since "these comings and goings can only be harmful both for the children and the community."[34]

Almost immediately the first injurious effect of cloister manifested itself. Although the Indian children endeared themselves to their mistresses, the end they had hoped for was seldom achieved. The Indian children, skillful mimics as they were, loved to watch and imitate the devotions of the sisters and were delighted to learn to

---

33. *Relation of 1654*, pp. 137.
34. *Constitutions et règlements*, p. 102.

genuflect, to bow, to say the same prayer a hundred times over. Yet their devotion to this new religion and to the nuns themselves was rarely strong enough to keep them within the palisade. Cloister was unendurable for them, so unendurable that they would fall into so profound a melancholy that their parents, fearing for their lives, would take them away, back to the forests where they regained their freedom. Even those who did not fall ill would sneak away, "like squirrels," Marie writes, or be taken away when it was time for the seminomadic Algonquins to leave for the forests. There could be little continuity in such education, for each time the errant pupil returned one must begin over again.

Even when faced with these continuing disappointments there seems to have been no thought that some mitigation in the cloister might be sought, even though such mitigation might broaden their successes and enable them to fulfill their avowed vocation: to win souls redeemed by the blood of Jesus Christ. Years later Marie wrote wistfully of the Jesuits' courageous explorations into Indian territory but with no complaint that her own missionary endeavors were limited by strict enclosure. It is even more remarkable that such cloister would continue—almost unchanged—for three hundred years. That a rule shaped for an entirely different culture and made sacrosanct by tradition should so take precedence over the very ministry which had motivated the foundation is a telling symbol of the relationship of Old World to New, and brings into relief one aspect of the constant struggle in the development of European congregations of women in North America.

Whatever the efforts of the missionaries—and their efforts were heroic—their success with the Indians was relatively meager. Although there were infant baptisms and adult conversions, the life of the forest was a strong counterforce. There were, of course, always some who persevered, were raised "in the French manner," and married a Frenchman; but these seem to have been the exception. Even when the Jesuits left their mission compound and journeyed with the Indians, they were sustained in their labors not so much by success as by the conviction that their sufferings would have value before the throne of God. In time, disease (brought by the White Man) and tribal wars reduced the Indian population dramatically, and Marie noted with regret that there were fewer and fewer Indian children in the school.

While the Indian population was decreasing, however, Quebec was growing rapidly, and soon the Ursuline school was filled to capacity with the children of the colonists. At first this was a disappointment; this was not why they had come. These were souls already baptized, safely gathered into the kingdom of Jesus Christ. In time, however, they saw this work to have an importance of its own. "I can assure you," Marie wrote to her son, "that were it not for the Ursulines their salvation would be in constant danger. . . . The girls of this country are, for the most part, more knowledgeable in many danger-ous ways than those of France. Thirty girls give us more work in our boarding school than sixty would in France."[35]

By the year of Marie's death, 1672, there seemed to be little doubt about the continuance of the Ursuline monastery in Quebec. It was a fine large building now, situated on extensive grounds in the Upper City. It had burned to the ground once but had been rebuilt on the same foundations. It had weathered its financial storms and although still dependent on divine providence, it no longer lived in fear of economic failure. They now had sufficient personnel, too, for Quebec had begun to provide its own vocations, both choir and lay sisters. Although there must have been some regret that their work with the Indians had not flourished as they had dreamed, yet the value to the colony of the education they provided was beyond question.

Marie herself had found in Canada all that her dream had prom-ised. It was here that those extraordinary mystic graces of her youth had coalesced with her powerful apostolic passion so that she could say, "I am like one of those birds which finds its nourishment while flying." Canada had become, in every sense, her home.

THE TEXTS

When Marie Guyart, known in religion as Marie of the Incarna-tion, died on April 30, 1672, she left behind a considerable body of writing:

1. An account of her spiritual life from her childhood up to 1633, written at the command of her spiritual director, Georges de la Haye, S.J.;
2. Notes from two retreats (c. 1633–35) and various other spiritual notes, also written for Father de la Haye;
3. An account of her vocation to Canada (c. 1636) written for her then director, Jacques Dinet, S.J.;

---

35. Letter to her son, August 9, 1668, *Letters,* p. 271.

4. Notes from instructions on the catechism given to the Ursuline novices at Tours (c. 1635);

5. Notes from conferences on the Song of Songs dating from the same period;

6. An account of her spiritual life from the beginning to 1654, requested by her son; a "Supplement" to this account written two years later (1656);

7. An extensive correspondence written largely after her arrival in Canada;

8. Several dictionaries: an Iroquois dictionary, a French-Algonquin dictionary, an Algonquin-French dictionary, and a catechism in Huron.

Except for the last-mentioned, which never left Quebec and which were eventually lost, these were the materials available to Dom Claude Martin when he began the publication of his mother's writings shortly after her death. Within the next ten years he had produced four volumes:

> *La Vie de la Vénérable Mère Marie de l'Incarnation, Première Supérieure des Ursulines de la Nouvelle-France, tirée de ses lettres et de ses écrits,* Paris, 1677.

> *Lettres de la Vénérable Mère Marie de l'Incarnation, Première Supérieure des Ursulines de la Nouvelle-France, divisée en deux parties,* Paris, 1681.

> *Retraites de la Vénérable Mère Marie de l'Incarnation, Religieuse Ursuline,* Paris, 1682.

> *L'École sainte, ou Explication Familière des mystères de la Foy, Par la Vénérable Mère Marie de l'Incarnation, Religieuse Ursuline,* Paris, 1684.

In 1654, Claude had received the most important of these documents, a text commonly identified as the *Relation of 1654*. As early as 1646 Claude had begun his persistent request for an account of his mother's spiritual life, and with the approval of her spiritual director, Jérôme Lalement, S.J., she had begun to comply. It is a revealing sign of her devotion to her son that she would undertake a task so contrary to her sense of privacy and humility, to say nothing of the difficulty of such a labor when the work of the mission was so encompassing. In winter it was almost impossible to write because of the extreme cold; in summer, in addition to the usual labors, there was the overwhelming task of correspondence. "I am exhausted," Marie wrote in the fall of 1644, "by the number of letters I have written. I think I must have written more than two hundred." Nonetheless, by 1650 the work was completed and she intended to send it to Claude the following spring. It was in December of that year, however, that the monastery burned to the ground and with it all of Marie's papers.

Once again, Claude pressed and Father Lalemant encouraged her. This time she was further urged by a clear interior light showing her that this was something God wanted of her. Without further thought she wrote a detailed outline of her proposed account and sent it to Claude in a letter of October 1653. It is this document which forms the basis of the life Claude published in 1677.

His original plan had been to write a biography. Influenced by the advice of his friends, however, who suggested that he let his mother speak for herself, Dom Claude devised a compromise.[36] Beginning each chapter with a section reproduced from the 1654 *Relation,* he amplified this by what he termed an "Addition," comprised of his own pious reflections and bolstered by further quotations from portions of his mother's other writings. Thus various texts were woven together with no effort to identify one from the other; and since—with the exception of a small number of letters—none of the originals is extant, the task of distinguishing and validating individual texts became close to impossible.

For the next 250 years Marie's biographers (Charlevoix, Casgrain, Richaudeau) were content, perforce, to use Claude Martin's life as their principal source.[37] Although Henri Brémond's volume opened up a new perspective on Marie of the Incarnation, it was only in the 1920's that a full-fledged critical investigation got underway under the editorship of Albert Jamet, O.S.B. Jamet, a Benedictine monk of Solesmes (and therefore a spiritual relative of Dom Claude) set out to publish an edition of the writings left by Marie according to the standards of modern critical scholarship. Between the years 1929 and his death in 1948 Dom Jamet published four volumes. The first volume comprised what is known as the *Relation of 1633,* some early "con-

---

36. "There is more than one author; there are two for both were necessary to accomplish this work. This great servant of God has herself worked and her son has put the final touch but only in such a way as to be an echo of her own words." Dom Claude Martin, *La Vie de la Vénérable Mère Marie de l'Incarnation* (facsimile edition, Solesmes, 1981), p. ii.

37. See the bibliography.

science" letters, a few pages of spiritual notes, and her "treatise" on the Song of Songs. The second volume included her notes from two retreats and the text of the *Relation of 1654*. Volumes three and four covered the letters up to 1652.

For the *Relation of 1654* Dom Jamet was fortunate in having a source not available to his predecessors: this is the copy of the *Relation of 1654* found in the archives of the Ursuline monastery at Three Rivers. A quarto manuscript of ninety-nine pages, it is written in an unidentified seventeenth century hand. Who wrote it and where remains conjectural but its importance is unquestionable: it is a control against which to read Claude's published text.[38] This manuscript copy provides evidence of what Claude had admitted in his introduction: that his mother was often writing at white heat and that this led her into repetitions and obscure constructions; that, accordingly, for the comfort of the reader, he has made some little changes in certain places where Marie's own expression seemed less clear and less appropriate to her thought. In fact, the Three Rivers manuscript indicates that Claude is guilty of far more tampering than he acknowledges. Jamet, after a careful study of both texts, made the decision to follow the Three Rivers manuscript for his own edition, since this appears to be a faithful copy of Marie's original manuscript. It is this text provided by Dom Jamet which I have followed for my translation.

Establishing a text for the 1654 *Relation* was the least thorny of Jamet's tasks. For Marie's other writings he had no source beyond that provided by Dom Claude; for when Claude completed his work, he apparently gave away—or at least made no suitable effort to preserve —the documents he had used. The *Relation of 1633,* which Dom Claude reproduced only in part, had been undertaken at the request of Georges de la Haye who as Marie's director was attempting to assess her spiritual state during this period of intense trial. On Good Friday 1633, Marie tells us, she began to compose her account, detailing both her sins and her graces. It was March 25, just thirteen years since the grace of her "conversion." By careful sorting and piecing, Jamet was able to establish seventy-two fragments from this early account. Although only a portion of the document, these fragments provide interesting psychological insights when read in tandem with the *Relation of 1654.*

With the two retreats written in 1633 and 1635 and the material

---

38. Jamet and Oury differ as to the source of this manuscript. See Albert Jamet, O.S.B., *Ecrits spirituels et historiques* (Paris, 1929–39), II, pp. 141–44. Guy Oury, O.S.B., *Marie,* II, pp. 480–81.

on the Song of Songs, the effort to provide a pure text becomes impossible. In both cases Claude was working only from notes. In the first case, these were notes written by Marie for her director at the close of her meditations. By their very nature and purpose such notes are incomplete. It is not a question of providing a "meditation" which others might profitably follow, but simply a matter of noting one's personal responses. Claude, however, was not content until he had transformed the series of private notes into a meditation manual. "I found these meditations rather vacuous and defective," he wrote; he then comforts the reader with this dubious assurance, "I have filled them in so that nothing is left unclear." Henri Brémond is much closer to the spirit of the text when he writes: "If there is profit for souls in reading these and being inspired for their own meditations, first they must enable us to approach as close as possible to Marie de l'Incarnation at the privileged moment of her prayer. More than anything else, the texts of this precious collection give us the opportunity of observing a great soul in prayer."[39]

In turning to Marie's correspondence, we are faced with problems of a different nature. In 1681 Dom Claude published a volume of his mother's letters. It was divided into two parts: spiritual letters and historical letters. From the start the structure was defective; such a distinction is impossible. Undaunted, however, Claude held stubbornly to his plan, even dividing individual letters into two sections in order to fit them into his schema. The initial problem for the editor, then, was to abandon this arbitrary division and establish a valid chronology for the letters. It was not until 1876—almost two hundred years after Claude's initial publication—that a zealous editor, Abbé Richaudeau, chaplain of the Ursulines at Blois, discarded Dom Claude's structure and put the letters into chronological order, without making any other significant changes.[40]

It was part of Dom Jamet's ambition to provide a critical edition of these letters. At his death, however, he had published only those through 1652, leaving behind a collection of scholarly but arcane notes for the later letters. It was not until several years later that Dom Oury, like Jamet a monk of Solesmes, began his edition of the letters. At that time the decision was made to undertake a completely new edition rather than attempt to complete Jamet's edition. In 1971 Dom Oury's edition of Marie's letters was published at Solesmes. It is a work of

---

39. Dom Claude quoted in Oury, *Marie,* I, p. 249; Brémond VI, 144.
40. See the bibliography.

meticulous scholarship, increasing the number of known letters to 277—far from the 12,000–13,000 conjectured by Dom Jamet—but well above the number included in Dom Claude's edition. Although Oury is necessarily dependent upon Claude's text, he has made a judicious use of other materials from Marie's correspondence, thus providing variant readings whenever possible.

For my translation I have used the text provided by Dom Jamet for the *Relation of 1654,* the *Relation of 1633,* and the retreat notes. For the letters I have used the text provided by Dom Oury.

Nothing seems more arbitrary than the picking and choosing one must do when faced with a large body of significant writing. There was no doubt in my mind that the *Relation of 1654* must appear in its entirety. The decision concerning the use of the 1633 *Relation* was more difficult. Ultimately I decided to include those fragments dealing with Marie's desire for religious life and her first years as an Ursuline since it is this which leads her to the mission of Canada. Although in one sense this material will seem repetitive after reading the *Relation of 1654,* yet it has a psychological importance. In 1633 Marie was very close in time to the events she is describing. It is a document of a woman in her late twenties and early thirties. The future is not clear to her and the tone of uncertainty and anxiety is palpable. The repetition itself is often significant. In places the language of the *Relation of 1654* and that of 1633 is almost identical. We can have no clearer evidence of the profound impression and decisive influence these events had on her than this identical language. The notes from the ten-day retreat, although regrettably altered, do provide another perspective on Marie's life of prayer. As Brémond points out, they give us the valuable opportunity of witnessing a privileged soul at prayer.

It was in the choice of the letters that I faced my greatest difficulty. Almost all are interesting; all provide new light on Marie, on her relationships, her dreams, her temptations—as well as on Canada itself. Choices here are necessarily arbitrary. I wanted my selection to provide some chronological progression. Originally I had planned to use fewer letters addressed to Claude. This, I soon discovered, would have made my choices even more arbitrary. The majority of the letters available are written to Claude, and it is to him that Marie reveals herself most completely.

There is much that we regret in Dom Claude Martin's work: his inadequate efforts to collect more of his mother's correspondence; his failure to provide adequately for the preservation of the materials he gathered; his tampering with the style and at times even with the structure of his mother's writing. Yet ultimately we must admit that without his efforts, we might well be left with nothing at all. Except for the manuscript of the *Relation of 1654* at Three Rivers and a very small number of letters preserved in various archives, nothing remains of Marie of the Incarnation except what has been preserved through her son's efforts. Although he lacked the sensitivity and perspicacity we would have wished for him, it was his persistence—albeit heavy-handed—that enables us to restore the image of this extraordinary woman who blended so uniquely the vocation of mystic and missionary.

THE RELATION OF 1654

PROLOGUE
JESUS, MARY, JOSEPH

Having been ordered by him who holds the place of God for me—in order to guide me in his ways—to write whatever is possible concerning the graces it has pleased his Divine Majesty to give me in prayer, I shall begin my obedience for his honor and glory, in the name of the adorable Word Incarnate, my heavenly and divine Spouse.[1]

FIRST STATE OF PRAYER
I.

From my earliest years the Divine Majesty filled my soul with those tendencies which would make it his temple and the vessel of his mercies. During my sleep one night when I was about seven years old, it seemed to me that I was playing some childhood game with one of my companions in the yard of a country school. I was looking upward when I saw the heavens open and Our Lord Jesus Christ in human form emerge and come toward me. "Look!" I cried to my companion, "There's Our Lord and he is coming to me!" It seemed to me that he had chosen me rather than her because she had been guilty of some imperfection, although she was, nevertheless, a good girl. However, there was a secret involved which I did not know then. As this most adorable Majesty approached me, my heart felt on fire with love for him and I started to open my arms to embrace him. Then he, the most beautiful of all the children of men, took me in his arms and with a look full of indescribable sweetness and charm, kissed me with great

---

1. Jérôme Lalemant, uncle of the martyr, Gabriel Lalemant, was Marie's director from 1645 until her death in 1672.

love and asked me, "Will you be mine?" I answered, "Yes!" Then when he heard my answer, we saw him return to heaven.[2]

Upon awakening my heart was so enraptured by this extraordinary grace that I naively told it to anyone who would listen. The result of this visitation was an inclination to do good. On account of my inexperience, it never occurred to me that this inclination to do good had come from an interior source. However, I did sometimes feel drawn to talk my little needs over with Our Lord. I did this very simply, unable to imagine that he would refuse anything asked with humility. This is why when I was in church, I used to watch the posture of people who were praying. When I noticed those who seemed to have a humble attitude, I would say to myself, "Surely God will hear this person, for his attitude shows that he is praying with humility."

All this made a great impression on me, and I would often feel urged by an interior spirit to withdraw to pray without even knowing what the interior spirit was or being acquainted with the words, "interior spirit," as I have already said. But that is how God's goodness led me. Since I was still only a child I didn't distinguish my prayer from my recreation, since they both seemed very compatible to me. I passed my time this way until I was about sixteen years old and remorse of conscience pressed upon me when I went to make my confession. I sensed that the Divine Majesty wanted me to distance myself from my childish attitudes and to realize that now I should pay more attention to what was happening to me interiorly.[3]

But I did not dare to—I was ashamed—and I told myself that I did not believe that I had offended God in this matter, for there can be no sin unless one believes there is sin while one is acting. Thus I opposed the Spirit of God which actually possessed me with such strength and hidden efficacy in order to win me entirely to him. The

---

2. Although there is some division in assessing the supernatural quality of this dream, no one doubts its importance for Marie. Dom Claude provides no explanation, noting only that "the kiss of God is the Holy Spirit," thus leading us, quite correctly, to see her life as peculiarly under the direction of the Holy Spirit from its very beginnings. Dom Jamet refuses to accept the word "dream" as appropriate, preferring "imaginary and symbolic vision." Contemporary commentators such as Klein, Renaudin and Oury sidestep classification, content with pointing out that it was an event that changed her life, "that first conversion which turns everything toward God." Joseph Klein, M.S.C., *L'Itinéraire mystique de la Vénérable Mère Marie de l'Incarnation* (Rome, 1937), pp. 14–15; Paul Renaudin, *Marie de l'Incarnation* (Paris, 1935), pp. 15–20; Oury, *Marie*, I, pp. 23–25.

3. Dom Claude specifies these "childish games" as a kind of "playing church"—a normal childhood activity. Martin, *Vie*, p. 6. Marie's concern over this is not scrupulosity but, as throughout her life, a delicate concern for the promptings of the Spirit.

charm of this attraction was for me far sweeter than anything else I had experienced, and whatever good I saw I gave myself to without any great effort on my part. Yet I continued to believe that in confession I was doing the right thing, even though I was not acting according to the light of the Holy Spirit who urged me to confess.

This was the only time I hesitated about following his inspiration. For more than a year I concluded that there was no need to confess my childhood games, and thus I delayed his great mercies until that time when he triumphed over me in an instant, as I shall explain further on.

II.

Our Lord let my parents put me in a situation where the pastimes which had been denied me in their house became available to me.[4] At the same time he removed all my desire for them and, instead, filled me with a desire for seclusion. Thus I was preoccupied with the love of a good which I did not yet understand, shunning the companionship of my peers in order to remain at home reading books of devotion. I gave up entirely those books which dealt with frivolous matters to which I had been attached simply for the sake of amusement.

Our whole neighborhood was amazed, bewildered by my withdrawal and by the attraction I had to go to church every day, as well as my inclination for the practice of virtue, especially the virtues of patience; for they could not see what I was experiencing interiorly and how the goodness of God was working in me. Even I myself did not understand how this happened except that I followed his lead in prayer and obeyed him in practicing those virtues for which he provided the opportunity.

For almost two years his divine goodness allowed me to endure great suffering, for it was during this period that he tried my soul.[5] Yet he never abandoned me, for this interior support of which I have

---

4. The oblique reference is to her marriage to Claude Martin, a young silk merchant of Tours. Marie's attraction for religious life had not been taken seriously by her parents who had arranged a marriage for their daughter who was just seventeen. Marie's attitude toward her marriage is ambivalent. She speaks of her husband as a good man whom she "loved dearly" but also writes that she felt that God's purpose in her marriage was to give her a son who would become a priest. Jamet, II, p. 483.

5. Jamet suggests that her mother-in-law is the cause of her suffering; this seems unlikely since the latter is very anxious for Marie to continue living with her after the death of her son. Dom Claude suggests that "a certain jealous woman" did everything she could to ruin both Marie and her husband. Jamet, II, p. 483 n.b (Jamet provides a double set of notes: numerical notes at end of chapter; alphabetical notes at bottom of page.); Martin, *Vie*, p. 638.

spoken gave me both strength and great patience and gentleness in the most painful assaults. Prayer was my recourse, for it seemed to me that in these sufferings God wished to prepare my soul and purify it through tribulation.

I often reflected on the caresses Our Lord had given me when I was a child, and this inspired a desire to belong completely to him.[6] I longed for this union with him and tried to do everything that my limited understanding suggested to achieve it. From the time of my first grace I often experienced this desire. I remember that shortly after I had received this grace, drawn by a sense of the goodness of God who hears those who pray to him with love, I would go to church and hide in a remote corner so as not to be seen. There I would stay for part of the day, longing passionately for union with him. I was so naive that I didn't even know that this was prayer. I experienced the same yearning to see the Blessed Virgin, at least before I died, so that she would be there to protect me when the moment of my death came. I prayed every day for this.

This is how the Divine Goodness would have gently wanted to direct me had I been faithful from the beginning to his inspirations.

III.

The Divine Majesty, not satisfied with having given me a distaste for worldly things and the strength to carry the crosses which he had permitted, strengthened me interiorly and gave me a profound desire for the reception of the sacraments. I was about eighteen years old at this time. This frequent reception gave me great courage and gentleness and a very lively faith which confirmed my belief in the divine mysteries. The good education I had received from my parents who were good Christians formed a solid foundation for everything related to the Christian life. When I reflect on this, I bless God who in his mercy did all this by disposing me to lead a virtuous life.

This lively faith helped me perform many good works and develop a spirit of prayer. The good qualities which I had received through previous graces and favors were thus perfected. I no longer had the heart for anything except for what was good. The more I

---

6. In the "Supplément" to the *Relation of 1654* she makes it clear that consecration to God would have been her first choice: "Had I had spiritual direction, I would never have consented [to marriage] but I was entirely deprived of this. . . . I let myself be led blindly by my parents. . . ." Jamet, II, p. 482.

approached the sacraments, the more I desired them, for there I found life and goodness and a longing for prayer. I wanted everyone whom Our Lord let me encounter to experience this love. I feared for them because there were certain serious sins which they failed to confess fully, and I knew that it was through the sacrament of confession that one was washed clean in the blood of Jesus Christ. I was also aware that the penance imposed must be carefully performed. This led me to talk to these people and urge them to try to do what this matter required.

Had I been convinced that my childish games and the pastimes I had engaged in with my companions had been real sins, I would very quickly have confessed them; but since I wasn't convinced of this, I did nothing about it. Yet the Spirit of God inspired me to see that they were faults and that in his eyes there was nothing slight where imperfections or minor sins were concerned, even though they might be regarded as nothing in the eyes of creatures. All this led me to ask pardon willingly and contritely, making use of holy water, for I had been told that this washed away venial sins.

One time when I was at the foot of the altar of Our Lady, I saw very clearly, by an inner light, the importance of confessing fully; I felt that I must do so, for my doubts had been removed. I prepared to make my confession, but once in the confessional I found that the priest was one of those who heard confessions routinely. At this my heart constricted and I could not confess according to my inspirations. I answered his questions and listened to his exhortations but I myself could say nothing. Having performed my penance, I went to Communion without the least scruple or sense of reproach, for Communion always inclined me toward virtue and trust in the goodness of God.

I had read the psalms in French and having heard that it was the Spirit of God who dictated them, they aroused in me various thoughts and reflections. I made use of them, convinced that whatever was said by the Spirit of God was infallibly true and that everything else would cease to exist before these words would ever fail me. This led me to believe that my hope in him would give me everything I asked for. I entrusted myself entirely to his word and therefore I would never be disappointed in my expectations.

IV.

From my childhood on I had a strong desire to listen to preachers since I had been told that God spoke through them, and I thought this was wonderful. I was too young to understand much of what was said except for the stories which I recounted on my return home. As I grew older, my instinctive faith, coupled with what I heard of the Divine Word, produced a greater and greater love in me which led me to go to listen to sermons. I had such esteem for the preachers that when I would see one of them in the streets, I wanted to run after him and kiss his footsteps. Prudence restrained me but I continued to gaze after him until he was out of sight.

I thought there was nothing more wonderful than to preach the word of God.[7] It was this which evoked my esteem for those to whom Our Lord had given the grace to proclaim his word. When I heard this word it seemed that my heart was like a vessel in which this divine word flowed like liquid. This was not my imagination but rather the power of the Spirit of God who himself was in this divine word and who, by a movement of grace, produced this effect in my soul.

Having received this fullness of grace, my soul could not contain it except by pouring it forth with God in prayer. Such was my nature that I even had to break into speech because I could not contain this abundance. With great ardor I would relate quite eloquently to the people of our household what the preachers had said, as well as my reflections on it. One time, hearing a sermon on the holy name of Jesus in which the preacher had repeated the holy name frequently, this divine word, like some heavenly food, filled my heart so completely that all day I could say nothing but "Jesus, Jesus!" without being able to stop.

God gave me powerful lights when I listened attentively to his holy word and my heart was on fire both day and night. This led me to speak to him in a new way—a way hitherto unknown to me. I had heard that one must meditate in order to practice mental prayer, but I did not feel that I was doing this when, following his inner call to me, I poured out my heart to God. I knew only that these were good impulses which the word of God stirred up in my soul and which urged me more and more to listen and to lead a life of virtue compatible with the vocation to which his Divine Majesty called me. One Lent when a Capuchin Father preached on the passion of Our Lord, my soul was so deeply plunged into this mystery that I could pay attention to nothing else day or night.

Now that I am more knowledgeable and experienced in the spiri-

---

7. This admiration for those who preach the word of God is often seen as an early hint of her mission vocation.

tual life, I see that the goodness of God predisposed me by his graces and filled me with "the blessings of his grace." At this time I had heavy crosses to bear, for the state I was in was constantly at odds with the Spirit who wished to win my heart and spirit completely. It was not that I was restricted in my devotions; on the contrary, the person to whom I was united sustained me in them and he himself derived great satisfaction from them. This was a merciful providence of God, for without this acceptance my duress and its consequent crosses would have been unendurable; it seems to me that I was not sufficiently rooted in virtue to sustain this. Since that time Our Lord has always given me a desire to hear his divine word and has given me very great graces through it. May he be blessed eternally.

V.

The ceremonies of the Church, to which I had had a strong attraction from childhood, were among the things I found helpful in inspiring devotion. I found them incomparably beautiful and holy. When I grew up and was able to understand their meaning, my love for them increased, along with the admiration I felt for the holiness and majesty of the Church. This developed my faith and united me to Our Lord in an extraordinary way. My gratitude overflowed for being born of Christian parents and for being called to be a daughter of the Church. The more I understood them, the more I was filled with love for these holy ceremonies of the Church.

When I saw processions of the cross and the banner behind which Christians walked, my heart leaped with joy. There was a captain who lived in our neighborhood whose soldiers marched behind him with their flag. Seeing the crucifix and the banner with its various figures, I used to say to myself: "There is my captain and there is his standard. I want to follow him just the way soldiers follow their leader." Thus I would follow the procession with great fervor. My eyes were riveted on the crucifix and I walked along, saying in my heart, "This is my captain. I want to follow him."

I had such an ardent faith for everything the Church did that it seemed to be my life and my food. One time I thought I would be suffocated during a procession for a Jubilee Year, for I was among the first to enter the church in order to see the ceremonies and the solemn office which were performed on this occasion. Everything I saw and heard led me deeper into my soul. One time during a procession of the Blessed Sacrament I was so enraptured at the thought of this sacrament of love that I did not see where I was going but walked randomly like someone drunk. I don't know if anyone noticed this or what they thought about it.

I thought this was true devotion because I did not know that there was any other way to pray to God and to serve him while frequenting the sacraments and earnestly avoiding sin. Thus when I made my confession I felt quite righteous, and my spirit was satisfied from one confession to the next. Yet the Spirit of God continued to urge me to confess everything I had done from my childhood. As I have said, he exacted of me a purity of soul that I did not understand any more than I understood the reason for his request.

When I was nineteen years old, Our Lord brought about a separation in my life, calling to himself the person with whom, by his will, I had been united.[8] Various matters, following upon this loss, brought me new crosses, greater—naturally speaking—than a person of my age and sex and ability would have been able to bear. But the extravagance of the divine goodness effected such strength and courage in my heart that I was able to endure everything. My mainstay was in his holy words: "I am with those who are in tribulation." I firmly believed that he was with me because he had said so, so that the loss of temporal goods, the lawsuit I was engaged in, actual want, even the care of my son who was only six months old and whom I saw stripped of everything—even as I was myself—none of these things were able to upset me.

Inexperienced as I was, the Holy Spirit drew me interiorly, filling me with faith, with hope, and with trust—thus bringing to a successful conclusion everything I undertook.

---

8. After only two years of marriage Claude Martin died, leaving his widow with a six-month-old son (Claude) and a business close to bankruptcy. Although legally Marie could not have been held responsible for her husband's death, she determined to salvage what she could of the business and pay his creditors. Cf. Jamet, II, p. 483; Martin, *Vie,* p. 24.

After all the inner promptings which the goodness of God had given me to draw me to true purity of soul—which I could not reach through my own efforts—his Divine Majesty delivered the *coup de grâce*. At this time I had no spiritual director and was not aware that these matters should be discussed with anyone but God—except to tell one's sins to one's confessor. God freed me from my ignorance and led me where he desired to manifest his grace to me. This happened on the eve of the Incarnation of Our Lord, March 24, 1620.

That morning on my way to work I was earnestly commending my business affairs to God with my usual prayer: "In Thee, O Lord, I have put my trust; let me never be disappointed." I had this invocation imprinted on my soul with the certitude of faith that he would help me without fail. Suddenly I was brought stock-still, both inwardly and outwardly. Even my thoughts were abruptly brushed aside. Then, in an instant, my inner eyes were opened and all the faults, sins, and imperfections that I had committed since my birth were shown to me in the most vivid detail: so clear and distinct were they that no human certainty could have expressed them thus. At the same moment I saw myself immersed in the blood of the Son of God, shed because of the sins which had been shown to me; and furthermore, realizing that it was for my salvation that this Precious Blood had been shed. I think I would have died of terror had God's goodness not sustained me, so frightful and shocking is the sight of sin, no matter how slight.[1]

No human language can express this: to look upon a God of infinite goodness and purity offended by a mere worm exceeds even horror itself. And then to think of a God made man, dying to atone for sin, shedding his precious blood to satisfy his Father and thus reconcile sinners to himself! In a word, it is impossible to express what the soul comes to understand in this marvel. And even beyond all this, to realize that one is personally guilty and that if one had been entirely

---

1. This experience Marie calls her "conversion." In referring to it as the "Vision of the Precious Blood," one must be careful to remember Marie's own warning that she saw nothing with her "bodily eyes." "Supplément," Jamet, II, pp. 483–84. Renaudin, in explaining Marie's use of "vision," notes: "an intuitive knowledge which sees everything in an instant." Renaudin, *Marie de l'Incarnation,* p. 43, n. 1. It is clearly Marie's initiation into the mystic way.

alone the Son of God would have done exactly what he did for everyone. This truly wastes and, as it were, destroys the soul.

These visions and what they evoke penetrate so deeply that in an instant they communicate everything with their own perfect efficacy. At that very moment I felt transported beyond myself and transformed through the mercy of him who had wrought this wonderful grace. Yet even while experiencing this love, I suffered an unimaginable sadness and regret at having offended him. It is impossible to imagine what the soul experiences. So penetrating and pitiless was this shaft of love that I would have thrown myself into the fire in order to satisfy him. Yet the strangest thing of all is that its very harshness seemed gentle to me. It had both its charms and its chains, binding the soul so that it considered itself fortunate to be led captive. In all this excess of emotion, I did not lose sight of the fact that I was plunged in the Precious Blood for the shedding of which I myself was guilty. It was this realization that caused my extreme sorrow, my intense love, and my urge to confess my sins.

When I came to myself I was standing in front of the little chapel of the Feuillant Fathers who had just established themselves at Tours. I was delighted to find my remedy so near at hand, for as I entered I found a priest standing alone in the middle of the chapel as though waiting for me. Urged forward by the Spirit, I accosted him, saying, "Father, I want to go to confession for I have committed such and such faults and sins." With great eagerness and a flood of tears bearing witness to the sorrow I felt in my heart, I started to confess all the sins which had been revealed to me.

There was a woman kneeling before the Blessed Sacrament who could easily have heard all I was saying quite audibly. But I cared about nothing except to appease the one whom I had offended. When I had finished I saw that the priest was astonished at the way I had introduced myself and poured out my sins in this unusual way, so that by my manner he recognized that this was something out of the ordinary. He spoke to me very gently, saying, "Go home now and come back to see me tomorrow in the confessional." I did not even stop to think that he had not given me absolution. I left and returned to him the next day when I repeated everything I had said. He then gave me absolution for my sins.

From that time on I made my confession to him as long as he was in Tours. I had never before confessed to a priest belonging to a religious order. His name was Dom François de Saint-Bernard.[2] Nevertheless, I did not tell him about what had happened to me nor about my inner life, but only recounted my sins, not believing it necessary to speak about anything else to one's confessor. I continued in this way for more than a year whenever I made my confession. Having heard a young woman say that one should ask permission from one's confessor to perform penances and not simply undertake them on one's own, I asked permission. At the beginning I was allowed the use of a hair shirt and discipline; he regulated my confessions and also my Communions, which he permitted on feast days, Sundays, and Thursdays during the first year. However, when I desired to go more often, he permitted me to do so.

Let me return now to what had happened to me. I came home changed into another person—and so powerfully changed that I did not even recognize myself. My ignorance, which had led me to think that I was perfect, that my actions were all innocent, and that I was quite a fine person, was now unmasked and I acknowledged that all my righteousness was, in fact, only sinfulness.

VII.

For over a year, following this action of God in my soul, I was closely united to the blood of Our Lord by a fresh realization of his sufferings. I constantly received new insights which revealed to me the tiniest particle of imperfection, which I was then moved to confess. I experienced a spirit of profound obedience and submission to God and I followed this inclination. It is not that I was scrupulous; in fact, I was deeply at peace. But what was shown to me as sin and imperfection was so clearly delineated that I was fully persuaded. I spoke about this to Our Lord, offering the shedding of his own Precious Blood. My comings and goings, my work, my waking and sleeping were all engaged in this activity. I had no need to reflect on what I should do: the Spirit who led me taught me everything and led me wherever he wished.

I still had some material affairs to attend to for which Our Lord

---

2. Dom François belonged to a group of rigorously reformed Cistercians known as Feuillants. They had been established in Tours since 1620 and would be Marie's spiritual directors for the next twelve years.

gave me the necessary grace. After dismissing the other domestics, I kept only a single servant because I felt called to solitude. I wanted to withdraw from all this bustle. During this period I had no interest in any temporal success—although my relatives urged me to consider it since God had given me an ability for business. They wanted to advance me some money for this purpose, but my heart was filled with very different feelings and my spirit with very different concerns, preferring solitude to all the benefits they suggested to me. I dressed unattractively to convince my acquaintances that my life in the world was finished.[3]

I was at this time only twenty years old and my son less than a year.[4] My father invited me back home where it was easier to be alone. I lived on the top floor of the house, where, while doing some quiet needle work, my spirit was absorbed in its usual activity and my heart spoke constantly to God. I myself was astonished at what my heart said, for it spoke not by its own power but was moved by a superior force which stirred it constantly. I saw clearly that this power sprang from the impression I had received of the Precious Blood and of the sufferings of Our Lord. This was so new to me that I marveled at it. My admiration produced a profound esteem for the goodness and mercy of God who had set aside his greatness, wishing to give himself to me, the least of all creatures, for whom he had so lovingly shed his Precious Blood.

It was utterly incomprehensible to me that my heart was able to speak to him so familiarly and so eloquently. Nevertheless, far from demurring, I let myself follow this attraction which produced in me more and more a hatred of self, a forgetfulness of my own interests and those of my son, and an aversion for the world and all its doings. I was like a turtle dove hidden in its nest in solitude. My regret was not for the loss of worldly goods but only for the time I had wasted, for I realized that the goodness and mercy of God were my portion and that he would take care of me. This made me zealous in his service.

I found my real life in the reception of the sacraments, in attending sermons, in acts of penance, and in my solitude where, through the divine mercy, I experienced the effect of these words: "I have led her

---

3. Dom Claude explains that at this time she was strongly urged to remarry: she was young, she had an infant for whom she must provide, and she could not expect her father to live forever. He concludes, however, "She remained strong in her resolution and in her hope in God." Martin, *Vie,* pp. 33, 39.

4. As was often the custom of the time, the infant Claude had been put with a wet-nurse shortly after his birth, but it is clear that Marie had him with her while living in her father's house.

into solitude and there I will speak to her heart." One must admit that the Spirit of God is a great master. Without my ever having been instructed in prayer and mortification—I did not even know these terms—he taught me everything, letting me experience the one and practice the other.

My sight was mortified; my ears were blocked against worldly conversation. I was silent, able to speak only of God and of virtue—except for necessary business which I dispatched as quickly as possible. I reflected only on this Spirit who so absorbed my soul and on my sins and imperfections. My heart poured forth words of gratitude, of blessing God, of praise of God, of abhorrence of everything that was not he, of loving sorrow, of promises of fidelity to follow whatever the Divine Goodness wished of me, and, finally, of my desire to hide myself in the sacred wounds of Jesus, who, through the effect wrought in me by his Precious Blood, had thrust a dart into my heart which consumed me in loving gratitude. Without any reflection my soul understood the four last things and saw in the shedding of the blood of God the means of arriving at its blessed end. My whole soul yearned to be bathed in it, constantly drawing me closer to this supreme remedy which was my life and my food.

VIII.

After about a year God drew me from my solitude in order that I go to live with my sister. She was overwhelmed with business and she and her husband wanted me to help them with it.[5] At first this seemed such a burden that I could not bear to think about it. Finally, however, I consented, provided that they would guarantee me the freedom needed for my devotions. I made this sacrifice willingly in order to help my sister.

At this time Our Lord who had led me there bestowed on me a fresh gift of prayer: a union with Our Lord Jesus Christ in all his sacred mysteries from his birth to his death. With this gift of prayer I experienced that this divine Savior was truly the Way, the Truth, and the

---

5. Marie's sister Claude was married to Paul Buisson, the owner of a successful carting business. Dom Claude identifies him as the commissioner for the transportation of merchandise throughout the kingdom. The group of men working for him would, according to custom, be part of the extended Buisson household. This explains Madame Buisson's need for help as well as some of the tasks Marie later describes. Martin, *Vie,* pp. 53, 636.

Life. He was the Way my soul constantly desired to follow; he was the Truth which my soul believed with such certainty that I said, "I no longer have faith, O my God, for you show your gifts to me, the truth of what you are, and of what you have revealed to me in a way that tells me everything in an indescribable manner. You are the Life which fills me. Yes, I have 'opened my mouth and you have filled it with your life and with your divine Spirit.' "

This is what I experienced of this blessed Savior who was for me both life and divine nourishment and who made me realize his words: "I am the door; if anyone enters through me he will be saved. He will go in and out the door and will find pasture for his soul." I was united to him who revealed to me the divine mysteries by which I lived, and my soul was satisfied. Filled with this food I went forth to the duties he had assigned me without ever leaving him. Then I returned to him with a redoubling of love which prompted me to seek my food in the pastures of this divine Shepherd who was constantly renewing his life and spirit in me.

During this time I came across some books which taught the practice of mental prayer, beginning with the preparation, the preludes, the divisions of point and subject matter, and the method of meditating, etc.[6] I was able to understand it all quite well, and I determined to follow this method since the books explained that to do otherwise would put one in imminent danger of being tricked by the devil.

I undertook this as my duty and spent many hours meditating and reflecting on the mysteries of the humanity of Our Lord which, had I followed my usual way, I would have seen immediately by an inner glance. But I resisted this attraction, using my imagination instead, reasoning with my understanding, turning over all the circumstances, weighing all the arguments, and determining what one should reap from all this for the practice of virtue. I worked so hard to do this well that the violence I did to myself gave me a headache that injured me considerably and from which I suffered intensely. My insistence in following this book point by point led me to begin each day by strictly disciplining myself, which only intensified my pain. I fell into a kind of

---

6. Marie's description bears all the earmarks of Ignatian prayer (rigorously explained) which was very popular at the time, especially in monasteries where the practice of mental prayer was being renewed after a period of disuse. It is clear that for Marie it ran counter to the spirit of contemplation with which she had been gifted. "Poor woman! Trying to raise herself to contemplation with the wings borrowed from the theologians and foundering miserably." Renaudin, *Marie de l'Incarnation,* p. 53. Not quite accurate; she was already raised to contemplation.

apathy which, along with my headache, I accepted as a means of suffering. Nevertheless, I felt a great inner tranquillity and peace accompanied by the presence of God to whom my will was peacefully linked.

At this period I had a book entitled *Introduction to the Devout Life* which enlightened me on many aspects of the interior life, among others, what one should do to make a vow of chastity—something which Our Lord was urging me to do.[7] I finally spoke about this to my confessor, Dom François, although I still did not speak to him of my prayer since I did not know that one ought to do so. He was a very reticent person, concerned only with the exact subject being discussed. He listened to me concerning this vow and for three months tested me in various ways. Following this, he let me make a vow of perpetual chastity, telling me what to say as well as the intentions I ought to have.

Our Lord gave me great graces through this sacrifice, strengthening me powerfully against the efforts that were being made to involve me in another marriage—a state from which his divine goodness had freed me. I was then twenty-one years old.

At this time Father Raymond de Saint-Bernard was sent to Tours to replace Dom François.[8] The latter put me under Dom Raymond's direction and enjoined me to take him as my director. In fact, it was God who favored me by introducing me to his servant who was a deeply spiritual man and experienced in the direction of souls. He questioned me on my manner of life and wished to know me through and through. He regulated everything for me and in directing my prayer forbade me to meditate any longer, but had me abandon myself entirely to the Spirit of God who until then had been my only director. He required me to give him an account of everything that happened to me, which I did very exactly during the whole time I was under his direction.

---

7. St. Francis de Sales' *Introduction to the Devout Life,* published in 1609, had been written especially to provide a spirituality for lay people. It must have helped Marie in suggesting the difference between a spirituality practiced in the cloister and that practiced in the world, as well as in affirming the necessity for spiritual direction.

8. Dom Raymond de Saint-Bernard is undoubtedly one of the most powerful influences in Marie's life. For the first time she experiences spiritual direction properly so called; Dom François had been content simply to hear her confession. Dom Raymond is a man universally praised as prudent, learned, and experienced. Although his treatment of Marie seems harsh and arrogant, this was an accepted treatment of penitents. Claude calls him "one of the most skillful directors of his day." Martin, *Vie,* p. 331.

IX.

Having found a guide to lead me in the ways of God, I felt deeply comforted. Had Our Lord not sent me this help by means of his servant, I would not have been good for anything. My violent headaches continued for more than two years after Dom Raymond forbade me to meditate, but this suffering was no obstacle to the action of his Divine Majesty. As soon as I knelt before my crucifix my spirit was carried away to him. All I could do was to say: "It is love which has brought you to this state. If you were not love you would never have suffered like this." Then my heart could do nothing but submit to the effects of this love, finding relief in uttering these words: "Ah, no, if you were not love, you would never have done these wonderful things for love of me."

On a similar occasion I found my heart beating so strangely that I was completely powerless. Had it burst open I would have found consolation in death, united to him whom I could conceive and imagine only as love.

Besides all this, my heart was constantly drawn to his goodness so that he would give me his spirit, for I could conceive nothing as being good or beautiful or desirable except possessing the spirit of Jesus Christ.[1] Words are ineffectual, but the desires of the soul speak and conceive great and limitless things concerning the spirit of Jesus. It wants to follow him according to the attraction of this same spirit. It says with the Spouse: "Draw me and we will run in the odor of your perfumes" (Song 2:14). All the powers of the soul yearn and hunger only to be in Jesus, through the spirit of Jesus, following him in his life and his spirit.

Although the soul experiences these ardent desires, nevertheless it remains in a state of profound humility, knowing itself to be most unworthy to possess what it aspires to. It does its best to weaken its lower nature, hoping to destroy its influence altogether. This lower nature permits itself to be guided and subdued so that the spirit of God may lead it where he wishes. The spirit imparts its gifts to the soul

---

1. As Jamet points out, this expression "the spirit of Jesus Christ" is found frequently throughout Marie's writings, "but not always in the same sense." Jamet, II, p. 203, n. 1. The fullest treatment of the use of "spirit" in Marie's writings is found in Robert Michel, *Living in the Spirit with Marie of the Incarnation* (Montreal, 1986). See especially chapter II, which distinguishes between "spirit of Jesus" and "Spirit of Jesus."

through an unction which sweetens all its labors. The soul then hastens in the way of humiliations as though it were pursuing something very precious, so dear to it that it has no other anxiety than the fear that people might notice that it is suffering too much, and thus deprive it of its happiness.

While living in my brother-in-law's house during the next three or four years, I dwelt in an awareness of the humility of the Son of God. The spirit of grace which guided me had me hide all the natural abilities which God had given me for various kinds of business, etc. I was reduced to the state of a poor person who knew nothing and was capable of nothing except to be the servant of the domestics and servants of the house where I performed the most menial and lowly tasks. The goodness of God allowed me to be so treated by people who behaved toward me in the most imperative and astonishing way.[2] I loved these humble tasks so dearly that one time I told my director that I was afraid of being attached to them. He smiled as he listened to me, for he knew very well where this would lead and that my real fear was that he would withdraw me from this humble condition—which he could do very easily through certain channels.

Now that I reflect on this state, I consider it infinitely valuable. It is only the spirit of Jesus Christ which can impart it. The soul is truly hidden "in the clefts of the living rock and in the recesses of this divine dwelling" (Song 2:14) where it is so united to the Spirit that it lives and subsists only in his life. These are its habitual dispositions while in this state.*

---

2. Dom Claude writes that at first she was so successful in hiding her abilities that she was not thought capable of any other tasks. Martin, *Vie,* p. 42. For further details of these years, see fragments from the *Relation of 1633* in Jamet, I, pp. 150–51 and II, p. 483.
   * Marie quotes Scripture from memory; it is frequently an inaccurate rendering of the text, and in some cases cannot be verified.

X.

Immediately after the Divine Majesty had given me the gift of prayer, he gave me the grace of his holy presence. This confirmed and established me in a continual colloquy with Our Lord. Even though I perceived him interiorly as the God-Man, my imagination was not at all involved. Everything occurred in my understanding and will, very spiritually and purely.[1] I sometimes felt that Our Lord Jesus Christ was very close to me, accompanying me, at my side. This divine presence and companionship were so sweet that I cannot describe what it was like. In this state everything which happens in the soul is very spiritual and free from the senses.

God lets the soul understand that he wants to withdraw from it all material support in order to place it in a state of greater detachment and purity than ever. So far it has been supported to some extent by the senses, filled with exuberance, springing from the holy humanity of Our Lord. In fact, while enjoying his presence, it had experienced his sweetness which made it exclaim, "Your name is a spreading perfume; that is why the maidens love you. They have leapt and sighed with joy after tasting your sweetness" (Song 1:2–3).

All the most sensitive faculties of the soul rejoiced at the sweetness of his tender approach. My soul shed floods of tears more precious than all imaginable riches which, had it possessed them, it would have relinquished to buy these gifts. And when it had done so it would have acknowledged that it had paid only a paltry price. As I have said, the soul feels called to the purest things without knowing where it will be led. Inclined toward things which it has never imagined or experienced, it abandons itself, wishing only to follow along the way the Beloved leads.

The soul now becomes increasingly receptive and enters into a new state of enlightenment. God shows it that he is like a great sea, rejecting all lifeless, lax, and impure souls. Just as the real sea cannot bear any impurity in it, neither can the God of infinite purity.[2] This

---

1. Marie's insistence that the imagination plays no part in these graces remains a constant in her spiritual life. Everything is perceived "very spiritually," as she tells us again and again. See p. 49, n. 1.

2. This image of God as a sea of purity becomes a key concept in her spiritual life. There is for Marie a strong correlation between "purity of heart" and "poverty of spirit." See her comments in the Thirteenth State of Prayer, pp. 170–71.

light produces profound effects in the soul. I must acknowledge that when I had done everything possible to confess and to destroy anything impure in me, I was overwhelmed by the inadequacy of the human spirit in its attempt to enter into union and converse with the Divine Majesty. O my God! what impurities there are to purge in order to arrive at that point where the soul, pierced with love, has a fervent and constant desire for its sovereign and single good. This defies imagination, as does the importance of purity of heart in both interior and exterior acts, for the spirit of God is a demanding master. And, in fact, the state I am speaking of is only the first step, for the soul who has achieved this can fall in a single moment. I shudder when I realize this and reflect on how important it is to be faithful.

It is true that the creature can do nothing of itself, but when God calls it to this kind of inner life, he demands absolute consent as well as total abandonment of self to divine providence. This supposes the guidance of a director whose orders must be followed blindly—provided that he is a good person. This is very easy to recognize, for Our Lord himself provides for those souls who have willingly surrendered to his guidance. Dear God! If I were able I would like to shout aloud the importance of this point. It will lead the soul to that true simplicity which forms saints. I have sometimes tried to tell this to the novices so that they will become simple and open. I can envision nothing better to lead or dispose the soul to profound graces and ultimately to put it on the path to God himself.[3]

XI.

This state of prayer which withdraws the support coming from the sacred humanity of Our Lord is at first unsettling until the soul comes to realize and experience what it has gained. The reason for the withdrawal is to enable the soul to advance in the good graces of the Divine Majesty through the virtues bestowed by the spirit of Jesus Christ on all who, with patient humility, work lovingly for their neighbor.

At this time I was about twenty-three years old and thought the best thing that could happen to me was to have some cause for humiliation. I felt a remarkable love for the persons responsible for this,

---

3. Marie, once aware of the importance of spiritual direction, remains zealous throughout her life. This blind obedience to directors and superiors was a strong characteristic of the spirituality of her day. Her allusion to the novices probably refers to those years in Tours when she held the position of assistant mistress of novices.

submitting myself to them with sincere affection. As soon as I had committed some imperfection, I was put in my place interiorly. Once when I was praying I felt a reproach—although a loving one—and these words were spoken to me: Would you be happy if you had a pearl or precious stone and someone spattered it with mud? These words made me sink in confusion before the God I conceived of only as purity. They produced a great hatred of self so that I considered myself more worthy than anyone to be scorned and cast aside. As often as my soul approached God and saw the disproportion between the creature and his infinite purity, my self-hatred and humility increased and induced me to perform acts increasingly humiliating to nature.

My soul was constantly impelled toward God in a purely spiritual way. I longed for him in a way hitherto utterly unknown to me. I found him in all creatures and in the purpose for which he created them. Yet all this was completely spiritual, for my contemplation was so purified that these creatures could not distract me from God. I was given infused knowledge concerning their nature and sometimes I spoke of this with great simplicity, unaware that this was in any way unusual. In speaking to his Divine Majesty with this passage in mind, "O God, you have made all things and by your will they have been created" (Rv 4:11), my soul discerned more than all these words express and it broke forth in praise and thanksgiving. Although it recognized that it was the lowliest and most worthless creature at the feet of this supreme majesty, nevertheless it longed to possess him by a title as yet unknown to the soul but of which it had an intuition.

I was shown that there were still some dispositions I did not yet possess—adornments required for the possession of so exalted and sublime a state. I would have walked through fire to reach what I aspired to, willing to work night and day, undertaking any labor to acquire what I lacked. I saw, however, that I could only reach this goal through the sheer goodness and greatness of God.

I did everything possible to win his heart and he on his part gave me a new spirit of penance which demanded that I treat my body like a slave. I burdened it with hair shirts and chains; I had it sleep on wooden planks, spending part of the night using a discipline until it drew blood. I put wormwood in my food, fearing to enjoy the taste of what I ate. I allowed myself only as much sleep as would keep me alive because I wanted to go on suffering. Along with these penances, as well as the domestic work of the house and the labor involved in the business, I also dressed the most foul-smelling wounds of the sick, making myself come close so that I would smell the odor. I forced myself to go where there were infected corpses in order to fully endure the stench. Not satisfied with all this, I begged a person in whom I confided to strike me roughly. I gave myself no quarter but constantly invented new means of suffering.[4]

If I were engaged in some recreation, the Spirit demanded that I leave to go to take the discipline or to ask for some new penance from my director. Or he would demand that I withdraw into solitude to engage more freely with God. He even had me leave the table for this purpose. My poor body allowed itself to be guided like someone dead, suffering everything without a word because the Spirit had conquered and vanquished it.

Yet this is not all. The Spirit made me see afresh the inner purity needed so that I went once more to my director to confess all the sins and imperfections of my life. After giving them to him in writing, I asked that he post them on the door of the church, with my name, so that everyone could see how unfaithful I had been to God. I had to obey this inspiration, for my extreme sorrow came from the love of God. My director, seeing such a flood of tears, was moved to agree and let me do this. In this state the soul suffers from a wound which causes it to sigh constantly after its Divine Object who has given it a taste of his great purity; thus the least atom of imperfection seems to it like a mountain, depriving it of the enjoyment of this sovereign good.

Concerning this matter, my director sent me away quite severely several times, but finally he saw that my tears came from a source other than nature. He listened to me and took my paper which I earnestly begged him to put on the door of the church. He took it without a word but I believe he burned it, for I never saw it on the door as I had requested. When I obeyed the Spirit thus, he gave himself over lavishly with new favors for me. May he be eternally blessed for having had such love for my weakness.

XII.

While I was in this state of self-sacrifice, of which I have spoken, I was often fearful that my director—who was also the director

---

4. This period of extraordinary penance is relatively short. As a religious, Marie's penances will be determined by the common rule. She says very little about them here; the *Relation of 1633*, written much closer to the period involved, provides graphic and horrifying details. Jamet, I, pp. 172–74.

of my brother[-in-law] and my sister—would decide to withdraw me from this way. I don't know if this is what actually happened, but I saw that they intended to employ me in their very strenuous business.[5] This actually happened, compelling me to deal with many outside persons and undertake great responsibilities. Yet all this never deprived me of my means of practicing charity. On the contrary, I had even more opportunities, for Our Lord gave me an increase of grace and strength for everything he wished of me. My penances continued, while the Spirit urged me to increase them and I had substantial opportunities for practicing patience. Yet all this was sweet to me in the sight of him who gave me such easy access to his Divine Majesty.

As I have said, I dearly loved those who gave me an opportunity to suffer. I looked upon them as persons chosen by God to provide me with the great benefits which I feared to lose because of my sins. Furthermore, I saw myself as an absolute nothing, deserving every sort of scorn. Whenever I had feelings contrary to this, I was deeply ashamed and punished myself rigorously. I was amazed that Our Lord gave me so many graces and anticipated my desires so lovingly, letting me dare to aspire to be his spouse, to be consumed in his divine embrace, and to speak to him with great familiarity, saying, "Ah, my love, when will this marriage be accomplished?" He delighted my spirit and thrilled my heart, wanting to grant my request but finding some finishing touches still wanting. My soul was dejected because of this even though I remained united to the will of him who, despite all my sighing, still did not grant my request.

I did everything I could to win his heart, for only this could satisfy my ardent yearning. I tried in many ways to please him whom I wished to possess. While in this mood, I suddenly remembered the first verse of the psalm: "Unless the Lord build the house, they labor in vain who build it" (Ps 127:1), and my mind was enlightened to see the nothingness and powerlessness of the creature to lift itself to God or to advance in his good graces. Finally, I realized how useless are all the efforts to possess him if he himself does not build the house and provide the appropriate adornments for so exalted a plan. This noth-

---

5. Dom Oury suggests that the occasion for this was the birth of a son to the Buissons. Madame Buisson could no longer give her time to her husband's business, and since he was unable to write, he needed someone skillful in business to be his assistant. Oury, *Marie,* I, p. 93.

ingness of the creature appeared so terrifying and so inescapable to me that I would not plumb its depths.[6]

All this brought me to a state of abnegation and such profound humility that I expected nothing from self and awaited everything from God. I was sure that I possessed him in that intimate union for which he had given me such a powerful attraction. I was submissive to all the orders of his Divine Majesty but, like the Spouse of the Canticle, my soul sighed for the kiss of his mouth.

It is impossible to say how agonizing this love is and yet the soul has no desire to free itself, except to possess him whom she loves. It seems to it that it has spiritual arms which are constantly extended to embrace him. It speaks as though it already possessed him totally, saying, "My Beloved is mine and I, I am all his" (Song 2:16). He is my only good, he is my true self, he is my all and my life. It is ceaselessly in this state. All its sighing, all its attention, even its life are constantly in this state of predilection for its well-beloved. It is in the humblest actions that it embraces him most closely. I cannot explain to what the Beloved reduces the soul in order to make it pursue him all the more. He secures it by double chains. He holds it captive under his own loving laws and despoils it completely in order to make it follow him.

It considers its own life as nothing in order to possess its Well-Beloved in the way he attracts it, for it cannot be satisfied with less. "No," it says. "No, my most chaste Love. I don't want only a portion. I want the whole of you. If it is my life that keeps you from coming to me, then take it away, for it is harmful if it hinders me from possessing you. You are so good and so powerful in your love and yet you take pleasure in my pain. You can deliver me by death. Alas! Why don't you do this? You can have me die from one of my sighs and then you can draw my spirit into your own since you so delay in coming to me. Yet you are everywhere and I know that you are in me. Alas! Why do you take pleasure in my suffering? What can I do to please you? Only command and your words will work wonders in me, wonders that will please you and make you more responsive."

---

6. "Nothingness of the creature" is a very Bérullian theme. Henri Daniel-Rops, in commenting on the essentials of Bérullian spirituality, writes: "Man is composed of two very different elements. On one hand he is a miracle; on the other, pure nothing. . . . He is an angel, he is an animal. . . . He is a god, he is a pure nothing surrounded by God; he is destitute of God yet capable of God and filled with God if he so wishes." For Marie this is a theme of increasing importance. In time it loses its terror and she comes to rejoice in her "nothingness" since this is how she will acknowledge the All-ness of God. Daniel-Rops, *Mystiques de France* (Paris, 1958), p. 137.

I experienced this in the streets, in the bustle of business, in conversation with numerous people, with as much application and attention of spirit as if it happened in an oratory because the soul is passively borne away by an attraction which in its depths brings profound peace. Yet in another respect divine love keeps it in agony, an agony which it feels keenly but cannot express.

XIII.

I haven't mentioned previously that as soon as my bonds were broken and I began to taste the good things of the spirit and to recognize the vanity of worldly things, I felt myself called to religious life. There was, however, one remaining hindrance which, in my director's judgment, was also God's will for me, although he believed that the Divine Majesty would give me this grace in his own good time. Thus I bore this inevitable burden in conformity to God's commands, keeping my heart in a cloister while my body remained in the world.[1]

In God's overwhelming love for my lowliness (which seemed to be satisfied only by showering me with new mercies), he let me see and experience—according to my burning desire to possess the spirit of Jesus Christ—the great and infinite riches hidden in the evangelical counsels to which he called chosen souls, especially those of poverty, chastity, and obedience. These I saw to be the preeminent virtues that Our Lord Jesus Christ had chosen and practiced during his mortal life in order to give us an example, thus making himself our divine exemplary cause as he would become our meritorious cause.

In this poverty of spirit I came to understand things so exalted and divine that all the kingdoms of the earth and everything material, everything conceived by the human spirit seemed to be only refuse and worthlessness—the very nothingness of things. I was so captivated and charmed by this that if it had been something that could be bought with my life—even if I had had a million lives, I would have given them all to possess it. I realized, however, that the price is not of this world but something divine which only the Eternal Father can bestow, according to the words of Our Lord: "No one can come to me unless the Father draw him" (Jn 6:44). For this call is nothing other than the communication of Jesus Christ. Oh, my God! Here all words and thoughts must come to a stop, for there is nothing that can be said or thought about what was revealed to me concerning this glorious and wonderful poverty of spirit as well as of the two other virtues which follow, for these are so linked that they cannot be separated.

---

1. The "one remaining hindrance" was, of course, her son. Marie's language is unfortunate here, as it was in the death of her husband. Her account of what it cost her to leave her son and her affectionate letters from Canada are strong indications of her very deep love. Later she will tell us that she refrained from affectionate gestures so that Claude would feel less deprived when it was time for her to leave him. Martin, *Vie,* p. 36.

Although these preeminent virtues refer to religious vows and are, in fact, essential to them, nevertheless, at closer look there are other virtues that make us realize that the vows are only the first step with regard to the spirit of these virtues. This spirit, as I have already said, is none other than the spirit of Jesus Christ. For as this divine Savior is the head of the Church and all the faithful are under his rule, because the Eternal Father has given them all to him, so there are in this kingdom certain chosen souls: these are religious. And among these there are many dwelling places which constitute the most noble part of his spiritual kingdom. These belong to those souls to whom this divine leader pours his life and his spirit in abundance—to some more, to some less, according to his divine choice and pleasure. Ah! "He will have mercy on those whom he wishes, as he is the absolute master of his gifts" (Rom 9:15). It is, then, to these souls that he communicates this living spirit in the wake of the gifts, communications, and impressions that he bestows on them in order to bring them at last to this true poverty of spirit which can only be the work of his all-powerful hand. If it pleases our divine Benefactor to give me the grace to accomplish what has been asked of me, what follows will show what occurs between God and the soul in order to lead it to this true poverty of spirit—at once so solid and so spiritual.

Yet even though all these lights diffused themselves in my soul, I did not see how I could arrive at the possession of the immense riches hidden in these virtues—virtues to which I was drawn as if they were the royal couch of the Spouse whose embrace my soul was longing for continually. I wished, nevertheless, to do what I could to win his heart and his love.

Then, having already made a vow of chastity, I felt strongly inspired to make those of obedience and poverty, according to what my present state would permit. My director, having carefully examined me, permitted me to do so. Yet everything else depended on God, for his creature is too stupid to take a single step by herself in such an important matter. What she can do is to consent, obey, and abandon herself, submitting to everything his Divine Majesty wishes of her. Despite the fact that he is the absolute master, having created the soul, he is so wonderfully good that he treats it nobly, never withdrawing its free will. But the soul, completely overcome, gives him everything because when it sees him so gracious in its regard, it wants nothing but to be entirely despoiled so that he may have everything and the soul nothing.

My vow was related to my director and to those he appointed in his place—that is, to my brother[-in-law] and to my sister whom I obeyed as though they were my superiors, or as a child would obey its father and mother.[2] God knows what there was to suffer in this, but in his goodness he treated me very gently. As for poverty, I had nothing for my use except what my sister gave me, but she was so kind and charitable that she gave me more than I wished.

Everything concerning my son was in the hands of Providence who lovingly impelled me to deal with him thus. Since I found infinite riches in poverty of spirit, I could ask my divine Spouse for nothing else but this invaluable treasure for my son. Thus I did nothing for myself or for him because I wanted us to share the same treasure. I persisted in asking for this constantly as something meriting such petition until one is granted the joy of possession.

XIV.

Following this sacrifice, Our Lord seemed happy to continue his sweet intimacy, but there was a dull suffering in this love. Although in this condition the soul dwells in God and speaks with him, because his spirit stirs up a loving movement which enables it to speak a language beyond the natural ability of the creature, yet it doesn't possess the treasures it hopes for from the enjoyment of the celestial Spouse who seems to take pleasure in having it die and die again.

The greatest comfort it can find is in daily Communion, where it is certain she possesses his life. Not only does its faith tell it so but it also experiences that this is he through a bonding and union of love which brings it an inexplicable joy. Even though everyone in the world would have said that the host does not contain the adorable Word Incarnate, it would have died to prove that it is he.

After all the labors that I undertook for my neighbor, my body, broken by my penances, regained its strength through eating this divine bread and gathered new courage to begin all over again—something I could not naturally have accomplished. Although I rejoiced in

---

2. "By this vow of obedience everything became easier for me than before." Jamet, I, p. 164. Such vows of obedience to a director were not unusual; what makes Marie's vow unique is that she was also vowed to obey her sister and brother-in-law, although they had no knowledge of her vow. Jamet remarks, "she became the slave of their caprices" (I, p. 164, n. 4). Dom Claude comments: "Her brother and sister who knew nothing of her vow were amazed to see her more obedient and submissive to their orders than the last servant in the house; and because she was always smiling and ready to obey, they believed that this submission was the result of her natural love and affection." Martin, *Vie,* p. 491.

this Holy Communion with my Beloved, with the certitude of faith and realization, yet nevertheless as soon as the sacred species was consumed, my soul returned to its desire to possess him without interruption, which filled me with a strong desire to die. "Tell me, you whom my soul loves, where you pasture your flock, where you make it lie down at noon" (Song 1:7). Lead me into your gardens and into your solitude where nothing will hinder our embraces. Although I knew he was in me, it seemed that he fled from me and dwelt in inaccessible light where even the seraphim could not reach him.

I sometimes felt myself abandoned. When in the chill of winter, during the darkness of the night, I wanted to chastise my body—which I always deprived of bed coverings—I could hardly move my arm. Then I would say to this divine lover, "My Beloved, put your own power into my arm so that I will have the strength to chastise this wretched body." Then he gave me such strength that I lacerated my body. Immediately I would put on a hair shirt, so that the knots and thorns would be as painful as possible. Only then would I throw myself on my bed for a few hours. I understood clearly that I was following his direction, and his spirit would not permit me to do otherwise. If I didn't obey, he would reprimand me sharply; or if I fell into some imperfection, he would humiliate me roundly to punish me; and thus, through my own weakness, I learned to my cost the nothingness of the creature.

XV.

Our Lord let me undergo all sorts of temptations. The devil conjured up a whole troup of foolish thoughts for me. Concerning my body, he made me feel that I was very silly to make it suffer so much, reminding me that there were many people who were Christians who kept the commandments and who would be saved without so much suffering. And further, what good was there in submission to a director? That this was much too harsh and that there was nothing wrong in following one's own will. At one point this attack was so severe that when I was with a young woman I involuntarily let some words slip: "What use is all this! I can't be subject to this sort of thing any longer!" But I was so ashamed after I said this that it was a very good penance for me.

In addition, my imagination was filled with my son—and this stirred up terrible trouble in me. I felt that I was bound in conscience, that God would hold me to account for the fact that I lived as if neither my son nor I had need of anything for the future. I was in anguish on that point, for I loved my son dearly and I had thought that I wished for him true wealth, obtaining for him and for myself poverty in the sight of God, and that I had acted with this end in view. I went to my director to determine if, in fact, I was bound in conscience. He assured me on that point but this did not alleviate my temptation. I was also tempted to think that it had been very simple-minded to bind myself in this way so that I was no more than a servant. In a word, I was in turmoil, even more because God let many people speak to me in this same vein, which made me suffer very deeply.

I had no inner comfort, for all the powers of my soul were as though numbed and I lacked the strength and vitality to pull myself out of this; and, as I have already said, my senses suffered from a great restlessness.[3] It seemed that my imagination was like an eloquent lawyer stirring up everything. Among other things, I thought I was a hypocrite and that all along right up to the present I had fooled my director, telling him tales and fantasies instead of the truth. My reason was affected but it was not so deeply troubled that it did not realize that I had always believed that I was searching for God and that, even in the worst of my temptations, I had never omitted any of my penances. Despite all this I was shaken with fear and told myself that I was deluded. In this affliction I abandoned myself to God and did not deviate from my regular pace.

It is true that at this point the powers of the soul are seized and bound so that they are immobilized and powerless to help either themselves or the inferior part of the soul which is left to undergo this temptation. The pain of this is intense, and the soul realizes that of itself it would not be able even to resist this temptation. I acknowledged completely that if the word of God were not in me I would be weakness itself. "I am with those who are in tribulation" (Ps 91:15). Not that this help is in any way felt, but it is the in-pouring of a secret strength which helps in bearing the weight of this temptation and makes one invincible. I remember that at this point the physical condition to which I was reduced by my mortifications was a heavy bur-

---

3. This is the first of the periods of terrible trials in her life: worn out by penances, by the vow that bound her in such an extraordinary way, by work that demanded an attention that tested all her powers, her concern about the manner in which she was bringing up her child, her continued longing for religious life and, worst of all, a feeling that she had deceived others, having herself been deceived. It's easy to believe her when she says, "My reason was affected." This foreshadows the trials she will undergo in religious life—but even more importantly, it leads her further into that poverty of spirit which acknowledges that God alone is savior.

den. It seemed to me that I was like those poor ragged beggars who go trembling from door to door. All this made me realize that "we cannot do anything of ourselves as of ourselves; for all our strength comes from God, the Father of mercies" (2 Cor 3:5).

Thus while still living in the world, I have undergone various trials like these from which God in his goodness suddenly and lovingly rescued me, making me realize that it is he who "lifts up the poor from the dung-heap and makes them sit with princes and inherit a seat of honor" (1 Sm 2:8).

XVI.

I was about twenty-five years old when I went through the trial I have just described, as well as others resulting from my neighbor. After this Our Lord increased the wonders of his mercies toward me, making me realize that the condition he had permitted me to suffer was only to purify my soul so that it would be fashioned as a vessel of his graces. Since he was a God of infinite purity I must endure fire in order to be admitted to his embrace.

Then my soul, seized by a power that rendered it utterly passive, spoke to God in such great intimacy that nothing in the world could stop it. There follow tender complaints, inexpressible moanings. It seemed that each fresh recurrence would devastate the soul. It yearns to cherish the Well-Beloved of the Father; yet, when it thinks it is about to possess him and be lost in his bosom, a powerful light from his majesty conceals him. He, as it were, says to the soul, "Turn your eyes from me, for they disturb me" (Song 6:4).

It is the alternation of possession and negation that evokes this anguish, but its purpose is only to goad the soul on. In these withdrawals the soul suffers once again from apathy. If I could have cried aloud this would have relieved me. The heart seems to swell enormously, filled with a fire that might erupt at any moment. This fire comes from those ardent affections which cannot be described. I hid myself in an out-of-the-way place, prostrating myself so as to stifle my sobs; and at the same time, by my abasement before the Divine Majesty to win over him for whom my soul yearned. Neither my love nor my familiarity ever diminished my sense of reverence, for one of these feelings did not exclude the other.

I found no consolation except in works of charity. It was these that enabled me to live, cherishing and seeking occasions of them when they were not available to me, as well as intensifying my penances and mortifications. I also instructed the servants, questioning them about their faults so that they would be able to confess them. I was able to guide them where I wished. I spoke to them only about what concerned them, for only to my director did I mention what was happening to me. This was fortunate, for, had I spoken according to what I felt interiorly, it might have caused me some injury, for my senses were not capable of sustaining this. In addition, bodily mortification helped me, although this was not the reason why I performed them but rather to chastise my body—since I was a great sinner I had a deadly hatred of it—and also to honor the sufferings of the adorable Word Incarnate whose heart I wanted to win to compensate for his having captured mine.

In addition, one time I felt that my heart was taken away and enclosed in another heart so that although there were still two hearts, they were so closely fitted together that they were like one. Then an inner voice said to me: "It is thus that a union of hearts is accomplished." I don't know if I was asleep or awake; but when I came to myself my heart was, for many days, in such a state of union with Our Lord that humanly speaking, without extraordinary help, I would have fainted at every moment because this divine pleasure flowed through my soul in a way that was impossible for my body to sustain.[4] Although this divine goodness accommodated itself when I was in conversation with my neighbor, nevertheless there were certain times of such extraordinary favor that I needed very special help.

XVII.

Although I have said that Our Lord made my interior state compatible with my external life, just the same I suffered very much in the world, for I saw it as completely contrary to the spirit of Jesus Christ. My spirit, which saw nothing as lovely or lovable except the blessed and divine precepts of the Son of God, could not understand how they were not followed by those who called themselves good Christians. This made me suffer a real martyrdom. Once during Lent as I was enduring these feelings, Our Lord with infinite kindness revealed to me what he had done for everyone and to what state his love had reduced him. He revealed the sacred mystery of his Incarnation in a

---

4. This same grace is explained in the *Relation of 1633* in almost identical terms. Jamet, I, p. 191. It is further elaborated on in the "Supplément," II, p. 485.

way I had never understood, but since then I have read something akin to this. Although what I read doesn't approach the effect made by God's visitation, nevertheless it is comforting to see that what one is experiencing is linked to and conformable with the faith of the Church.

This constant awareness gave me a new love for religious life where, beyond the obstacles of the world, the counsels of the Son of God were observed. This made me sigh after them, and the bonds which kept me in the world were very painful. Yet I felt that Our Lord wished me to be attached in this way, and he sweetened my suffering by the remembrance of his words: "My yoke is sweet and my burden light" (Mt 11:30). Then he poured the effect of these words into my soul so that my pain was alleviated.

Thus I ran in his ways; even among the coarsest and most material things which absorbed the body, my spirit was bound to the adorable Word Incarnate.

If the clock struck, I had to count it on my fingers because this interval of counting, although necessary, interrupted my loving conversation with my Beloved. If I had to speak with my neighbor, my gaze never left him whom I loved. And when my neighbor answered me, my conversation recommenced and my attention to what was necessary never took me away from him. It's the same with writing where one's attention is twofold: it is on the divine object and also on the matter in question. The time I have to dip my pen in ink is precious, for then the spirit and the heart make their colloquy. Even if the whole world were present, nothing could distract me.[5]

It is true that as peace wells up in the heart, and since the object one is linked to is itself very enjoyable, one's appearance seems joyful and one's conversation pleasant. The world calls this good humor because it judges it only humanly and doesn't understand that it is the infinite Good which has captured the soul that is responsible for this kind of appearance. I have noticed that the sufferings and austerities consequent upon my penances have never made me morose or sad but have united me to God in so gentle a way that it has led me to treat my neighbor with great kindness. It was the same when I had to correct one of the servants.

One time a person deeply insulted me during a business matter that I had to discuss with someone of importance. This seemed to be

---

5. A clear statement of the relation between her contemplation and action and a foreshadowing of her future active/contemplative vocation.

done in order to discredit me, although perhaps this had not been his intention; he may simply have acted through imprudence. Nevertheless, this made a great impression on the person with whom I was dealing so that I had to choke down my embarrassment in the face of several people. I bore no grudge against this poor man nor did I ever say a word about it. Our Lord gave me the grace to endure this little insult for love of him, along with many others on various occasions. But, alas, this has not kept me from committing serious imperfections which could be the reason why I have not made haste despite all the opportunities I have had to suffer. I very humbly ask pardon of my Divine Spouse for all my lack of correspondence with his constant grace and favors.

The Divine Majesty in his desire to give me extraordinary favors pursued me constantly with his graces and lights, leading me to a state of humiliation and self-abasement and thus disposing me for an unusual purity.

One morning, the Monday after Pentecost, while I was hearing Mass in the chapel of the Feuillant Fathers where I usually went for my devotions and where Our Lord had given me exceptional graces, as my eyes were fixed on the altar, gazing without any particular attention on the little images of the seraphim attached to the base of the candles, my eyes suddenly closed and my spirit was raised and absorbed into a vision of the Most Holy and August Trinity, in a way I cannot express.[1]

At that moment all the powers of my soul were arrested, receiving the imprint of this sacred mystery. This imprint was without form or figure, yet clearer and more intelligible than light itself which assured me that my soul was in truth. In a moment I saw the divine interchange among the three divine Persons: the love of the Father who in contemplating himself begets his Son in an eternal generation. My soul was penetrated by this truth in a manner so ineffable that I was made speechless, engulfed in light. Then I understood the mutual love of Father and Son which generates the Holy Spirit by a reciprocal immersion of love, yet without any confusion of persons. I received this revelation and understood the meaning of both spiration and generation; but the whole exchange is so sublime that I have no words to express it. Even as I saw the distinctions of person, I understood the unity existing among the three divine Persons. Although a description of this would require many words, in a flash I understood the unity, the distinctions, and the operations both within the divine Persons and those which culminate outside of them. Little by little I was enlightened in a very spiritual way concerning those acts of the divine Persons

---

1. This vision, the first of Marie's three "visions" of the Trinity, took place in May 1625, when Marie was already engaged in Paul Buisson's business. She has left two full accounts of it: the *Relation of 1654* and a letter to her son, written in the fall of 1671 (Oury, *Correspondance,* pp. 928–32). A fragment, adding a few details, appears in the "Supplément," Jamet, II, p. 486. Undoubtedly she included an account of this extraordinary grace in the *Relation of 1633;* unhappily, Dom Claude did not include this in his biography.

which lead beyond themselves. I found no confusion in any of the knowledge I received, for everything was shown to me in a very clear light.

During that same impression, the Most Holy Trinity taught me how it acts through the supreme hierarchy of angels, cherubim, seraphim, and thrones to whom it makes its holy will known without the intermediary of any created spirit. I learned clearly the operations of each of the divine Persons of the most august Trinity in each of the choirs of this supreme hierarchy: that the Eternal Father dwelt among the thrones, which signified to me the purity and stability of his eternal thoughts; that the Word, through the splendor of his lights, communicates himself to the cherubim; and that the Holy Spirit dwells among the seraphim, filling them with his ardent love. And, finally, that the entire Trinity, in the unity of its divine essence, communicates itself to this supreme hierarchy which makes the divine will known to the other heavenly spirits according to their rank.

My soul was completely lost in these splendors, and it seemed that the Divine Majesty wished to enlighten it more and more on those matters which creatures are too dull-witted to express. Once again I was shown that the Divinity had designated a gradation among the angels so that by degrees they would be enlightened by each other; but that he himself could enlighten them whenever he wished. I also understood that this is how he acted with some chosen souls in the world, and although I knew that I was only dust and mire, yet I felt certain that I was among this number. As I was enlightened, I understood and experienced how I was created in the image of God: that the memory is related to the Eternal Father, the understanding to the Son, and the will to the Holy Spirit; and that just as the Holy Trinity is three in person but one in divine essence, just so the soul is three according to its faculties but one in substance.

This vision lasted for the duration of several Masses. When I came to myself I was kneeling in the same posture as when it began.

XIX.

This great light led me into an entirely new state. For a long time I was unable to turn from my absorption in the three divine Persons. Then a great fear came over me that I was being deceived, that this was some snare of the devil or of the imagination—although the imagination had had nothing to do with it—in order to divert and retard me in the spiritual life and in the practice of virtue. Although Father Dom

Raymond reassured me, nevertheless I still remained fearful until one time while I was at prayer, skeptical and anxious about this matter, an inner voice said to me: "Stay as you are; this is your resting place." This word brought peace and confidence to my heart and I was immediately reassured. Thus I lived in this divine mystery as in a place where I found both rest and nourishment.

I was so deeply absorbed in my thoughts that not even business transactions with the neighbor could distract me. One time when I was with some Huguenots in a store, transacting some business with them, I felt in the depths of my soul a kind of heaven, experiencing a movement which bound me to this divine mystery. All this was still the effect of that most important visitation.

It must be noted that these movements and lights which come from God by a powerful impression are, as I have said before, not like the things one reads in books or which come from human instruction; for, naturally speaking, these are soon forgotten. But these others make such an impression on the soul that they are always remembered and one becomes rooted in them. After these lights, when one reads or hears the mysteries of faith spoken of, one recognizes that one has understood all this, that it is true, and that one would be ready to die for these truths. This is a great consolation to the soul who feared being deluded, for now it sees that everything that has happened to it falls within the faith of the Church. It experiences profound peace and great happiness to be the daughter of the Church.

It is also true that these lights from God (here I make a distinction between what is purely light, what is light and love intermingled, and what is purely love—an attraction for God which enraptures the soul in a single stroke)—that these lights succeed so well in their revelation to the soul that it is now freed from doubt and even from curiosity to know more. It is filled with a sense of reverence which gently prevents it from going further. Or to put it better: it is satisfied. Although it sees the truth of these words of Scripture: "He who searches into the majesty of God will be overwhelmed by his glory" (Prv 25:2) this is not what stops it. Rather, in its fulfillment it cannot wish for anything more nor indulge in mere curiosity.

As for those graces which are a combination of light and love, with love always in first place, one doesn't think in terms of seeing but rather of always loving more and of being rooted in him whom she loves. What I have referred to as "purely love" occurs when God at a single stroke possesses the soul, engaging it in an intimate exchange. In this state the soul's only desire is to enjoy. It is enough for it to know that he is in it and with it and that he is God. It is happy, yet not completely satisfied, for as he is infinite goodness and an abyss of love whose depths it cannot plumb, it longs to be absorbed into this abyss and thus to be so lost that it will no longer see anything but its Beloved who through love transforms the soul into himself. If formerly she had asked him "where he reposes and where he takes his rest at noon" (Song 1:6), now, in this allurement of love the soul understands that he is in the bosom of the Eternal Father where he rests in the mutual love from Father to Son and from Son to Father and that their delight—this very breath of love—is God the Holy Spirit.

It has no desire to know anything more but rather, as I have said, to be lost in the Beloved and in losing itself to possess him completely. The soul sings to him: "Who will help me find you, my Beloved, so that I will kiss you and embrace you at leisure and give you the juice of my pomegranates to eat?" (Song 8:1–2). It wishes to find him beyond all the aspects of his majesty which make him so formidable and thus she says, "Flee, my Beloved, go among the spices." Go among the cherubim, to those who alone can bear your light. Then come, O my Love, that I may overflow within you, by an exchange of love—so far as my lowliness permits and your love allows. "This is why I have longed to see you, my little brother, who sucked at my mother's breasts," O adorable Word Incarnate, "may I embrace you at my leisure and may no one be scandalized," for you have made yourself as you are for this purpose and this is why I long for you (Song 8:14, 1). Thus, the soul is not prompted by curiosity to see but is insatiable in its desire to love.

In some cases light produces love but in the case of pure love it is love that produces light. The soul is passive, realizing that it is God who enables it to experience this love. It is not that the other two states are not passive but that of pure love is the very best. Still the spiritual marriage is not consummated. Although in a certain way the soul is in God, yet it still sighs and yearns. Although it is already in the wine cellar, wholly filled with love, yet there still remain some necessary preparations for the marriage. For its part, the soul does everything it can, so far as its weakness permits. This is such an exalted and sublime matter that the Beloved leads the soul by secret paths and hidden places so that when it comes to the full possession of its happiness, it will confess that everything has been the work of the Beloved.

I did not intend to write all this but the Spirit led me to do so. May he be eternally blessed.

XX.

I have already described the great anguish the soul experiences on account of its yearning for this [spiritual] marriage to which it feels drawn. Reverence for the Divine Majesty, perceived in former visions, blends with love. This love has now blossomed into intimacy and, as I have mentioned before, the Beloved guides the soul in such secret and hidden ways that they are barely perceptible.

These are those interior caresses and divine movements—so subtle, so intense, and so removed from the soul's awareness that it seems that it is separated from its Beloved. Nevertheless, he is near. The soul yearns for the Spouse. It beckons to him, saying, "Come, my Beloved, come into the garden." Then it realizes he is close to it; and it hears his voice which is a secret sign that makes it thrill with joy, saying with a surge of love: "I hear the voice of my Beloved. See how he looks. He is behind the wall. He looks at me through the trellis" (Song 2:9). This is the meaning: the wall and the trellis are the great distance between God in his greatness and the soul in its lowliness. Yet in spite of this, he is so filled with love that he wants to draw near. The soul, on the other hand, feels itself drawn by this outpouring of love. Aware of its nothingness, yet unable to resist, it yields to these impulses and follows its yearnings.

I must confess that I only stammer when I speak of what happens between God and the soul in this exchange in which he honors it, uniting it to himself—the Infinite Majesty. I have never read or heard anything similar concerning these states, which leads me to think that those who have written of the interior life, from their own experience or otherwise, have preferred not to speak of them, either out of reverence for God or because it is beyond human ability to do so. Or better still: although able to speak, they prefer not to, fearing that those who are not led in these ways might be scandalized. However, since I have been ordered to write I am setting down on paper whatever the Spirit of grace leads or compels me to write.

I will say, then, that these caresses—at once delicate yet painful —are a purification of the most profound part of the soul to make it worthy to be the royal couch of the Spouse. I have found myself fainting at the sight of the splendor of his majesty which is so incompatible with the soul. It finds itself lost in this ocean, then returns to itself, then once again is lost; and this continues for a long time. You must not think there is anything imaginary in this, for the imagination has nothing to do with it. The powers of the soul are held in unity— motionless and silent. All is passive in order to receive the imprint of the Divine Majesty who wishes to make this innermost part of the soul the object of his pleasure as well as of his mercy. The soul thus becomes more pleasing in proportion to its purification, and its daring increases in accordance with its lights which engender love.

XXI.

Following this state, the Divine Majesty effected in my soul a sense of his divine perfections which included love as well as light—although in this state it seemed that love gave rise to light. When my soul contemplated God as life, it could only sigh, "O Life, O Love!" Thus, in its profound love of this divine source of life, it longs for its own life to be entirely absorbed. It believes and understands those sublime truths found in the first chapter of St. John's Gospel which speak of the Word as light as well as life; and of the abundance and fullness of this divine life, the Word of the Father, who has made us sharers in his abundance. It sees also the infinite happiness of souls that are born of God and not of the flesh or of blood. These distinctions are full of an inexplicable extravagance of love emanating from the Word in his role as head of all Christians and especially of holy souls.

This emanation derives from the fact that his Father has not measured out his grace to him but, insofar as he is our head, pours forth grace into holy souls just as the ointment of Aaron ran down from his head onto the hem of his garments. What can be said of the outpouring from this adorable Head—I mean this communication as I have experienced it? No human language can express it.

From what I have said it is easy to see that these impressions are not simply speculative but are a matter of divine nourishment. If the impression is of the being of God, then the spirit can say only, "O Being!" Then the soul adores, filled with a very great reverence and esteem for the sublimity of this divine attribute. If the impression is of purity and holiness, it can say only, "O Purity, O Clarity, O Bottomless Abyss!" The soul loves this great God who is an abyss of perfection.

I think I spent almost a year in the effects of these divine attributes with such clarity and simplicity that all the distinctions were yoked together although remaining distinct. When the knowledge of the Most Holy Trinity was given me, although I understood the distinctions and the unity, yet my soul was merely instructed; however, in the matter of the divine attributes, as I have already said, love and light became a divine food. Otherwise it would have been impossible to sustain this experience without dying because of the grandeur of his majesty which, in some way, love made approachable.

None of this kept me from carrying on the ordinary business affairs which were entrusted to me or from performing those acts of charity which in a way sustained my natural life. For as I was never distracted from what was happening interiorly, these acts of charity served as a diversion. They enabled me to endure the fatigue with which I was burdened by my spiritual life because of my austerities and penances, as well as all the rest.

I have said that I spent close to a year in the experience of these divine attributes. It is not that finally it was taken from me; on the contrary, my soul was rooted in this by its constant effects. It was no longer a matter of repeated instruction which held the spirit in wonder, but of a habitual depth which I shall call "beatitude" because of the enjoyment of unspeakable blessings which provide food for the soul. I was then about twenty-six or twenty-seven years old. Had I tried to find comparisons in order to express myself in some way other than I have done, I might have gone astray. I have said simply what I believe to be the truth and what the Spirit has led me and urged me to say.[2] Nevertheless, I experience some fear and embarrassment in writing this because I am sure that my very imperfect life has not corresponded—nor does it correspond now—with such exalted grace and so I write only in a spirit of humility. I am upheld only by obedience and by the Spirit who tells me what I am to say.

---

2. This is to be a characteristic of Marie's writing—a determination to speak directly of what, of course, cannot be said directly. Her problem is that which confronts all mystics in attempting to narrate their experiences: uttering the unutterable. Even so, it is true that there is a marked clarity in most of her exposition. To Dom Claude, of course, it is perfection: "This chapter contains the most sublime theology, but described and explained so clearly and in such appropriate terms that it is not possible to say anything that would make it more clear." Martin, *Vie,* p. 79.

XXII.

It has always been my experience that when the Divine Majesty wished to bestow some unusual grace on me, in addition to the remote preparations, I would feel, as the time drew near, that he was disposing me in a special way by a foretaste which was like the peace of paradise. The dignity of this makes it impossible for me to express myself otherwise. With these premonitions I would say to him: "What do you want of me, my Love?" And then I would feel his action and, generally, he would effect a change in my state.

Following the preceding events, one morning while I was in prayer God drew my spirit into himself by an unusually powerful attraction.[1] I do not know in what position my body remained. The vision of the most august Trinity was once again communicated to me and its movements shown to me in a more exalted and distinct manner than before. The first time, the impression I received principally affected my understanding and, as I have said, it seemed that the Divine Majesty had acted in order to instruct me and dispose me for what was to follow. This time, although my understanding was enlightened even more than before, it was the will which was important because this grace was concerned entirely with love, and through love my soul found itself wholly in the intimacy and enjoyment of a God of love.

Then, engulfed in the presence of this adorable Majesty, Father, Son, and Holy Spirit, adoring him in the awareness and acknowledgement of my lowliness, the Sacred Person of the Divine Word revealed to me that he was in truth the spouse of the faithful soul. I understood this truth with absolute certainty, and this very understanding became the imminent preparation for this grace to be effected in me. At that moment, this adorable Person seized my soul and embracing it with indescribable love united it to himself, taking it as his spouse.[2]

When I say he embraced it, this was not in the manner of human embraces. There is nothing sensual which approximates this divine action, but I must express myself in these earthly terms since we are

---

1. This second vision of the Trinity occurred about two years after the first, May 1627. In addition to the account in the *Relation of 1654,* Claude also quoted fragments from the *Relation of 1633.* Jamet, I, pp. 204–05.

2. For the place of the spiritual marriage in Marie's mystic ascesis, see the introduction, pp. 11–12.

composed of matter. It was through his divine touches and by being enfolded in his love that I in return loved him, in a union so complete that I was no longer aware of myself, having become one with him.

Then for a few moments I returned to myself and saw the Eternal Father and the Holy Spirit, and then the unity of the Divine Persons. Absorbed in the splendors and love of the Word, I realized that I was powerless to pay homage to the Father and the Holy Spirit, for my soul with all its powers was like a captive in him who was my spouse and my love and who wanted me wholly for himself.

Yet even in the extravagance of his divine love and his embraces, from time to time he permitted me to see the Father and the Holy Spirit, and these glimpses convinced me of my dependence on the other Persons of the Trinity, although nothing occurred in the imagination either by comparisons or other means. This time my soul recognized the distinct actions of the three divine Persons. When the Sacred Word acted in me, the Father and the Holy Spirit contemplated his action, but this did not hinder their unity because in the Trinity unity and diversity coexist without difficulty and in an indescribable manner so that each Person is free to act of itself.

I would have to have the ability of the seraphim and the other blessed spirits to express what occurred during this ecstasy and rapturous love which so absorbed the understanding, that it was powerless to see anything except the treasures it possessed in the Sacred Person of the Eternal Word. Or to express it better: the powers of the soul were completely engulfed and absorbed in the Word who, as its spouse, bestowed on the soul the intimacy and right to be his bride. The soul realizes that in all this, it is the Holy Spirit who is the moving power, enabling it to act thus with the Word; for it would be impossible for a mere creature, so narrow and limited, to dare to deal thus with God. Even were it to become forgetful of self and desirous to undertake such a course, it would not have the ability to do it. These actions being entirely supernatural, the soul can only receive them, powerless either to augment or diminish them or even to distract itself from them. The consequences which result will show the truth of this. The soul has been granted this exalted grace and received it even before it could be made ready for its reception; so suddenly does this happen that only a god of goodness and infinite power could so act on a creature.

The soul constantly experiences the action of this gracious initiator who by this spiritual marriage has taken possession of it with so gentle and sweet a fire that it cannot be described. He makes it sing a constant bridal hymn just as he wishes. Neither books nor study can teach this language which is completely divine and heavenly. It comes from that sweet melody of the mutual embrace of the soul and the adorable Word which, through the kisses of his divine mouth, fills her with his spirit and his life. Thus this bridal hymn is the return and requital of the soul to its beloved Spouse.

XXIII.

With the spiritual marriage the soul has completely changed its state. Hitherto it had been in continual longing and expectation of this exalted grace which had been shown to it from afar to arouse in it the dispositions and preparations for receiving it. Now the soul has no further longing because it possesses him whom it loves.[3] The soul is all his. Now there follow caresses and a love which consumes the soul, making it die in him the gentlest of deaths; yet this death is sweetness itself.

I paused for a moment to think if I could find some earthly comparison, but I find nothing that can help me explain the embraces of the Word and the soul. Although the soul recognizes him as its great God, equal to the Father, eternal, by whom all things have been made and subsist; yet it embraces him and speaks to him face to face. Seeing itself raised to this dignity where the Word is its spouse and the soul his, it says to him: "You are my very self; you are mine. Let us go, my Spouse, to the business affairs you have entrusted to me." The soul has no further desires; it possesses its Beloved. It speaks to him because he has spoken to it, but the language it uses is not its own. It goes about its business, faithful to the revelation given it. It seeks his glory in all and through all so that he may reign, absolute master of all hearts.

I redoubled my penances and consumed myself in acts of charity for my neighbor, making myself all to all in order to win them for my Beloved. I sometimes spent time with a group of men, servants of my brother-in-law, sitting alone at table with twenty or so of these simple people (depending on the number who gathered together, coming in from the country), to have the opportunity of instructing them about their salvation. They would give me very simply and intimately an account of their actions, pointing out to each other the faults they had committed when, through forgetfulness, someone had neglected to

---

3. "Tendance"—rendered here as longing—is a word frequently used by Marie. It is difficult to find an accurate translation. Jamet suggests that it is an inclination "to something that she does not know and which can be satisfied by no created object." Jamet, I, p. 157, n.a.

mention something. I brought them together from time to time to speak of God and teach them how to keep the commandments. I reprimanded them openly, for these poor fellows were as submissive to me as children. I even made them get out of bed if they had retired without praying to God.[4]

They came to me for help in all their needs, above all in their sickness, or to have me make peace with my brother[-in-law] when they had displeased him. I felt impelled to do all this and to take care of them in their sickness. Sometimes I had such a group of them lingering on that it seemed like a hospital with me as the nurse. In all this, I was convinced that what I did, I did for my divine Spouse. I had such energy that everything was easy for me in these circumstances. In making the beds of both the sick and the healthy, I was often—even continuously—moved to yield to the caresses which he who possessed my soul bestowed on me to ease the weariness to which I was reduced for love of him. I fell to my knees in order to humble myself, for I felt infinitely indebted to him for providing opportunities of offering him some small services. In these lowly actions in which I found my riches he continued and redoubled his caresses.

I hid myself, then, for fear of being seen, and since the excess of his love burned me like a fire that smothered my sighs, I spoke to him aloud to give vent to this fire, being moved to say: "O my Love, I can bear no more. Leave me for a little while. My weakness cannot bear the excess of your love. Or else take my life for your love makes me suffer more than a soul, bound in prison, can endure." I sensed that he was pleased with what I said, for it was his own spirit which would not let me be silent.

XXIV.

In this state of prayer, since the spirit is entirely withdrawn from earthly things, there follows an ecstasy of love with the Second Divine Person. This leaves one's lower nature alone, without support, to suffer and carry the weight of daily work. The higher part [of the soul] shows no more concern for the body than if it were its mortal enemy and its greatest obstacle, responsible for holding it back and hindering

---

4. Later Marie sees this as part of her preparation for Canada, where she must deal with "all kinds of people."

it from flying away with its Beloved, free of this mortal life in which it can no longer be immersed.

In order to be eternally absorbed in his bosom, the soul yearns to be separated [from the body], for although it dwells in the love of this divine and adorable object, yet these divine embraces must have little interludes for sleep and business. These are like little clouds which, carried along by a strong wind, pass beneath the sun, forming shadows. Then, too, bodily needs creep in, creating intervals which, short as they may be, are a kind of martyrdom for the soul that cannot bear to be separated for a moment from the caresses or the vision of its Beloved.[5]

The greatest hindrance of all is sleep—no matter how short—which impels the soul to say: "O my Beloved, when shall I be able to sleep no more!" Completely awake as I was—for I lay on a couch in my hair shirt—I sang a song to my divine Spouse, inspired by his spirit. This song would have divided my soul in two had I not been sustained in an extraordinary way. Thus my body became so weary that I was forced to say: "My Divine Love, I beg you to let me sleep a little so that being rested, I can serve you again tomorrow since it is your will that I go on living." Then I slept a little. As soon as I awoke I returned to that very love which sleep had stolen away from me. "Alas, my dear Love," I said, "when shall I be able to sleep no more? I must begin now to mortify my body." Then I left my hard bed and put on a hair shirt or some other instrument of penance.

When in the midst of my business affairs this divine Spouse would sweep me away, I would say to him: "My Beloved, let me take care of this matter and then I will embrace you at my leisure, for my soul longs to be consumed in your pure love." If I tried to pick up a book, love engrossed me and I had to put it down in order to rest in the love which bound me so that I could sustain no other effect but its own. Sometimes I did read a little, particularly when I had to stay in my brother-in-law's office, waiting for him while he was conducting business with someone. This, however, did me violence and gave me a headache because it forced me to stop my interior colloquy; in this state the struggle of spirit against spirit is violent.

What I read was beautiful and my inclination would have been to reflect on it and linger over it, but the Spirit which absorbed me kept me from doing so. However, I did force myself to read, for it was a holy

---

5. For this period see the "Supplément," Jamet, II, p. 591.

occupation. (On the other hand, I had strong desires to follow the ordinary paths of devout souls, feeling that this was the surest way and this was one of the things which made me do the most violence to myself.) Thus, too, when I was in public, if I could not take up some needlework to occupy myself, I would take up a book rather than let people know that I was immersed in prayer. This never showed in the bustle of affairs, where, to all appearances, those who saw me believed that I was completely engrossed. This was because my bodily movements were extremely quick and my soul found itself freer than ever because my body was thus occupied.

This was how I was in those two kinds of situations; but when I could free myself, the Spirit had its turn. It took no account either of the pain of the body or its posture. This state was known only to my heavenly Spouse, who knew very well that I could not act otherwise.

I had great difficulty with vocal prayer. As soon as I began my rosary, paying attention to the meaning of the words, my spirit was carried up to God. Either I had to stop or, sometimes, to say it in stages. It was the same with the Office of Our Lady, except that when I was in the country, in an isolated place, I sang it.[6] This singing soothed me, and whenever I had the opportunity I recited it—but this was very seldom. In order to relax I would sometimes look out over the fields and the shrubbery; yet my bridal song with my divine Spouse continued despite whatever else I looked at. I catered to the lower feelings of my nature so that they would serve the spirit and not hinder its movements.

XXV.

The soul, then, kept continually in this loving ecstasy, no longer lives in itself but in him who keeps it wholly absorbed in his love. It is transformed by the Spirit who possesses it—sometimes it is languid, sometimes kept in suspense. He leads the soul where he wishes and it is powerless to resist, for the will is his captive so that should this captive —by some secret inclination or inadvertence—be held back, this divine Spirit, at that very moment, jealous of what he wishes to possess, draws the will to himself; and by this divine action bestows on the soul a loving movement which leads it to proclaim his love.

---

6. This is doubtless a reference to "La Charpraie," a country house owned by the Buissons, situated about five miles from Tours. See Oury, *Marie,* I, pp. 68–69.

Since that time I have read the Song of Songs in Holy Scripture. I can find nothing better related to my experience, yet the depths which is experienced creates a very different impression from the sound of the words. There is a meaning which brings a divine nourishment that human language cannot express, a familiarity and daring, an inexplicable return of love from the soul to the Word and from the Word to the soul.

When I had to go to our country house, my spirit rejoiced to see myself free of the great bustle of affairs. Then, in silence, my divine Spouse let me experience a new martyrdom in his loving touch and embrace. He kept me thus for several days without permitting me a single respite or pause. I experienced the effect of which St. Paul speaks: "The Word of God is efficacious; it divides soul from spirit; it penetrates to the very depths of being" (Heb 4:12).

In this sense, this grace is in truth a sword which cleaves and cleanses with a fiery purification. I dislike using words like this, but I see no other meaning in this spiritual suffering caused by the Spirit of the adorable and divine Word. In this suffering he fills me in a way that is more difficult for nature to endure than all the pain of a very cruel death. I set out to distract myself, but this only affected my body. Mindlessly I walked in the woodland paths or in the vineyards, like one unconscious; and afterwards, returning to myself, he so struck my body through the Spirit that I fell where I was. Had I been able to speak during this loving activity, this would ordinarily have relieved me, but I was bound in all my faculties. There is nothing to do but submit to this divine mastery on the part of the sacred Person of the Word.

The soul, while suffering, loves with an unwavering love which overwhelms her. Nonetheless, she sees very clearly that she must make a return for this intimacy with which she has been graced; but it is not time for this in her present condition. With her steadfast gaze she desires this suffering because she is only able to want what her Beloved desires and accomplishes in her by his loving law.

XXVI.

After this suffering, the soul in a single moment regains its freedom. The riches with which the adorable Spirit of the Word has filled it, now, by another kind of suffering, become like fire and flame. These, as though they were arrows, the soul launches back to him, crying, "O Love, it has pleased you to make me suffer; now I must avenge myself by inflicting on you those same wounds which you have inflicted on me. Still more: had you by these wounds taken away my soul, freeing it from its prison, you would have made me happy; but instead you have left me to go on living, to endure these sharp and fiery darts. Thus, I must avenge myself." Then it seems that these lightning flashes speed from the heart to be hurled at the Beloved— and that these are exactly the same as those which had been hurled at the soul. After this, through another kind of suffering, the soul languishes totally, swooning on the breast of the Beloved as though it would die in him.

Who can express this loving intimacy? I will say nothing, although I might be able to say something akin to this.

Without these momentary respites—respites which provide relief from the overflowing presence of the Beloved, this divine outpouring would destroy the body, for the impact caused by the Spirit is beyond imagination. It is not the body that finds it difficult to sustain the burden of this love, for the senses have no part in this. The body undergoes only the physical penances, not the purely spiritual suffering.

What assuaged me, body and soul, as I have already mentioned, were deeds performed for the neighbor. This was food for my soul, even if it meant being up all night. In fact, charity often required that I be up late at night; then, afterwards, I would take the discipline. Looking back now, I can't imagine how I could have found the means to do this in the midst of such a large family as that of my brother-in-law. I went everywhere without using a candle because of my fear of being seen or heard. The cellars, the attics, the courtyard, the stable—full of horses—this was where I went. At night there was always the danger that I might hurt myself, but I was blind to everything. Provided that I found some place to hide, this was enough for me.

My brother sometimes laughingly mentioned these things, which made me think he knew something about my penances. But taking this only as a joke, I was blind and oblivious to it all; my only intention being to give happiness to my heavenly Spouse who asked my obedience to his inspiration.

So well did my Spouse protect me that I never met anyone. Twice, however, a servant took me unawares upon entering my room and saw the table and the bench where I slept and also my hair shirt. I think she told my father and my sister about this, but they had the discretion never to mention it, for they had a great love of virtue and esteemed and admired even the smallest virtuous act.

XXVII.

At other times I felt that the adorable Spirit of Jesus wanted to separate me from my body. This experience is so painful to nature that if it had continued for three successive days, I would have died.[7] For my part, I longed to follow this Holy Spirit which seemed to want to lead me away. Thus the poor body suffered the violence of a spirit which wanted to be rid of it, enduring a division which cast it into a terrifying solitude. This was more painful for me when I was alone than when I was busy. In this condition the spirit has an advantage over the body, happy with this separation, longing to be freed from its prison in the enjoyment of the blessedness it possesses which is beyond all description. It has no interest in what the body suffers, preferring to have nothing to do with it. I would never have believed what occurs in this suspension of the spirit had I not experienced it.

Finally, I was freed from this state through the sweetness of my union with the Sacred Person of the Word, a sweetness which seeped into my lower nature, producing a serenity which drew it from its suffering so that my whole being experienced what the Spouse says in the Song: "My soul melted with love when my Beloved spoke."

Then I turned to another kind of union which led me to a loving activity and gentle intimacy with my divine Spouse. In this state my lower nature was not excluded, for although it did not share in any of the feelings, it was sustained in some mysterious way. It is impossible to evaluate the resources in these spiritual paths, for it would not be possible to continue without them. This is particularly true in that constant state of love in which the Spirit of God is pleased to manifest his riches and his divine splendors to the soul. It is true to say that he pursues the soul (although in truth never separated from it) as though desirous to have it enjoy everything that he has. Thus the soul says to him: "My Beloved, you are my delight. You pursue me constantly, as though you have only me to love and provide for." Then, as though infinitely pleased with what the soul (urged by God himself) has said, he redoubles his divine love so that it becomes an inexhaustible source, pouring into the soul which, in its turn, like a little stream, flows back

---

7. Dom Claude notes that at this time she fell physically ill. Doctors were consulted but they were baffled by her description of the pains in her heart. "This was a wound of divine love," Claude explains, adding that only He who had wounded her was capable of curing her. Martin, *Vie,* p. 151.

to the divine source. Thus it loses itself so that it seems that the soul is the Beloved in this mutual interchange.

Perhaps it seems that I exaggerate, but no human language can express the excess of mercy of so great and good a God on my behalf, or reveal what it has pleased him to communicate to me. Although I have spoken of the relation of spirit to Spirit, of my being plunged into this abyss, of the loss of myself in him, as well as of the most intimate revelations, yet I was always aware that I was a mere nothing to whom this All was pleased to show mercy because he makes no exception of persons. I have always believed and witnessed the nothingness of the creature, happy to be this nothing and to have this God be all. In my loving activity, this was one of the songs I sang to him: "My chaste love, it is my glory that you be all and that I be nothing. May you be blessed in this, O my Love." These sentiments of my lowliness some-times made me fear, seeing a disposition involving two such opposite things. One day as I spoke with my divine Spouse, he said to me interiorly: "It is my will that you glorify me and sing my praises as do the blessed in heaven." This answer reassured me and so my soul continued its constant bridal song: "You are blessed, O my Love, O my God, O my God! You are blessed and glorified, O my sweet Love!" This continued unchanged except during the periods of new graces, after which I returned to my song. I was at this time about twenty-eight or twenty-nine years old.

XXVIII.

I think I have spoken before of the strong desire I felt for religious life from the time I was freed, but my affairs did not permit this. This vocation was always with me, and I spoke of it to my divine Spouse in those intimate colloquies I had with him. He assured me that this would come about.

This assurance gave me confidence and peace during the delay which was caused by my son.[8] Nevertheless, from time to time my desire was so strong that secular life seemed unendurable to me, not understanding that one could follow the counsels of the Gospel just as in the cloister. This led me to urge the Divine Majesty in quite another

---

8. Once again, Marie's words seem harsh and unfeeling toward those she professes to love so deeply.

way. One day, being with some people who spoke a little too freely and whom I could neither reprimand nor leave, I spoke of this to my divine Spouse. He urged me to leave and go with him to my room. Human respect held me back but he urged me anew with a loving movement to leave with him. Thus, following his loving reprimand, I withdrew.

As soon as I entered my room, his Spirit took possession of mine. My body unable to sustain me, I fell to the ground, so sudden and powerful was this attraction. Through his Spirit I experienced the words of St. Paul: "The Spirit asks for us with unspeakable groanings" (Rom 8:16). Since it was the Spirit of my dear Spouse who was present, it pleased him to hear my sighs and laments: "How is it possible, my Love, for you to endure my sighs and laments? You have let me see and taste the blessings hidden in your Gospel treasures. You have captivated my soul with them. Yet you let me languish by delaying to give me what you want me to have. My chaste Spouse, my Beloved, what pleasure do you take in having me suffer? You must put me in this home of blessed souls, drawing me from the corruption of the world whose spirit is so contrary to your own. Ah, chaste Love, please do this or otherwise take my life, for in many ways this is martyrdom to me. You want me to possess this happiness; you do not want me to die—and yet you act thus! I love your good pleasure but just the same I do not understand why you let me languish here, for it is you who make me suffer thus."

What I said is only a shadow of what the Spirit moved me to say, with an astonishing familiarity and daring. Without this Spirit I would not have been able to wish for anything, for this Spirit had seized my soul with all its powers. This is why in such raptures there are no studied words, no reflections, no movements of the will or human reasoning. It is a captivating inner language fashioned by a supreme power, spirit to Spirit, which may last for half an hour.

After this, my divine Spouse, who had been pleased to see me suffer, united me to himself in an indescribable way; and for some time I remained as though I had fainted in him. Then, as though wishing to console me, he indicated very clearly and lovingly that if I would have a little patience he would grant me my desire. Then it seemed he wanted to consume me in his pure, divine love—and afterward he confirmed his promise to me.

My son's affairs were in the same condition as my own, for as far as my divine Spouse was concerned, it was all one, and he reproached me whenever I had even the slightest doubt that he would provide for us.[9] Actually, as far as this matter is concerned, it never occurred to me to doubt.

Following this experience, I remained in profound peace and certainty without at all knowing how Our Lord would draw me from the world or into what religious order he would lead me, for everything was to come from his Providence, since I was devoid of all temporal goods. I had a strong attraction to the Feuillantines because of their great seclusion and austerities. The Father General of the Feuillants had promised to give me the first available place, and the Fathers planned to take care of my son. Some good people would have liked to see me a Carmelite and, for my part, I dearly loved this holy order.[10] Nevertheless, Our Lord did not wish me in either of these holy orders. Meanwhile, I awaited from him, as from a good Father and my divine Spouse, his plan for me, keeping as well as I could the vows of poverty, obedience, and chastity that I had already made.

XXIX.

Ever since my strong desire to leave the world, I wanted to be an Ursuline because they were instituted to help souls, something which powerfully attracted me. But the Ursulines were not established at Tours at this time, and I knew nothing about where they were.[11] I had only heard them spoken about. Since my goal was not attainable, I stopped thinking about it for the present so that had the opportunity arisen, I would have gone to one of the two orders I have mentioned. In effect, this was what I was inclined to do while awaiting God's action.

Dom Raymond, who was certain that I would be a religious, was thinking of the necessary means, without telling me. Meanwhile the Ursulines had been established at Tours, but he did not think God wanted me there. For my part, I believed that the divine goodness

---

9. Marie is determined throughout this period that her son will share what she considers her greatest treasure: poverty and consequent trust in God. See especially her letter to her son, September 4, 1641, in which she explains herself at length. "I have never loved you except in the poverty of Jesus Christ in whom I have found all riches. . . ." "Letters," p. 222.

10. At this time the Feuillantines had three houses: at Toulouse, Luxembourg, and Paris. The Carmelites had been established in Tours since 1608. Marie knew them not only through the works of Teresa of Avila and John of the Cross but also through two of her cousins who were Carmelites. See Oury, *Marie,* I, p. 145.

11. On the Ursuline foundation at Tours, see the introduction, p. 15 and Gueudré, I, pp. 131–32.

would inspire my director about what he wanted me to do and so I remained at peace, conversing with God so that he would dispose of me and my son in whatever way he wished. Thus my spirit was free and resigned, unable to wish or to choose.

In the meantime the Ursulines had moved to their present location, and everytime I passed the monastery my spirit and my heart gave a subtle leap which seemed to pull me into this holy house. This happened without any preceding reflection on my part. This movement impressed me with the fact that God wanted me there; and as many times a day as I passed this place, it was always the same. I told this to my director, who answered that this was not the place I should think of going, and I left him believing that it was to be as he said. Yet this call and impression remained and I recommended it to my divine Spouse, telling him that he must choose for me.

Finally God revealed to my director that this was the place for me. The latter then began to take this affair to heart and to discuss it with Reverend Mother Françoise de St. Bernard, then assistant prioress of the Ursulines.[12] She agreed with him and resolved to work toward this as soon as she found the opportunity. I watched all this very confidently but without saying anything, convinced that one should leave it all to God.

Time passed while I remained in the usual union with which the Divine Majesty honored me. Finally, when I was thirty years old, he gave me a special intuition that the time had come. I sensed that it was a matter of great importance, requiring great preparations, yet externally it did not seem that anything had changed. An inner voice pursued me everywhere, saying, "Hurry; it's time; there's nothing more for you to do in the world." I told all this to my director who also felt himself urged by God. At this time I was working for my brother, who wanted to employ me more and more in his business. I could tell that I would meet with strong opposition from him; and, in fact, it was just as I predicted.

XXX.

In that same year, 1630, Mother Françoise de St. Bernard was elected prioress of the Ursuline convent in Tours. Immediately God

---

12. Françoise de St. Bernard was one of the foundresses of the Ursuline monastery in Tours. As prioress she will be the one who offers Marie a place in the community. There will always be a close bond between them.

inspired her to accept me into the community. She summoned me that same day, thus indicating her good will. I understood very well what she wanted to tell me, but I pretended not to understand, for I wanted to consult my director about my answer. So I simply said "Thank you."

What concerned me, humanly speaking, was my son. He was not yet twelve years old and without material resources. The devil plagued me on this matter, pointing out that I lacked judgment in not holding on to my own interests and in doing nothing for either myself or my son, that leaving him in this condition was to destroy him and thus to act very much against my conscience. These arguments were the more persuasive since I was considering the good of the present moment and since, humanly speaking, this way of thinking was most convincing. But at once God filled me with confidence that he would take care of him whom I wanted to leave for love of God in order to follow his divine counsels more perfectly. These counsels were perfectly engraved on my spirit: first, those concerning the vows, then those of leaving one's relatives, and the unhappiness of those who, being called, do not obey.

All this was so tenderly impressed on my soul that I was determined to follow and to lose my life, as the adorable Word Incarnate had preached. I loved my son deeply; leaving him constituted my sacrifice. Since God wished this, I blindly and willingly committed everything to his providence.

My director consulted with the Ursuline nuns as well as with the archbishop, for since they were receiving me without a dowry, his permission was necessary. My brother and sister were the greatest obstacles but since my director was also theirs, he was able to win them over. He had them promise they would take care of my son.

The arrangements were completed and the day set for my entrance, when something happened which almost ruined everything. My son, unaware of my plans, and although only twelve years old, fancied to go to Paris to become a religious in company with a Feuillant Father whom he knew. This priest, in order to get rid of the child who was always after him, pretended that he would take the child with him but then left without telling him. When my son learned this, without mentioning his plans to me, he left. He was in boarding school at that time. For three days he remained lost without my being able to find him no matter what I did, for I had everyone alerted. All my friends blamed me for this loss, saying that it was a clear sign that God did not want me to be a religious.

I was harassed on all sides. This was a heavy cross because the devil, also intervening, did what he could to upset me, insinuating that I was responsible for this loss. At the end of three days, after I had prayed urgently to God, along with some of my friends who shared deeply in my sorrow, a good man, finding my son at the port of Blois, brought him back to me.

It was then that everyone came up with fresh objections, pointing out that leaving him so young would be on my conscience, that what had happened before would happen again, and that I would be responsible for this and that God would certainly punish me. In a word, I was besieged on all sides and my natural love pressed upon me so sharply that it was as though my soul were being wrenched from my body. Nothing about my obligations concerned me except my love for my son. Furthermore, I never stopped hearing an inner voice which pursued me everywhere, saying, "Hurry! It's time. It's not good for you to be in the world any longer." These words made their point.[13]

Putting my son into the hands of God and of the Blessed Virgin, I left him, as well as my elderly father, who cried pitifully. When I said goodbye to him he found every possible argument to stop me, but my heart remained unshaken. I had discussed this matter with my divine Spouse several days before, unable to say anything to him but this: "My chaste love, I do not wish to strike this blow if you do not wish it. Choose for me yourself. I will accept anything as long as you will it." Then there flowed into my heart an inner sustenance which would have enabled me to pass through fire, giving me courage to surmount all and accomplish all. Then he transported my spirit where he wanted it to be.

One morning on the feast of the Conversion of St. Paul 1631, I left what I loved the most. My son came with me, crying bitterly in leaving me. Watching him, it seemed to me that I was being cut in two. Nevertheless, I did not let my emotions show. Dom Raymond presented me to Reverend Mother St. Bernard who, with the whole community, received me with extraordinary charity. Previously I had received the blessing of the archbishop of Tours, who wished to see me before my entrance.

---

13. For a more detailed account of this painful separation, see the fragments from the *Relation of 1633* in this volume, pp. 185–86. Dom Claude dramatizes the event by including a "remembered" conversation with his mother on the night before her departure. The hortatory tone seems closer to Claude's rhetoric than to his mother's. Martin, *Vie,* p. 176. See also Brémond, VI, p. 55.

XXXI.

There is no way of expressing how peaceful religious life seemed after the sort of worries I had left, especially as a novice who is not supposed to be concerned with anything except the observance of the Rule.[1] All this curtailment was perfectly adapted to my spirit and nature which, of itself, had no love for commotion. One of the first points of observance was to follow the common life, to put aside my ordinary dress, leaving me only what was conformable to the Rule. Although I had dearly loved all these little mortifications while I was still in the world, nevertheless, on this occasion I did not experience a single thought or emotion contrary to obedience. Our Lord gave me a love for the common life and since that time he has always led me according to it, except when, occasionally, obedience has demanded something else of me.

As the very beginning of my religious life Our Lord permitted me to suffer a real trial. This was when a crowd of little school boys, companions of my son, gathered together and began to hoot and cry that he had been silly to let me enter a convent and that now that he was without both father and mother he would be disdained and abandoned. "Let's go find her," they said to him; "let's go and make so much noise that they will have to give her back to you." This upset this poor child so deeply that he cried grievously. Then a whole gang came to the gate of the monastery, making a hullaballoo and crying that I be given back to my son. This could be heard everywhere. At first I didn't know what it was, but then among the other voices I could distinguish the voice of my son who was crying, "Give me back my mother! I want my mother!" This pierced me to the heart and made me fear that the community, being so harassed, might get tired and reach the point of sending me away.

At this point I spoke humbly and lovingly about it to Our Lord for whose love I had abandoned this child in order to follow his holy will and divine counsels. Thus my soul remained in peace. Our sisters wept with compassion on hearing his cries. He came to the church when Mass was going on, putting his head through the opening of the com-

---

1. Although the Ursuline monastery had been established at Tours for just ten years, it already had about thirty professed sisters and about the same number of novices. See Oury, *Marie,* I, p. 169.

munion grille. "Give me back my mother!" he would cry. He went to the parlor and begged the tourière sister to give me back to him or to let him enter the monastery with me. I was sent to the parlor to see him and I tried to console and appease him, giving him some little gifts that I had been given.

When he was leaving he thought that I was returning to the dormitory, and the tourière sister noticed that he kept walking backwards, his eyes fixed on the windows to see if I was there. He kept this up until the monastery was lost from sight. They told me all this and I was amazed at his deep affection, for since his infancy I had been determined to leave him in obedience to God. I had never fondled him as one does with children, despite my deep love. My intention was to detach him from me in view of the time when he would be old enough for me to leave him.[2]

The act of leaving my son was variously interpreted so that I needed great courage—courage which it pleased my divine Spouse to give me. Ceaselessly I begged his goodness to have compassion on this poor abandoned child who was not yet twelve years old. I saw that he would have a great deal to suffer, for ordinarily relatives lack the tenderness of a mother nor does a child so confidently seek their help. Finally, I foresaw all that could happen by way of conflict, and I bore this cross lovingly out of love for my dear Jesus who, one day as I was climbing the steps of our novitiate, assured me inwardly and with deep love that he would take care of my son. This comforted me so tenderly that all my pain was changed into peace and a certainty that my son would be dedicated to God's holy service since God was taking care of him.

Almost immediately an opportunity came to send him to Rennes in Brittany to the Jesuit seminary. The archbishop of Tours and Dom Raymond had explained my son's situation upon my entering religious life to Father Dinet, who arranged to send him to Rennes where he was rector.[3] My sister provided for his needs as she continued to do until he finished his studies.

I was subject to one more assault. My father who was elderly when I left him warned me that he would die if I departed. Since I wanted only to obey God and, on the other hand, having three sisters capable of helping him if he needed it, I rose above human affection,

---

2. For further details of this difficult period, see Martin, *Vie,* pp. 184–87.

3. Jacques Dinet, S.J., was later transferred to Tours and acted as Marie's director around 1634. It is probably for him that she wrote her retreat notes. See the introduction, pp. 37–38.

leaning on the words of Our Lord: "He who loves father and mother more than me is not worthy of me" (Mt 10:37). In fact he died about six months later. Nevertheless, I was on good terms with him. He gave me his blessing and came to the cloister grille to visit me. Some people of worldly judgment had a very different feeling about this, but my divine Spouse let me experience that it is good to leave everything for love of him.

XXXII.

After these events some people who had found fault with my entrance into religious life changed their minds and admitted that the divine goodness guided all my affairs. Had they witnessed what was happening in my soul, they would have joined me in singing his mercies, but this was a secret hidden from them. The state of union in which I was held at this time kept my soul silent about the loving activity of which I have spoken earlier. The soul is like someone withdrawn from the battlefield for whom a bed of sweet-smelling flowers has been prepared. This comparison is unsuitable but I know of no other which would be more adequate. The soul is at rest, cleaving to the tender impressions of the Spirit of the Sacred Word Incarnate who is preparing it for marvelous things, the secret of which has not yet been revealed. The soul has no desire to know more than the divine Spirit lets it understand. It can only love.

I think I have already said that in the way in which God has led me, I have never had any curiosity to know more than he reveals and I have considered it a serious imperfection to use one's own efforts to know more. It is not the same with loving. The soul has an inclination always to love more. I am not speaking of what one must know in order to live well and be instructed in the ways of virtue and the avoidance of error. There are spiritual directors and books one should have recourse to for this. I am referring to extraordinary lights and graces in which, as I have already said, God leaves the soul fulfilled. It would be a grave fault if the spirit of nature wished to intrude itself, trying on its own to seek beyond its capacity. Sometimes this spirit of nature is so subtle that it induces the higher part of the soul to follow its inclination.

On this subject I have had in mind for a long time this passage of Holy Scripture: "How art thou fallen, Lucifer, who rose up in the morning" (Is 14:12). I saw that it was simply unadulterated curiosity to be and to know beyond what God had created him for. This is why the following line confirmed my feelings: "How are you fallen, you who have troubled and disturbed the people." There is nothing in those extraordinary matters so capable of ruining the soul as curiosity which at first is so illusory, but which then upsets and troubles the power of the soul so that the spirit of grace cannot be distinguished from that of nature. Thus it follows that the soul falls into grave faults and is constantly wandering astray on the path of the spirit.

Were I able to counsel souls whom God calls to contemplation, it would be to give a faithful account to their spiritual director of everything that happens, for candor blunts curiosity and makes the soul simple, drawing graces from God and uniting it to him who is pure simple being. He desires only souls who resemble him in this to receive his holy impressions which are the enemies of nature.

I have given in to the urge to make this little digression on the subject of curiosity which is so harmful to union. This union establishes such a calm that nothing troubles the soul in its attachment to its heavenly Spouse who makes it one spirit with himself. The rules, the choir, all the acts of obedience contribute to the perfection of this state because the spirit of God is there. I have experienced this truth which made me love my vocation and the religious life which I saw as superior to everything, and I could not understand the contempt of the world which values only emptiness and the dust of vanity.

XXXIII.

In this aforementioned union, I saw clearly that the Divine Majesty was preparing my soul for some great grace; and thus I spoke familiarly to my Spouse: "What do you want of me, my Beloved? Do with me whatever you wish. You have captivated my soul so that I can hardly endure it." For three days I remained in anticipation of what he intended to do, speaking to him of this preparation.

One day at evening prayer, just as the signal had been given to begin, I was kneeling in my place in choir when a sudden inner transport ravished my soul.[4] Then the three Persons of the Most Holy Trinity manifested themselves again through the words of the adorable

---

4. Feast of the Guardian Angels, March 17, 1631. See also her account in the *Relation of 1633* in this volume, pp. 192–93.

Word Incarnate: "If anyone loves me, my Father will love him; we will come to him and make our dwelling with him" (Jn 14:23). I then felt the effects of these divine words and the action of the three divine Persons in me more strongly than ever before. These words, by penetrating me with their meaning, brought me both to understand and to experience. Then the Most Holy Trinity, in its unity, took my soul to itself like a thing which already belonged to it, and which it had itself made capable of this divine imprint and the effects of this divine action.

In this great abyss it was shown to me that I was receiving the highest grace of all those communications of the three divine Persons which I had received in the past. This meaning was clearer and more intelligible than any words and occurred in this way: "The first time I revealed myself to you it was to instruct your soul in this great mystery; the second time was for the Word to take your soul for his spouse; this time, Father, Son, and Holy Spirit are giving themselves in order to possess your soul completely." The effect of this was immediate and as the three divine Persons possessed me, so I possessed them in the full participation of the treasures of the divine magnificence. The Eternal Father was my father; the adorable Word, my Spouse; and the Holy Spirit was he who by his action worked in my soul, fashioning it to support the divine impressions.

During all this I saw myself as a mere nothing which the Great All had chosen to bear the effects of his great mercy. I could say only: "O my God, O adorable abyss! I am absolute nothingness." And then he would reply: "Even though you are mere nothingness, yet you are all mine." This was repeated several times in proportion to my abasement. The more I humbled myself, the more I saw myself exalted, while my soul experienced a manifestation of love for which no human language has words. Who can express the honor with which God treats the soul created in his image when it pleases him to raise it into his divine embraces? When one considers the mere nothingness of the creature, it is something so astonishing that if the soul were not sustained by the tenderness of the spirit of God, it would be reduced to nothingness for all eternity. I can find no other way to express this.

This profound impression lasted for about half an hour. I found myself leaning against my chair in the choir. I had sufficient freedom to say Compline, although still enduring the impression that the divine activity had imprinted on my soul, which had been utterly vanquished.

XXXIV.

Following the events I have just described which occurred about two months after my entrance into religious life, my spirit, still bearing the imprint and unction of this great grace, was more withdrawn than ever from things of earth and drawn toward religious virtue and the Divine Office, where Our Lord bestowed on me a sweet and nourishing understanding of Holy Scripture.[5] While in choir I heard in French what I was chanting in Latin. This so captured my spirit that had I not rigorously controlled myself, this might have been noticeable. The act of singing soothed me and liberated my spirit, so engaging my senses that I had a strong impulse to leap and clap my hands and induce everyone to sing the praises of this great God, so worthy of everyone is being consumed for his love and service and with the bride of the Song "rejoicing and leaping with joy at the remembrance of the embraces of the Spouse." Thus I savored the spirit of these divine words and I would sing the "Eructavit" (Psalm 45), proclaiming in inexpressible exuberance the greatness and the prerogatives of my Spouse whose words were for me spirit and life.

In the psalms I saw his justice, his judgments, his grandeur, his love, his equity, his beauties, his magnificence, his generosity, and, finally, that he had (according to the sense of the Church, his spouse) "well-shaped hands, full of hyacinths" and other fruits appropriate for revealing the fullness of purity to souls, his beloved ones. I saw that the goodness of this divine spirit had established me in green and fertile pastures which kept my soul so nourished that it overflowed and I could not keep silent.

I had great simplicity in expressing my thoughts, and my sisters were amazed to hear me speak like this. One of them, having found a book containing a passage from the *Song* in French, said to me: "Instruct us a little; tell us what this means, 'May he kiss me with the kiss of his mouth' (Song 1:1)." Our mistress was there and had me bring a chair so that I could be more comfortable.[6] Without further ado I began with the first word which swept me along so that, no longer

---

5. Dom Oury suggests that this need not be interpreted as a supernatural gift; Marie's familiarity with the psalms in French may have made it possible for her to "hear" the French while she recited the Latin. Oury, *Marie,* I, p. 188.

6. It was these conferences which Claude organized and amplified into the *Exposition Succincte du Cantique des Cantiques,* which he published in 1682. For the text see Jamet, I, pp. 387–95.

conscious of myself, I spoke for a long time, according as this loving action took hold of me. Finally I became speechless, as though the Spirit of my Jesus wanted everything for himself. On this occasion I was unable to conceal these graces which embarrassed me deeply. This same thing took me by surprise on other occasions, too. My spirit was so filled with all that was sung in choir, that day and night this formed my colloquy with my heavenly spouse.

This took me so completely out of myself that as I went about the monastery I was in a constant state of ecstasy. It was the same while I was at work. Sometimes my thoughts were concentrated on the purity of God and how all things declare his glory. The psalm "The heavens declare the glory of God" (Ps 19) had an allure for me which pierced my heart and enraptured my spirit. "Yes, yes, O my Love! 'Your testimonies are true; they are justified of themselves. They give witness to the foolish' (Ps 19:8). Send me over the whole world to teach those who are ignorant of you." I would have liked everyone to know these things and to taste the delights my soul was experiencing. My spirit was led from one attraction to another in endless succession. One time, lost in such emotions, I spoke in French instead of Latin. This happened while praising the Sacred Person of the Word by whom all things have been made. This occurred during the recitation of the "Laudate" while I was in those transports which the psalms evoked in me.

As I walked it was as though I did not touch the ground. Seeing my religious habit, I put my hand to my head to touch my veil and assure myself that I was not mistaken in thinking I had the happiness of being in this house of God and sharing a portion of his inheritance. None of this was a feeling which emanated from the senses but stemmed rather from the strength and vigor of the Spirit which overwhelmed me. Everything I saw in religious life seemed to me to be full of the spirit of God: the rules, the ceremonies, the cloister, the vows—everything.

Some lay people who knew how I had been employed while still in the world and who had seen me perform my daily duties so wholeheartedly, and thinking I had been happy there, now expected that I would soon leave because, they said, it was impossible that the state I had left behind would not render that which I now wished to embrace unendurable because of the great disproportion between them. They instilled such a hope of this in my brother, who was traveling far away at that time, that he sent word to my sister to leave all their business in my hands. These good people did not know the great graces and mercies which the divine compassion had bestowed on me in my former state, nor those which he showered on me in the state to which he had been pleased to call me. May his name be eternally blessed!

As I have already said, I found only sweetness in obedience. I had a complete openness of heart toward my superior and my novice mistress. I was humiliated when they did not act toward me as they did with the other novices who were no more than sixteen years old. I admired these young girls, so mortified and disciplined in all the regular observances, and it was my opinion that I was very far from their virtue. It seemed that I had become a child again and I acted with them in a spirit of simplicity, although they showed me more honor and respect than I deserved. One of the things which made me happiest was that the novices did not get involved in activities. Thus I spoke with my divine Spouse of the mercy he had shown me in freeing me from the burden of being involved in everything, as had been necessary while I was a lay person. Oh, what a great relief! I could not contain my happiness in not having to be involved in activity or being spoken to about business.

XXXV.

Sometime after I had been clothed with the religious habit, temptations began to attack me on all sides, although I was not tempted to leave religious life.[7] I have never been tempted on that score. These were temptations to blasphemy, to immodesty, even to pride, despite the fact that I was experiencing both my weakness and poverty. I felt insensible and dull in the face of spiritual things and suffered from a spirit of contradiction toward my neighbor and an inclination to destroy myself. It seemed to me that I had been fooled by the devil and that I had deluded myself; I now believed that what had happened to me and what had been considered as coming from God, was mere imagination. Everything I had experienced, all that I have described above, rose up before me and caused me to suffer grievously.

Dom Raymond came to see me and gave me every possible help. At first the confidence I had in him made me believe that what he told me was the truth. But he had hardly left when I thought I had deceived him. My imagination was so aroused and all the objects in it in such

---

7. Marie's clothing took place on March 25, 1631, just two months after her entrance. The length of the postulantship was arbitrary, determined by the community. Two years of novitiate was required, however, counting from the date of entrance. Thus Marie will pronounce her vows on January 25, 1633.

turmoil that I suffered a migraine headache which never left me. In addition, obedience kept me engaged in needlework for the altar which demanded meticulous attention, contributing still further to my headache. My imagination made me suffer more than anything else, inasmuch as its restlessness was most unusual for me. Formerly it had been quieted by the activity of the spirit in which it played no part and, therefore, was silent. The reversal of this state led to many temptations.

All this never hindered my observance of the Rule. It was only my superior and Dom Raymond who were aware of my state and who feared that it might cause me to leave and return to the world because they had seen instances like this. But at the core of my soul there was a conformity to God, for I thought that his Divine Majesty was exercising his justice upon me, that he was dwelling in me in a region which seemed far away and that it pleased him, while looking at me, to see me suffer. For in my compliance to this suffering, I did not know in what part of my spirit he dwelt. I was hardly aware of him and I received no consolation, for I found myself alone in bearing my cross. (At least I was not aware of any other help.) Thus, the darkness I endured was very great. My whole inner task was to try to be patient and not fall into any voluntary imperfection.

At this time we heard of the possessions which had happened to our nuns at Loudun.[8] This filled me with compassion and a hatred of the devil who was so bold as to dare approach and trouble those servants of God; and I prayed often for these poor, afflicted people. One night, at midnight, as I went to see our mistress of novices who was ill, I remembered as I went through the dormitory to pay homage to the Most Holy Trinity through the intercession of the most holy Virgin and, in order to frustrate the devil, to say some vocal prayers for this cause. This I did. On my return, I was no sooner in bed (I had no candle) than there rose up in my imagination a horrifying specter in human form which I saw as clearly as in daylight, although my eyes were closed. He had a long face, of a bluish color, with huge eyes bigger than a cow's; in order to mock me he thrust out a long, ugly tongue and with a grimace gave a howl which I thought could be heard all over the dormitories. At first I was trembling, but then I made the sign of

---

8. This bizarre case which Aldous Huxley uses for the basis of his famous novel, *The Devils of Loudun,* created a great stir throughout France. With little knowledge of psychology at their command, the seventeenth century had no hesitation in reading the events of Loudun as a case of diabolical possession. Since the religious of Loudun were Ursulines, the monastery at Tours had a special interest in the case.

the cross and turned my back on him and I saw this image no more. I slept soundly until morning when I went to my superior to tell her all that had happened and to see if she had heard the howling, for her cell was just under mine.

She told me no, but that she had been uneasy and restless all night. On another night while I still heard some sisters walking through the dormitory, suddenly I felt this evil spirit slipping into my bones, into my very marrow and nerves to destroy and annihilate me. I was terrified and I could neither move nor call out to anyone. This went on for a long time. Then, having suffered grievously, I felt in myself a strength and vigor so powerful that it seemed like another spirit come to do battle against the first one, so that in no time it had been conquered and brought to naught. Then I was free.

When the Reverend Mother Prioress of Loudun spent some time with us here at Tours, I told her about this. She told me that often the devil did something similar to their exorcists. Since that time this has never happened to me again.

Returning to my interior sufferings: they lasted for almost two years with no respite except for a few moments. Dom Raymond was sent to be prior of the Feuillants, and this distance of 120 leagues deprived me of his help. One day, prostrate before the Blessed Sacrament, abandoning myself to Our Lord, I heard in my heart this verse of the psalm "in convertendo Dominus": "They who sow in tears will reap in joy" (Ps 126:5). Then the burden of my cross was lifted as though someone had removed a huge heavy garment; and instead of the weight of the cross, I experienced the words of Our Lord: "My yoke is sweet and my burden light" (Mt 11:30). I still had my crosses but they were sweet and easy to bear. They lasted until after my religious profession.

XXXVI.

Since Our Lord had taken away Dom Raymond who had been my director for about twelve years, I felt frequently impelled to seek help from the Fathers of the Company of Jesus.[9] They had not yet

---

9. In the spring of 1631, Dom Raymond was assigned to Toulouse. Another Feuillant, Dom Louis, replaced him. Marie was at this time going through a period of agonizing trials, and Dom Louis with his practical and rather opaque sensibility did nothing to relieve her. It was at this time that she first turned to the Jesuits for spiritual direction.

been established at Tours, but there was something in me which told me that the Divine Majesty wished me to be helped by them. However, I felt that Dom Raymond would return and that while I waited I ought to ask help from one of their priests whom I knew. I did this, yet I could get help from no one in my difficulties. I feared that it was some caprice which moved me so often to seek help from the Jesuits, so I said nothing about this out of respect for my absent director and also out of fear of acting capriciously.

The day of my profession arrived and I made this act wholeheartedly.[10] Our Lord visited me that day with some consolation—or better, he lifted my cross. After returning from the choir, I entered my cell and prostrated myself to offer to Our Lord once again the sacrifice I had just offered him publicly. While in this posture and in a state of great intimacy with his Divine Majesty, I heard interiorly that henceforth, in imitation of the seraphim mentioned by the prophet Isaiah, I would fly constantly in his presence and in his service with six wings: first, by a faithful observance of the vows I had just made; second, by constant adherence to divine love and divine union. Just as the movement of the wings of the seraphim was constant, my love and my correspondence with grace would have no truce, no boundary or limit, neither in the practice of my vows and virtues, nor in the use of the three powers of my soul—all of which were to be directed to a very close and intimate union.

Although this instruction was effective in nourishing me and inclining my soul completely to God, yet it was done in so secret a way that it did not free me from my sufferings except at the moment of this grace when I pronounced my vows. At that time I would willingly have gone through fire (had that been necessary) in order to offer my sacrifice with more purity and better interior and exterior dispositions. This was on the day of the Conversion of St. Paul, January 25, 1633, in the thirty-third year of my age. My son, having shrewdly managed to come from Rennes, was present. Since he had not been allowed to be present at my clothing, he had now made his own plans, for he did not intend to be fooled twice. At this time he was not yet fourteen years old. His pain over my leaving him had softened—or at least he made it appear thus.[11]

---

10. January 25, 1633.

11. Dom Oury conjectures that Claude had deliberately brought about his dismissal from the Jesuit school at Rennes in order to assure that he would be present for his mother's profession ceremony. Thus, Marie's use of the word "shrewdly." Oury, *Marie,* I, p. 207.

The following Lent Father Georges de la Haye of the Company of Jesus, who had preached the Advent devotions and was going to preach at St. Gatien, came to give instructions in our monastery from time to time. I had a strong impulse to speak with him but for the reasons mentioned above, I said nothing, leaving it all to God's providence. My superior, who knew the dispositions of my soul, asked me if I would like to see this priest and open my heart to him. I answered that I wanted to do this but that for various reasons I had never asked.

She asked him to see me frequently during his visit to Tours, which he promised to do—and did with great charity. When he heard me out, he required me to write down the way God had led me from my childhood, including everything that had happened in the course of the graces his Divine Majesty had been pleased to give me.[12] Although I had permission from my superior to do this, it gave me great repugnance unless I also wrote what I was able to remember of the sins and imperfections of my whole life so that by this he could better judge my disposition. I received permission and I did this as faithfully as possible, putting it in the hands of this priest. Following this, he assured me that it was indeed the Holy Spirit who had guided me and that I would be very guilty were I to have heart or love for anyone but him.

As soon as I began to open my heart to this good priest, all my pains disappeared as though I had been freed from my captivity and I knew for certain that God had wanted me to do this. Father de la Haye wanted to know all about my son's affairs and wished to oversee his progress in the studies which he had begun in Rennes. My sister did not wish to commit herself to paying his full board and tuition since he was living outside her house, but she indicated what she was able to pay and this kind, charitable priest found some devoted people who would provide for the rest. He took my son to Orléans, where he entrusted him to Father Poncet. He completed all his studies there with the exception of Rhetoric, which he did at Tours since the Jesuit Fathers had now established a house. Here my sister took care of him, having him live in her home. Then, ordered by Father de la Haye, he returned to Orléans to complete his philosophy.

Since that time, with my superiors' permission, my spiritual direction has always been in the hands of the Jesuits. They were established at Tours a little while after this.

---

12. For the events surrounding the writing of the *Relation of 1633,* see the Introduction, p. 37.

XXXVII.

Following the assurance that Father de la Haye gave me that I was on the right path, I remained in deep peace. One of the things which had upset me was that even during my sufferings, I experienced the continual presence of God. This seemed incompatible to me with the frivolity and wildness of my imagination; and there were other imperfections as well. In addition, ever since I had become a religious I had never been able, no matter how hard I tried, to follow the subjects of meditation which were read to us three times daily in community. Although I was reassured on this point and my judgment put to rest, yet once again fear seized me, warning me that if it were really the Spirit of God which led me I would certainly have been able to conform to the community since this was where God was to be found. But since I have been in contact with Father de la Haye, all these fears disappeared in a moment. My mind enjoyed its ordinary clarity and my imagination no longer troubled me.

I found myself in a new state, enjoying the same peace and exchange with the Divine Majesty which I had had before, but now with very special graces for understanding Holy Scripture which Father had told me I should read. My superior gave me a copy of the New Testament which I read a little, along with my breviary. Before this I had used Rodriquez for my reading of Rule, but my director had me stop this. As I have said, I read very little because I was too interiorly absorbed to permit this. I simply observed my obligation of Rule as well as I could.

During my second year of profession I was appointed assistant mistress of novices—of whom we had a good number. Some days before this, I had a premonition that Our Lord wanted to change my state, and during this period of anticipation I continued my usual colloquies with him. One night, after speaking intimately with him, I had a dream that I was with a secular woman whom I had somehow met.[1] Together we left our usual residence and, taking her by the hand, I led her along with me with giant strides. We experienced great fatigue

---

1. Four accounts of this dream are extant:
1. A letter to Dom Raymond, May, 1635 in Oury, *Correspondance,* pp. 42–43.
2. The *Relation of 1654;*
3. A fragment in Martin, *Vie,* p. 223;
4. An account in the *Jesuit Relation* for 1672.

because we encountered very severe obstacles along the way which hindered us from reaching our goal. I did not know where we were nor how to get where we were going, yet I was able to overcome all these obstacles, while drawing this good woman along with me.

Finally we arrived at the entrance to a very beautiful place. Here there was a man garbed in white, in clothes resembling those in which the Apostles are depicted. He was the caretaker and he admitted us, indicating with a gesture that we must go the way he pointed since there was no other way. And then, although he said nothing, I understood that we had reached our destination, and I entered with my companion. It was a beautiful place with no covering but the sky. The pavement was like white marble or alabaster, composed of squares, cemented together by a pretty red substance. It was very silent there and that was part of its beauty.

I entered further and saw in the distance, on my right, a little church of white marble, constructed in a pretty, ancient style. On top of the pinnacle was a chair in which the Blessed Virgin was seated, holding her little Jesus in her lap with her arms around him. The place was very elevated and beneath it lay a great, vast country, full of mountains and valleys and thick fog which covered everything except a tiny house which was the church for this country, and which alone was freed from the mists. The Blessed Virgin, Mother of God, gazed at this country which aroused as much compassion as fear.

When I first saw her she seemed as rigid as the marble on which she was seated. There was a narrow path leading into this vast country, along which I led my companion by the hand; but when I saw the Blessed Virgin, in a burst of affection, dropping this woman's hand, I ran toward the divine Mother, holding out my arms, so that they could touch both sides of this little church on which she was seated. There I waited, wanting something from her. As she gazed at this poor country, I could see only her back. In a minute I saw her bend and look at the Blessed Child, to whom, without speaking, she conveyed some important thought.

In my heart, I felt that she spoke to him of this country and of me and that she had some plan for me and thus I strained toward her with outstretched arms. With endearing grace she turned toward me, and with a smile full of love she kissed me without saying a word. Once

---

The accounts are very similar, each providing little details not present in the others. This dream which took place within the octave of Christmas 1633 is interpreted by most of her commentators as her definitive entrance into the apostolic way, just as her childhood dream may be seen as her initial call to the contemplative way.

more she turned to her Son and spoke to him as before; and once again I understood interiorly that she spoke to him of her plans for me. She turned for the second time and kissed me afresh. Again she spoke to her most adorable Son and then bestowed a third kiss on me. These caresses filled me with an indescribable sweetness. Then she began to speak about me again. I could never describe the beauty and sweetness of this divine Mother's face. She was the same age as when she was nursing our adorable little Jesus. My companion had stopped two or three steps down into this country from whence she looked at the Blessed Virgin whom she could see from the side.

When I awoke I had such a profound peace and sweetness in my heart that it lasted for several days, uniting me to Our Lord and to the love of the most holy Virgin. Nevertheless, I didn't know the meaning of what had happened and what had made such a deep impression on my soul. Everything remained a deep secret for me.

XXXVIII.

Following the events I have already mentioned, I was assigned to the novitiate to assist the Mistress of Novices. My task was to teach Christian doctrine in order to form the novices into capable members of the Institute. This I did with the great zeal which God gave me for proclaiming the mysteries of our holy faith. Many lights were imparted to me on this subject, and I bore in my soul a grace of wisdom which sometimes led me to say things which I would never have dared to say without the outpouring of the Spirit. One time while speaking on the "Hail Mary," my spirit was completely swept away.

It was concerning these words: "and blessed is the fruit of thy womb." This brought to mind that passage of Holy Scripture in which Our Lord is the "corn of the elect and wine bringing forth virgins" (Zec 9:17). I had to stop and let the Spirit have his will with me; or, to put it better, simply to endure what was happening in my soul. Concerning this "wine" there came to me a passage from the Song, "My beloved is a cluster of grapes to me" (Song 1:13). I saw him as this corn. I saw him as the nourishment of our souls in the Blessed Sacrament, crushed like the grapes in the winepress of the cross, thus producing that wine out of which virgins spring. When possible I would then withdraw to my cell to sustain this outpouring of divine nourishment. The same thing happened when explaining the creed. I told all this to Father Dinet, my director, who had me write out many of these things.[2]

Before beginning my instruction, I would read something from the little *Catechism of the Council of Trent* or that of Cardinal Bellarmine, although I did this rather seldom. When, after speaking of some article of faith, I would turn to questions of morality, I was amazed at the number of relevant passages of Holy Scripture which would come to mind. I could not remain silent, for I had to obey the Spirit who possessed me. I did this twice a week for almost three years for twenty or thirty sisters who came to the novitiate for this instruction.[3]

All my life I had had a great love for the salvation of souls, but since the kiss of the most holy Virgin I have had a consuming fire for this. Since I could not travel through the world as I would have wished to win souls, I did what I could in the novitiate, adjusting myself to each one's individual capability. There were some very fine souls there, hungry to learn what would serve them in their vocation of dedication to God. They would urge me more and more to continue my instruction. God also desired this of me, and I experienced interiorly that it was the Holy Spirit who had given me the key to the treasures of the Sacred Word Incarnate. He had opened them to me through the knowledge of Holy Scripture in those passages pertaining to him, although hitherto I had not studied or meditated on them.

What I had read or heard on various occasions provided me with good insights, but they were nothing like the impressions made on me in my prayer, during which my nature became more capable of sustaining those divine touches and outpourings concerning the kingdom of the Sacred Word Incarnate. These nourished me and revealed to me the blessings and sovereign domain that the Father had given him over hearts, through his victory over the empire of death and hell by the shedding of his Precious Blood.

Previously, in an intimate union with his Divine Majesty, I had learned that my Spouse was like the bosom of the Eternal Father from which flowed a great river and torrent of grace, which was the Holy

---

2. Jacques Dinet had assumed her direction following the departure of Georges de la Haye for Orléans in 1634.

3. It is notes from these conferences which Dom Claude gathers up and uses for the basis of his book, *L'École Sainte,* which appeared in 1684. Although it purports to be his mother's work, it is clear that Claude's hand guides it. Whatever notes he was able to collect would hardly have been sufficient for the volume he produces. It does, however, indicate the general structure of her instructions and her heavy reliance on Scripture.

Spirit, flooding all his saints and nourishing them with his divine life. It was the life of this Spirit which nourished my soul with such fullness and exuberance that I could not keep some flashes of this from appearing. Had I kept this in check, I myself would have been devoured by the subtlety of this impression. If someone came to see me while I was at work on some delicate needlework for the altar, my answers always had something of this inner fire so that I got the reputation of speaking only in maxims, maxims which were passages from Holy Scripture. Without premeditation on my part these fit appropriately into my replies.

XXXIX.

The spirit of grace which possessed me in the way I have described, along with the impression made on my soul by the sacred kisses of the Blessed Virgin, led me to understand that his Divine Majesty wanted to put me in a new state. All my longings and inclinations were directed toward entering into these divine plans; and my will was consumed in love for his commands no matter what happened to me. Beyond this, from the very time I had become an Ursuline there was something which told me that the Divine Goodness had hidden me away in this holy house as in a refuge, until such time as he would dispose of me according to his plans. I always rejected this intuition for fear that it was a temptation of the devil; just the same, it always returned. Finally, without reasoning about what this could mean, I simply abandoned myself to God.

Then at the age of thirty-four or thirty-five, I entered into that state which, as it were, had been shown me and of which I had remained in expectation. This was an outpouring of apostolic spirit (which is nothing else than the Spirit of Jesus Christ) which took possession of my soul so that it could no longer live except in him and by him. I was thus wholly dedicated to zeal for his glory so that he would be known, loved, and adored by all peoples whom he had redeemed by his Precious Blood.

My body was in our monastery but my spirit, united to that of Jesus, could not remain shut up there. This apostolic spirit carried me in thought to the Indies, to Japan, to America, to the East and to the West, to parts of Canada, to the country of the Hurons—in short, to every part of the inhabited world where there were human souls who belonged by right to Jesus Christ. With inner certainty I saw the demons gaining victory over these poor souls, whom they snatched from the domain of Jesus Christ, our divine Master and Sovereign Lord, who had redeemed them by his Precious Blood.[4]

As I watched this happen so surely, I became jealous, unable to endure the sight. I yearned for these poor souls; I gathered them to my heart; I presented them to the Eternal Father, telling him that it was time he exercised his justice in favor of my Spouse, to whom he had promised all nations for his inheritance. I reminded him that his Divine Son, through the shedding of his blood, had satisfied for all the sins of men who had previously been condemned to eternal death; yet there were still souls who did not live or belong to him. It was these souls whom I carried in my heart and whom I presented to the Eternal Father, begging that they all be given to Jesus Christ, to whom they rightfully belonged.

In spirit I roamed through the vast stretches of the Indies, of Japan and China, and kept company with those laboring to spread the Gospel there. I felt closely united to these workers because I felt that I was one with them in spirit. While it is true that in body I was bound by my rule of enclosure, nevertheless, my spirit did not cease its travels, nor did my heart cease its loving solicitations to the Eternal Father for the salvation of the many millions of souls whom I constantly offered him. The spirit of grace which acted in me moved me to such boldness and familiarity with the Eternal Father that it was impossible for me to do otherwise. "O Father, why do you delay? It is a long time since my Beloved shed his blood. I beg you in the interests of my Spouse," I would say to him, "be faithful to your word, O Father, for you have promised him all nations."

By a light infused into my soul, I saw more clearly than by any human light the meaning of this passage of Holy Scripture which speaks of the sovereign power which the Eternal Father has given the adorable Word Incarnate over all men, and this bright light which revealed so many wonders now kindled in my soul a love which consumed me and increased my longing that this Sacred Word would reign as absolute master—to the exclusion of all the demons—in the souls of all rational creatures. I felt that justice was on my side. The Spirit which possessed me made this clear and compelled me to say to the Eternal Father: "It is only just that my divine Spouse be master. I am wise enough to teach all nations about him. Give me a voice strong

---

4. The importance of the "Precious Blood" in Marie's spirituality had begun with her "conversion" (March 24, 1620). At this state, however, it has developed an apostolic dimension. See Guy Oury, "Le Sang de Jésus-Christ," in *Ce que croyait,* pp. 107–16.

enough to be heard to the ends of the earth to proclaim that my divine Spouse is worthy to reign and to be loved by all hearts."

In my eagerness and yearning toward the Eternal Father, I gave tongue, without any effort on my part, to passages from the Apocalypse which speak of this divine King of nations. I never sought out these passages, but they were urged on me and produced by the Spirit which possessed me. Turning to myself, I found myself in spirit among whole groups of souls who did not know my Spouse and who, therefore, did not pay him homage. I paid homage for all of them. I embraced them and longed to gather them all in the most Precious Blood of this adorable Lord and Master.

I never left off begging the Eternal Father on his Son's behalf that he would give him his inheritance, interceding as though I were his advocate. My spirit was wholly outside myself and my body became like a skeleton. My director, inquiring about my interior state, was fearful that this long-lasting preoccupation might cause my death. He ordered me to do everything I could to distract myself. I tried hard to obey but it was not in my power to change my disposition. He saw me about this matter several times but when he realized how powerless I was, he left me in peace under the direction of God who moved me so forcefully.

XL.

When Father Dinet (rector of the Company of Jesus who, as I have said, was given to me for my director by my superior) came to see me, I told him everything that had happened to me. He approved my attitude and said that what I had seen in my dream could be realized if I were to go to Canada. When I told him this, I had not even known that there was a Canada in the world. What I had seen had not given me any clear idea about it for, as I have said, I remained ignorant, leaving everything to the guidance of Divine Providence, letting myself be led by the Spirit who acted upon me so powerfully concerning the salvation of souls.

In view of my life as a religious in an enclosed monastery, I could not imagine that Our Lord would want me to be bodily present in a foreign country, to actually serve him there. My spirit, however, was continually present there, so that everything I did was fervently related to this. In fact, I felt that the duty Our Lord had assigned me was to do in spirit whatever I could for those poor souls and to animate each of the sisters, both the professed and the novices, to join their intentions to mine. Although I did my best to conduct myself prudently, I could not hide my feelings and some people got the impression that God wanted something very special of me, and that he would withdraw me from the monastery to work for his glory.

My constant supplication to the Eternal Father for the extension of the kingdom of Jesus Christ in those poor souls who did not know him grew in intensity. One night I once again presented this grave matter to him, but by an inner light I saw that the Divine Majesty was neither paying attention to me nor showing himself disposed to listen to my entreaties as he usually was. My heart was sharply pierced, and I experienced a sense of humiliation and submission to his divine justice concerning whatever was lacking on my part, since I saw nothing lacking on the part of my Spouse.

I would have been satisfied to be condemned to suffer every imaginable torment in order to achieve the purity necessary to win my point, softening the heart of the Eternal Father so that my beloved Spouse, whom he had constituted King of all nations, would by their conversion possess them in peace. I felt that the Eternal Father was pleased by my entreaties in so just a cause, but that there was something lacking which he wanted of me in order to grant my request. I cast myself at his feet, abasing myself to the very center of my lowliness so that his divine goodness would bestow on me whatever he wanted in order to hear me in the cause of my Spouse.

Then I felt in my soul an effusion and a ray of divine light followed by these words: "Ask of me by the heart of Jesus, my beloved Son; it is through him I will hear you and grant your requests."[5] At this moment the Spirit which moved me united me to this divine heart of Jesus so that I could neither speak nor breathe except in him. I experienced a fresh outpouring of grace through this divine heart and through the spirit of my Jesus which worked marvels in me for the spread of the kingdom of Jesus Christ. All this happened about 1635.

I addressed everything to the Eternal Father and my sighs—the external manifestation of what my soul was undergoing—were like flaming arrows aimed at the heart of the Eternal Father. (Not that I imagined anything material, but I don't know how else to express myself satisfactorily.) It seemed that I was aware of all the souls re-

---

5. Jamet comments that this is the beginning of Marie's "cult" of the heart of Jesus. "This revelation gives a new orientation to her life. . . . She offers nothing to God and asks nothing from him except through this adorable heart." Martin, *Vie,* p. 308. See also the fragment from the *Relation of 1633* in this volume, p. 191 See Oury, "Le Coeur du Fils de Dieu," in *Ce que croyait,* pp. 128–37.

deemed by the Precious Blood of Jesus in whatever corner of the earth they dwelt; and my love turned toward the most abandoned in the lands of the savages where I wandered endlessly.

XLI.

One day as I was praying in these dispositions before the Blessed Sacrament, leaning against my prie-dieu, my spirit was suddenly absorbed in God and there was again shown to me this vast country as I have described it before in all its details. Then this adorable Majesty said to me: "It is Canada that I have shown you; you must go there to build a house for Jesus and Mary."[6] These words vivified my soul while at the same time reducing me to indescribable abasement at the command of this infinite and adorable Majesty. He gave me sufficient strength to reply, however: "O my great God, you can do all and I, I can do nothing. If you will help me, I am ready. I promise to obey you. May your adorable will be done in me and through me." In this reply there was neither reasoning nor reflection: my response followed upon the heels of the command, my will being at that very moment united to the will of God. Then there followed an ecstasy of love in which this infinite Goodness caressed me in a way no human language can express and from which sprang a profound source of inner strength.

I no longer saw any country except Canada, and my greatest journeyings were in the land of the Hurons, accompanying those who were spreading the Gospel, united in spirit to the Eternal Father under the patronage of the Sacred Heart of Jesus, in order to win souls for him there. I stopped in many places throughout the world, but the country of Canada was my home and my country. My spirit, withdrawn from my body, seemed to have gone beyond me, which caused my body to suffer a great deal. Even while I ate, I was journeying through the country of the savages, working for their conversion and helping the missionaries. My days and nights were spent in this way.

At the very same time, Father Poncet sent me a *Relation* describing events in Canada.[7] Although unaware of my dispositions concerning this mission, he wrote telling me of the vocation God had given him to go to work there. He also sent me a picture of Mother Anne de

---

6. Oury suggests that this happened early in 1635 at about the same time that she spoke to Dinet. Oury, *Marie*, I, p. 209.

7. Antoine Poncet, S.J., a teacher at Orléans, and later a missionary in New France, will become a lifelong friend and correspondent.

Saint-Barthélemy, a Spaniard, in which Our Lord was depicted with his hand pointing toward Flanders, inviting her to go to serve him there where heresy was causing such ruin. "I'm sending you this picture," he wrote "to urge you to go to serve God in New France." I was amazed at this invitation for, as I have said, he knew nothing of what had happened to me, for I had kept this very secret. However, this was like a spur which activated still more powerfully the fire for the salvation of souls which consumed me. I dared not speak to anybody of the command the Divine Majesty had given me because it was such an extraordinary undertaking and, at least in appearance, so far from my condition, and without precedent. I begged the Eternal Father, reminding him of what he already knew of my inability to accomplish what it had pleased him to command me, telling him that he could do all while I could do nothing, and that I must act according to his good pleasure. Thus, I awaited his orders; but meanwhile I lived, as it were, in the missions, my heart consumed with zeal. A fragrant and fruitful peace sustained me, without which I could never have endured such a profound and constant absorption.

At the same time that the Divine Majesty kept me in this state of mind, he led Madame de la Peltrie, a woman of eminent virtue, to donate herself and all her goods to the Canadian Mission.[8] She had been deeply moved in reading a *Relation* in which Father Le Jeune wrote that he hoped to find some holy woman who would wish to come to gather up the blood of the Son of God for the salvation of the poor barbarians of Canada. This holy woman, won over by this invitation, sought every possible means to accomplish her desires. At this time God was pleased to order her affairs so that it became suitable to carry out her plan. Thus she fell mortally ill, so that the doctors awaited her death from moment to moment. While she was in this condition, she recalled her desires for Canada, which she considered to be her own beloved country. She was inspired to make a vow to the glorious St. Joseph that if he would obtain from God a return to health, she would build a school in Canada for the poor daughters of the savages. At the very moment she made her vow all her violent

---

8. Madeleine de la Peltrie (née Chauvigny), like Marie, had aspired to religious life, had been persuaded to marry, and had been left a widow while still young. Inspired by the *Jesuit Relations,* she determined to give her life and her fortune to the missions of New France. Unable to overcome the violent opposition of her family, she resorted to a ruse: she engaged in a formal marriage with Jean de Bernières, a devout man holding the office of Treasurer of France at Caen, where he had founded a small group of lay-contemplatives. The ruse worked and it was as Bernière's wife that Madeleine secretly made her preparations for Canada.

suffering, which had been considered mortal, ceased, leaving her only in a state of weakness. When the doctor arrived, he was astonished. "Madame," he asked her, "What has become of your pains?" She answered him innocently, "They have gone off to Canada." Since he knew nothing of what had happened, he took her answer as a kind of joke.

At the time this was happening we did not know each other nor had either one of us ever heard of the other. But the divine goodness was arranging everything very smoothly.

XLII.

The Divine Majesty wished to divest me of my own will even in what he commanded, for he wanted everything to come from him and not from any creature. I experienced this one day while praying before the Blessed Sacrament. I was praying for the salvation of souls in the familiar way that God generally permitted me. Suddenly I was stripped of my power to speak with him, and my soul, plunged in ecstasy, was absorbed into its sovereign and only good. Here it enjoyed his caresses and divine embraces in indescribable love and intimacy. In this state he showed me the value of winning souls for him and encouraged me to ask him for them. Then my soul, stung by the interests of its Spouse, the Sacred Word Incarnate, and full of loving impatience, longed to further his work. I would gladly be a victim, giving a thousand lives, if that were possible, for this cause. I begged the Eternal Father to enable me to carry out the command he had given me: to build a house in Canada in which he would be adored and praised in company with Jesus and Mary—along with St. Joseph who should never be separated from them. I said this because I had a very clear impression that it was he whom I had seen as the guardian of that place; thus I felt deeply that Jesus, Mary, and Joseph should never be separated.

One day while I was at table in the refectory, in a state of loving absorption, I could not help murmuring: "O my Love, this house must be for Jesus, Mary, and Joseph." I was sure that the Divine Majesty would receive my petitions favorably since I acted only through the Holy Spirit. He gazed at me while I, at the same moment, longed to prevail lovingly over his will, for I saw that I had justice on my side in the cause of my divine Spouse. Then this adorable Majesty, looking upon me, made me understand that while I had wished to triumph over his will, he, through love, willed to triumph over mine. What can ever express this interchange of love! Then he effected in my soul a blissful pain. I scarcely breathed, acknowledging myself vanquished, saying with what breath I still had, "O my Love, my great God, I want nothing; I can wish for nothing. You have triumphed over my will. How can I will since you have captured me and made me powerless to will? Then, O my Love, you yourself must will in the righteousness and justice of your divine will." At this my soul was wholly lost in this great ocean of love, the Divine Majesty of God.

119

At the conclusion of this indescribable state (about which I can only stammer), I found myself in a completely different attitude. Now there was peace, repose, indifference, and a habitual dwelling in the will of God with whom I discussed everything pertaining to the kingdom of the Sacred Word Incarnate. This divine will guided me and kept me in these peaceful ways in a manner hitherto unknown to me, although formerly I had been favored with great graces. I no longer experienced anguish over the salvation of souls or over anything else, for although I still had the same insight and sense of mission as before, now I felt that this divine will was doing everything for me.

Following this divine action, I remained in this state for almost a year.

XLIII.

After being in this state for about a year, the Divine Majesty strongly urged me to reveal everything which had happened to me concerning Canada. In order to obey him, I resolved to speak to Father Salin, to whom at that time I went for spiritual direction.[1] He silenced me at my very first word, mortifying me curtly and ridiculing me for being caught up, as he put it, in fantasies. I dared not say anything further, considering myself such a wretched creature that I would have been more surprised had he not sent me off in this way. Thus I continued to live in my humiliation. To the Sacred Word Incarnate I said, "My dear Love, if there is something to be done, do it, please. Since nothing is hidden from you, you know that I am such a poor creature that no one will ever believe me. They will say that I want to delude others, after having been deluded myself; this is especially true in something like this which seems quite out of the realm of common sense, considering what I am: a nun, who should live and die in her cloister. Nevertheless, I wish to obey you in all this. Please, then, arrange things yourself so that I shall be able to do whatever is your holy will."

After that I was in peace, awaiting the moment of the divine command. More than ever I felt that I was in our monastery in Tours

---

1. Michel Salin, S.J., was stationed at Tours 1634–39 and replaced Jacques Dinet as Marie's director. He was exactly the wrong person, especially during this period of uncertainty. Charlevoix describes him as "a man who believed you could never go wrong in rejecting the extraordinary." Pierre F.X. Charlevoix, *La Vie de la Mère Marie de l'Incarnation* (Paris, 1724), p. 204.

only until Our Lord would draw me from it and that he had put me there to train me in religious life and prepare me for what he planned for me. I usually banished these thoughts, but the last impressions I had received from Our Lord about Canada were immovably fixed in my spirit. Just the same, I struggled against them, fearful that I had been mistaken. In fact, I was so cowed that I did not dare say anything about my interest in Canada. This fear was increased by the way Father Salin had rebuffed me so sharply. I was not so successful, however, in hiding all this, for my special attraction for the Canadian Mission was discovered. Many devout people wrote to me about this while others came to speak to me. Yet I never revealed my secret to anyone, feeling in myself a very great reserve, restrained by the Holy Spirit who guided me. I spoke of it in general as a holy enterprise, greatly for God's glory, according to what the *Relations* reported. In our monastery I did what I could to get everyone to beg God for the conversion of the savages. I aroused the fervor of all my sisters so that there were constant prayers, penances, and Communions in the community.

After some time the Divine Majesty made it clear that he wanted me to do something about the command he had given me, and he strongly urged me to set aside my fear and rise above human respect in order to reveal all that was in my mind about Canada. It was this constant, interior impulse which finally urged me to write to Reverend Georges de la Haye. After all this, my fear of being deceived by the devil redoubled, so that I kept procrastinating, not daring to ask permission of Reverend Mother Françoise de St. Bernard, our prioress, nor to speak about it to Father Salin. This was where my childish lack of faith had brought me. Yet, on the other side, God threatened to abandon me if I did not obey, reminding me that it was not a question of a house of stone but of a spiritual edifice for his greater glory.

While I was in this state, not knowing to whom to open my heart, Father de Lidel of the Company of Jesus came to see me. I had a strong inclination to tell him my difficulty—which I did. After listening to me, he told me that I had a duty to tell everything to Father de la Haye. This I did with the permission of my superior who, recognizing that this was a matter of conscience, did not look at my letter. Father de la Haye, having reflected on the whole matter, urged me to prepare myself for whatever Divine Providence would demand of me, and he hoped that the moment for carrying out the project would soon arrive. He showed my papers (as I learned later) to Father Poncet, with whom I had already exchanged letters concerning the Canadian missions as well as other things—so that everything was done through the intervention of Father de la Haye.[2]

Once I revealed my secret to this priest, my soul was established in profound peace as I have hitherto described. I wanted nothing for myself but only what pertained to the divine will. As for the poor savages, here I knew no limits—they were my constant concern.

XLIV.

At the same time that I was speaking to Father de la Haye, I learned that a man of deep piety and virtue had been powerfully moved and inspired by God to work for the salvation of these poor savages, to the point of sacrificing his life for them.[3] At that time he was holding a position of importance in his order; however he had so advanced his plans that he was on the verge of concluding matters with those in charge of the mission country. The whole thing had been kept so secret, however, that only one person, a lay brother who was his companion, was aware of it. This brother was so upset that he did not know to whom to pour out his heart. He decided to write (he was at Paris at that time) to our Reverend Mother who knew the Father involved, so that she might write to dissuade him from his enterprise. At once she gave me the task of telling him about my own vocation in very general terms and showing him that we knew of his plan. Never was a man so surprised to learn that what he had kept so secret was discovered, and—even more—that I myself was considering going to Canada! He wrote to tell us how surprised he had been and to assure me that he would help in every way he could to facilitate my passage, provided he were certain that my vocation was from God. And, in fact, he did feel certain of this. He was a person of such virtue and ability that I was profoundly consoled that he approved my vocation and believed it to be from God.

Seeing his plan revealed, he knew that the news would spread and that it would be better to explain to some of his friends who might oppose him. He wrote to one of them who was then at Tours who,

---

2. These "papers" are undoubtedly what Oury refers to as the "Relation of 1636," a document available to Claude and which he uses extensively. See Oury, *Marie,* I, pp. 218–19.

3. The unidentified man is Marie's former director, Dom Raymond. This revelation initiates a series of letters about her own Canadian vocation, a valuable source of details for this period. Oury, *Correspondance,* pp. 24–74.

after reading the letter, came to me forthwith to tell me how shocked he was at his friend's plan and to say that he was going to have recourse to their Father General to stop him because of the injustice he was doing his order by leaving. I did my best to console and calm him, telling him how shocked I was at his opposition to such a holy enterprise and that he should bless God that N. wanted to sacrifice himself in so noble a plan as the conversion of the savages; and as for myself, I intended to use all my power to pray for him.

From the moment he heard me he became as stirred up as such a person can get and began to tell me bluntly that I had certainly known about N.'s plan, that N. had caused me to take leave of my senses, that I was on his side, that he had written to me and led me astray by his fantasies. On my part, far from being upset by his talk, I smiled to see him attacking me like this. He left still feeling the same way, and I wrote to N. warning him that he would have done better not to say anything to his friends, for the latter was going to reveal his plan and oppose it.

In fact, during this period, he never lost a chance of coming to torment me, urging me to tell him if I, too, wanted to go to Canada. Seeing his anxiety, I told him frankly that he was right, but that I was not worthy, being only a mere nothing. And, furthermore, that my vocation as a religious was at cross-purposes with such a plan. After this he persecuted me more than ever, giving me no rest, acting contrary to his natural disposition which was really very gentle. He was so angry that he frequently resorted to insults and invectives, even writing whole pages of them to me. What annoyed him most was that I continued in peace during all these contradictions. He even sent another priest whom I knew to argue with me—having first given him his own impressions of me. He got no further than before. I told them both that they would change their minds, that someday they themselves would want to go to Canada but that they would never get there. They both ridiculed me.

The second of the two went on his way to Paris and wrote to me at once, apologizing for all he had said and telling me that he was very much attracted to the Canadian Missions. I began to invoke the Holy Spirit for the other priest, not that he would go to Canada but that he might gain a little understanding of the effect this has on hearts for the salvation of souls. This happened during the feast of Pentecost.

This priest was so deeply touched that he could not sleep all night; he was seized with remorse for what he had done and had so vivid a longing for the salvation of these poor savages and such a desire to go to help them, if it should please God to grant him this grace, that he could not endure it any more. He came to see me in great humility, not daring to raise his eyes. Right from the start he said, "What have you done to me? I can't go on living. Ask God to be merciful to me. Never again in my life will I oppose the Canadian Mission. Alas! I am not worthy to go there to serve his Divine Majesty. What could I do there? No, I will never again say anything against such a holy vocation. I shall be careful not to oppose N.'s plans, neither will I blame you any more for your own devout feelings. I esteem them deeply and I ask God to pardon my resistance."

The next post from Paris brought me a letter from N. which read: "I think he [his original friend] has been profoundly changed in the last three days. I had a compelling vision at this time in which he seemed to be before his Sovereign Judge to receive the punishment due to his rebellion against the divine will, and that you were the one who was accusing him of this rebellion. Then this poor criminal, trembling with fright and half-dead, fell on his face at the feet of his Judge, crying, 'Be merciful!' He promised amends, saying like another St. Paul, 'Lord, what do you want me to do?' He was told to rise and then, his eyes falling on me, he said to me very gently, 'Why have you done this to me?' I answered him by pointing you out to him, telling him that this was your work and that he owed it to you. I do not know if he will be converted. If he is, as he was in my vision, my vision will have foretold the truth. Let me know what happens."

In fact the remorse of conscience and the pains of this other person were even worse than those he revealed to me, even though he told me a great deal more than I have mentioned here. This occurred at the time of N.'s vision. This person did not follow through with his desire to join the missionaries, but he never again reverted to the stubbornness and indignation he had shown me. His reversion concerned only himself, however, for he continued to respect the vocation to Canada in others. Nevertheless, he did hinder N.'s departure, for just as he was on the verge of leaving, he was assigned new duties which obliged him to remain. It was clear that Our Lord had given N. those devout sentiments to lead him to pray for the salvation of souls and to facilitate my vocation for Canada. Had he not approved it, neither his Eminence, the bishop of Tours, who freely followed his advice, would have given permission for my work nor would our community have consented.

XLV.

During this time Madame de la Peltrie, as I later learned, was trying zealously to find someone who could help her fulfill her vow to found a seminary for Indian girls in Canada. Her relatives were raising difficulties, however, so that unless she was able to get the help of some trustworthy person, she could not carry out her project. Someone put her in touch with Monsieur de Bernières, an honorable and virtuous man, treasurer for France at Caen, who in his unsparing charity was able to give her considerable help by appearing to seek a marriage with her.

He accompanied her to Paris to find some means of carrying out her plan where she begged him to get in touch with one of the fathers of the mission. At that time he knew that Father Poncet was in charge of everything involving mission affairs. He located him at the novitiate house where he was then living and confided to him Madame de la Peltrie's secret plans, especially how she wanted to take some Ursuline religious with her. Immediately Father recalled my vocation and said that he believed that I was the one whom God had chosen for this work, confidentially giving him his reasons for thinking so. This good man was comforted by this information and lost no time in recounting it all to Madame who, in her zeal for the salvation of souls, was overjoyed to learn that her plans seemed to be coming to a head.

She submitted her project to a number of important and learned servants of God who all approved it, assuring her that the Divine Majesty desired this sacrifice of herself and her fortune and that, even were she to perish, she should undertake this voyage for his glory. Fathers Dinet and de la Haye were among those she consulted. The latter asked Father Poncet to write to me explaining everything that had happened, for Madame and I did not know each other at all except for what the Jesuit Fathers had told her about me without my knowledge. All this occurred in November 1638.

Our Reverend Mother received letters from both Father Poncet and the above-mentioned lady which suggested me for this project which they planned for the first possible embarkation date. In this Madame de la Peltrie expressed her strong desire to have me to establish her school. As can be easily imagined, Reverend Mother was astonished and moved to see that my vocation for Canada seemed to have some foundation and that God himself was working to realize it.

She came to find me and kneeling with me, she told me everything. We thanked the Divine Majesty and she instructed me to answer the letters and to write to Monsieur de Bernières as well. All was carried on by letter until the very end and everything was kept secret from the community (except for three of us: Mother St. Bernard, prioress, Mother Ursule, and me)[1] until January because Madame did not want the affair revealed since her relatives would undoubtedly oppose it.

Even before I learned of these events, I had a strong interior sense that the end was approaching. We never wearied of marveling at the guidance of God: the meeting of this good lady, the meeting of Father Poncet with M. de Bernières—all without any effort on their part but through the pure providence of God. This made me sing his mercies, treating lovingly with him who is so infinitely faithful in his promises, his call, and his guidance.

Various disagreements with the Company were encountered concerning the details.[2] They preferred Madame to postpone her voyage to the following year or to go alone and send for religious afterwards. She didn't want to listen to this proposal, for she had no desire to go without us. To settle this affair it was decided to have a meeting in the house of Monsieur Fouquet, Counselor of State, where there gathered Fathers Dinet, de la Haye, and Lalemant, the leading men of the Company, and M. de Bernières and Madame de la Peltrie.[3]

During this meeting they pointed out to her that her request had come too late, that all the ships were already chartered so that there was no room for her baggage and provisions or for her companions. She must be patient and wait for a later embarkation. She persisted, however, saying she would charter a ship at her own expense, even though it was the regulation that everything be transported free for three consecutive years. To this suggestion of hers, they had no answer.

There remained only the question of which religious would be taken. She said that she wanted me and that she would not leave without me and that she intended to ask my superiors both for me and for a companion. It was pointed out that the bishop of Tours had the reputation for being a difficult prelate and that to be on the safe side she should rather take religious from the Ursulines of Faubourg St.

1. Ursule de Ste. Catherine had been the novice mistress during the period when Marie was the assistant. She herself had considered the Canadian mission but was instead elected prioress of Tours in 1639.

2. Concerning the role of the Company of One Hundred Associates, see the introduction, p. 24.

3. This is Charles Lalemant, S.J., who had recently returned from Canada. He is the brother of Jérôme and uncle of Gabriel who was later martyred.

Jacques at Paris.[4] But she persisted that it was me she wanted. Father de la Haye, seeing the disagreement, took the floor and spoke strongly and effectively, pointing out that it was a matter of justice to favor Madame in a project so pious and so clearly for the glory of God, and which had been judged to be so by capable people, etc. He carried the argument and it was concluded that they must agree to what she asked, and that in order to facilitate the question of which religious she should bring with her, she herself should go to Tours.

The principal members of this assembly—as well as Fathers Dinet, de la Haye, the Commander of Sillery, and M. Fouquet—wrote to his Eminence, the bishop of Tours. Father Dinet, Provincial of the Company of Jesus, wrote to Father Grand-Amy, the rector at Tours, with the result that Madame received a favorable answer from this prelate. Letters were also written to our Mother and to me.

Madame de la Peltrie, now very happy, generously consigned a considerable sum of money to charter a ship and prepare it for immediate departure. Father Charles Lalemant kindly undertook all the responsibilities for this. Madame immediately informed me about everything that happened. It was on January 22, 1639, feast of the Espousals of the Blessed Virgin and St. Joseph, that we received the news and that our Reverend Mother revealed the secret to the whole community while they were having special feastday devotions in a hermitage dedicated to St. Joseph. I had made the decision to be absent—and also it was my turn to serve in the kitchen. Everyone was so startled by the news that they could hardly believe it, persuaded that such an extraordinary thing could never happen. Nor could they believe that there was a sister so blessed as to be chosen by God for an enterprise of such consequence. They never tired of blessing God.

Madame de la Peltrie, having dispatched her affairs in Paris, left Paris for Tours, accompanied by M. de Bernières. On the morning that we received letters advising us of their departure, I was with the boarders of whom I had charge, when my intuition told me to leave everything and go to the hermitage of St. Joseph to thank him for the great grace he had obtained for me. I did not obey this inspiration because I did not think it proper to go through the garden where I would have to pass by some workmen. However, I was urged to do this by such a loving movement that I had to obey. Taking two boarders

---

4. This is Marie's first reference to the Ursulines of Paris who will play a major role in the Ursuline mission in Quebec. Many Jesuits favored them over the other Ursuline congregations. See the Introduction, pp. 25–26 and Jamet, II, p. 360, n. 6.

with me, I went to thank with special fervor this great saint for the grace he had obtained for me.

About an hour later Mother Ursule de Ste. Catherine came to find me saying, "Dear Sister, what graces God has given you! This lady is coming to see you. She will be here very shortly." This dear nun, who herself had a strong inclination to go to Canada, was so deeply touched by this news that she could hardly speak, for no matter what she was told she could not believe that this was actually happening. As for me, I believed it, for the goodness of God had given me signs, making me understand that like a good father and a good friend he was faithful to his promises and would manage everything very easily. After learning this news, I no longer doubted why I had been so strongly moved to thank St. Joseph to whom the seminary was to be dedicated. I resumed my thanksgiving to the Divine Majesty, submitting and abandoning myself to his divine command.

On February 19, 1639, Madame de la Peltrie and her party arrived at Tours. In order to keep matters as secret as possible she had assumed the name of Madame de la Croix. Meanwhile Father Grand-Amy had received the letters from Father Provincial Dinet. Madame having gone to see him, they conferred together about this project; then he alone went to see his Eminence the bishop and explain everything to him, especially that they wanted me and also hoped that I would be given a companion. This worthy prelate was totally amazed. Turning toward Father, he exclaimed, "Is it possible, Father Grand-Amy, that God is asking for my daughters for such a holy enterprise? I am not worthy of this grace! Can someone be found who would wish to venture into such a laudable prospect? Take this good lady to my daughters. Tell the Mother Superior for me that their gates are to be opened and that she and her party are to enter and be received as I myself would be." Having received such a favorable response, they came, very pleased, to our enclosure.

XLVI.

As Father Grand-Amy arrived at our monastery he met Madame de la Peltrie and M. de Bernières at the entrance. He told them that he had accomplished his task and that she could obtain whatever she wanted. He explained the result of his visit with the bishop, announcing that Madame had the bishop's permission to enter the monastery. She was inexpressibly relieved to find that what she had been warned

would be so difficult had in fact been so simple. She and M. de
Bernières marvelled as they praised God.

Meanwhile our Mother Prioress was told to open the gates to
admit Madame into the monastery. At once the whole community
ranged in choirs to receive her. We began with the "Veni Creator,"
etc., and then followed with the "Te Deum." It seemed that this dear
lady had brought the joy of paradise with her. Each one wanted to be
the first to cast herself at Madame's feet, offering herself to be her
companion in all the labors she would undertake. When I saw her I
remembered the woman who had been my companion in that vast
country which I had seen. The innocence and sweetness of her face
helped me recognize her, although she was not wearing the same
clothes. At once my heart and spirit felt united to hers for the enterprise she was about to undertake for the glory of God.

She stayed in our house for three days, deliberating on what
would be required for the choice of the person who would accompany
me. We had Forty Hours Devotion during this time to pray for this
intention. Following an inspiration, as well as the advice of a person of
trusted virtue, I asked for Mother St. Bernard, who was later named St.
Joseph. There was strong resistance to this because our superior said
that she was too young; she was then twenty-two and a half. However,
Madame, M. de Bernières, and I all persisted in our request. Finally, to
the exclusion of all the others who were offering themselves, she was
chosen. Her parents were then notified. They strongly opposed this
decision but Our Lord who had made the choice showed himself the
master. There were other circumstances involved in this choice of
which I have spoken elsewhere.[5] She was thus given to me as my
companion; and in order to fulfill the vow she had made should her
parents consent to her sacrifice, she took the name "St. Joseph."

My sister, learning that I was about to undertake this journey,
came with a notary in order to put a stop to it.[6] All her efforts, which
she believed were undertaken through zeal for justice, had no effect
nor were they any more successful with his Eminence, the bishop of
Tours. She tried everything imaginable, but our good God dispelled
it all.

Then something happened to me which lasted for the three days
preceding our departure. For these three days Our Lord possessed me

---

5. See Marie's letter to the community at Tours at the time of Mother Marie de St.
Joseph's death in 1652. Oury, *Correspondance*, pp. 436–66.

6. Her intention was to frighten Marie by threatening to cancel the annuity for
Claude that had been promised at the time of Marie's entrance.

so completely that I could neither eat nor sleep nor do anything else. I was totally withdrawn and separated from everything. I saw all that would happen in Canada. I saw crosses without end: interior abandonment by God, a crucifying trial from creatures, and a life in which I would be hidden and unknown. Then his Divine Majesty spoke to me, piercing me through with his words: "Go and serve me now at your own expense; go and give me proof of the fidelity you owe me in return for the great graces I have already given you." I cannot tell you the terror I felt at this thought.

During this period I felt impelled to do and to suffer generously whatever would be pleasing to the Divine Majesty. Thus I resolved to submit and follow his commands in this work which, humanly speaking, I could never undertake without his help. No one noticed what I was experiencing, for our sudden departure had me engaged in all kinds of business as well as making my farewells both inside the monastery and at the grill.

Sometime before this, I had an imaginary experience. It seemed I was on a street or in a completely new town where there was a building of extraordinary grandeur. All that I could see was that the building, instead of being constructed of stones, was fashioned of crucified bodies. Some had only their legs pierced; others were attached a little higher up. Some were crucified at the waist while others again had their whole body crucified. But it was only those who were entirely attached who bore it willingly. I found this so wonderful that I could not take my eyes away. Since that time this has made a deep impression on me and given me a strong love of the cross.

Let me return to what I was saying before. I found myself completely alone, already feeling that terrifying solitude which, in accordance with God's plan, I was to suffer. In this loneliness I found myself indifferent to leaving my sisters, my relatives, my friends, even to leaving France. It seemed that my soul had gone before me, unable to wait any longer to be where the Divine Majesty called it. I recognized that in all this God had put me among these religious women so that this life would prepare me in spirit to give myself wherever his Divine Majesty would call me. Had there been a question of going to the Indies, to Japan, to China, or Turkey, I would have gone, for my spirit was united to a Spirit that governed it in everything.

XLVII.

The day of our departure was February 22, 1639. His Eminence, the bishop of Tours, sent his carriage to take us to the episcopal palace for his blessing. He was not feeling well, but he gave us Holy Communion and we then had breakfast with him. Following this he gave us a beautiful exhortation on the words Our Lord spoke to the Apostles as he sent them on their mission. He pointed out our duties and had us give him our promise of obedience. Then my companion and I asked him to command us in holy obedience to undertake this mission so that in receiving this command from him who holds the place of God we would be generously blessed. He thus commanded us gently and lovingly. After this he had us sing the psalm "In exitu de Egypto" and the "Magnificat." We had with us our Reverend Mother Prioress and the sister with the best voice in our monastery, as his Eminence had wished. We returned then for our last goodbyes to our community, after which we took to the road with our foundress and M. de Bernières, who had with him his valet and his lackey. Madame had only a maid servant since she had come as inconspicuously as possible.

During our trip our time was carefully regulated since we were with prayerful people who nurtured our devotions. It was M. de Bernières who organized our time. On the fifth day of our journey we arrived at Paris where we were to stay because of Madame's business affairs.[7] We stayed outside the cloister of the Jesuit Fathers where M. de Meules, a royal steward, gave us his whole residence, which was like a little refuge for us except that business obliged us to see various people and receive important personages who honored us by their visits. Here we stayed until the feast of St. Joseph when we went to our monastery in the Faubourg St. Jacques, where we were in our own element, for it is very difficult for religious to live outside their cloister.

We did our best to get a choir religious from this house to come with us. She was given permission by everyone involved in our mission; but our joy was short-lived, for the very evening before we were to leave, his Eminence, the bishop of Paris, changed his mind and rescinded his permission, which left us in great difficulties. We had to leave without her but were still hopeful that we would receive her later. We availed ourselves of the influence of the Duchess of Aiguillon and

---

7. Marie here omits a painful episode in the journey. Marie's sister, having failed in her effort to dissuade Marie from going to Canada, notified Claude of his mother's departure. Upon her arrival at Orléans Marie was confronted by her son. At first hostile and angry, Claude, upon hearing his mother's explanation, "felt his heart lifted above material concerns" and when their conversation ended his anger and sense of loss were replaced by admiration. Martin, *Vie,* p. 375. This pious rendition, however, fails to explain or justify Marie's apparently heartless conduct. Claude is now close to twenty years old, old enough to be entitled to an explanation. It seems inconceivable that his mother would leave for Canada without telling him.

the Countess of Brienne, who approved our project. They did their best, but his Eminence, fearful of refusing them, withdrew so that they were unable to see him.

The queen had sent word that she wished to see us, and the Countess of Brienne brought us to St. Germain where her Majesty was.[8] In her goodness and piety she looked on us with very special love, indicating how very happy she was at our voyage to Canada and how deeply impressed she was by Madame de la Peltrie who, not satisfied in offering her fortune, was risking her life as well. She had us recount everything that had happened to bring us to the realization of our enterprise. We made one last effort with her Majesty to obtain Mother St. Jérôme whom his Eminence had refused. Immediately she sent a gentleman to find him and tell him that he was to let her come with us; but he had hidden himself so that he could not be found. Ultimately, we had to leave without this nun.

While at Dieppe, where we stayed until May 4, we lived with the Ursulines of Dieppe. They let us have one of their religious, a virtuous and wise person named Mother Cécile de Ste. Croix, who joined us although we were of different congregations.[9] Thus we were three choir religious. Madame left her maid in France because the latter dreaded the dangers. In her place she engaged a young woman from a good family in Tours who was ready to follow her in all perils. This maid was just nineteen. Now she is a choir religious, the first to make profession in Canada.[10]

XLVIII.

On the morning of May 4, 1639, we left the Ursulines to attend Mass at the hospital and to take three of their sisters who were to embark with us. They were going to found a monastery in Canada through the generosity of the Duchess of Aiguillon, who was to be their foundress.[11]

During all our comings and goings since we had left Tours, my

---

8. Anne of Austria, wife of Louis XIII. They saw the Dauphin, the future Louis XIV, who was just six months old.

9. The Dieppe monastery belonged to the Congregation of Paris.

10. This is Charlotte Barré who had been recommended by Father Salin. After seven years as Madame de la Peltrie's maid, she entered the Ursuline convent in Quebec in 1646.

11. These three Augustinian Hospital Sisters were the foundresses of the Hôtel-Dieu in Quebec, the first hospital in Canada.

spirit seemed never to be in my body. I was longing for that moment when I could actually risk my life for God, to give him some meager witness of my affection and acknowledgement of the immense mercies he had showered on his poor creature. I saw that I had nothing but my life to offer, but the nothing that I was could offer only this, along with my heart and my love.

Swept away by these feelings as I was about to embark and thus realize my desires, I prostrated myself before the Blessed Sacrament in the choir of the Hospitalières. There I remained for a long time. I felt, then, that the Holy Spirit possessed my soul and directed it towards emotions in accord with what I was about to do as a proof of my love for the adorable Word Incarnate to whom I was giving myself. Dear God! Who can say what happened during this total donation and abandonment of myself. I don't know how to express it. I felt then (and the Spirit who guided me was witness of this) that I had never done anything so gladly, and I felt that the Sacred Word Incarnate, king and ruler of all nations, was pleased with what I was doing.

While I was absorbed thus, the wife of the governor of Dieppe honored us by coming in her carriage to take us to the dock. Here we were completely surrounded by people, yet my soul was so caught up that it was only with difficulty that I could divert my attention from the adorable Word Incarnate. No one would have known this to look at me because I managed to do everything I was supposed to in a very normal manner. As I stepped into the launch which would take us out into the harbor, it seemed to me that I was entering paradise since I was taking the first step on the way to risking my life for love of him who had given it to me. I sang to myself the mercies of so good a God who had brought me with such love to where I had so long desired to be.

The whole period of our crossing was for me a continual sacrifice during which I offered myself day and night in our constant dangers, as a holocaust to our divine spouse. When a huge iceberg appeared out of the fog and like a fury came directly toward the hull of the ship as though it would cleave it in two, everyone was crying, "Have mercy! We are lost!" Thus surrounded by death, which to all human appearances seemed inevitable, Father Vimont gave general absolution to everyone.[12] Yet my heart and soul remained in the most profound peace and tranquillity. I did not feel a single movement of terror, but

---

12. Barthélemy Vimont, S.J., is going to Canada for the first time to take up his duties as superior of the Mission.

was ready to make a holocaust of myself even to the deprivation of seeing our dear savages.

I recalled all the graces and favors Our Lord had given me concerning Canada—all his commands and all his promises—and I found myself despoiled of all desire either to live or die. My whole inclination was to do the will of God which, as things appeared, seemed to be our death. Madame our foundress clung to me so that we might die together. I arranged my clothing so that when the crash came I would be decently covered. At this final moment Father Vimont made a vow to the Blessed Virgin in our name. My companion, Mother St. Joseph, began the litany of this Holy Mother and everyone took it up.

In a moment, the pilot who had been told to turn the rudder to one side, without his doing anything, found it turning in the opposite direction. This caused the vessel to veer so that the huge iceberg which at that very moment was no more than a pike's length from the ship, passed along our side. It was so close that we heard it scraping. It was clearly a miracle and everyone was crying, "Miracle!" I saw this frightful iceberg but the fog kept us from seeing its peak. What I saw was so appalling that I could not believe that the sea could sustain such a huge mass without its sinking to the bottom. This happened because the ship, buffeted by storms, had drifted northward.

During all this terror, I felt sure in the depths of my soul that we would arrive at Quebec, although this did not keep me from making those acts which God asked of me at the time. When this accident occurred, we had just gone to confession and Communion and were singing the canonical hours. It was Trinity Sunday.

During the entire crossing, we kept our rules exactly. We had a comfortable cabin, for although Madame de la Peltrie had chartered only a small vessel, the officers of the Company had put us aboard the flagship. Our cabin was large enough for us to say office in choir: the Hospitalières on one side and we on the other. Here we both slept and ate. It was closed off like a hall and it had some good windows which provided us with fresh air. There were eleven people comfortably accommodated here. Our voyage lasted three months. Our Lord gave us the grace of hearing Mass and receiving Communion every day except for thirteen days when storms rocked the vessel so violently that we could not even stand upright.

Twice we thought we would perish. Once when we first caught sight of land and disembarked in order to pay our vows to the Blessed Virgin as we had promised. The launch, overcrowded, almost overturned because all were eager to go and thank this divine Mother, and they forced their way into the boat so that it was almost sucked to the bottom under the ship. The second time we got off course because of the fog, and we sailed along a rocky coastline for almost sixty leagues without being able to steer away from it.

We met numbers of savages along the shore, which gave us great joy. These poor people who had never seen anyone like us were filled with awe. And when they were told that we were the daughters of a chief who, out of love of them, had left our own country, our relatives, and all our comforts, and still more that we had come to teach their daughters so that they would not burn in fire but would be instructed in what they must do to be happy forever—at this their astonishment knew no bounds. They could not understand it. They followed our ship, accompanying us as far as Quebec.

Let me return to my subject: one must admit that when God has won our hearts, there is pleasure in suffering. Although we were comfortably lodged and cared for as well as possible, and in a very fine ship, nevertheless there is still much to suffer for people of our sex and condition. One would have to experience this in order to believe it. As for me, I thought I would die of thirst. Our fresh water spoiled as soon as we left the harbor and my stomach could not sustain strong drink which produced a very painful sickness. I hardly slept during the whole voyage. I suffered such an agonizing headache that I don't think it could have been worse without killing me. Yet my heart and soul remained in profound peace in union with my sovereign and only good. I never neglected my duties or what charity to my neighbor demanded except for three days when everybody on board was sick because of the storm which rocked the vessel. May God be eternally blessed for the mercies granted me during that time.[13]

---

13. The fullest account of the voyage is found in a letter from Cécile de Ste. Croix to her community in Dieppe. For the text see Oury, *Correspondance,* pp. 951–58.

XLIX.

On August 1, 1639, we reached Quebec. Since the little ship of Madame de la Peltrie was the lightest, it took the lead and was the first to arrive, bringing news of our arrival. This was a source of special joy to the country, for in our company there were four priests of the Company of Jesus, a lay brother, and eleven other people, not counting the servants. Father Vimont, who was coming to be superior of the missions, was in charge of everything and thus was on board the flagship. The other priests were on the other ships where they could be of spiritual help to the passengers. While we were at Tadoussac, however, everyone gathered into our ship so that we had five Masses a day, since another priest had joined us. Thus we arrived in very good company.

Monsieur de Montmagny, governor of New France, who in anticipation of our arrival had already sent his launch filled with refreshments, received us and the priests with great affection. The colonists were so happy to see us that as a sign of joy they put aside all their work for the day. The first thing we did was to kiss the ground of this land to which we had come to give our lives for the service of God and the poor natives. We were then taken to the church for the solemn singing of the "Te Deum." After this the governor took us to the Fort for breakfast. Finally, the priests and the governor led us to the place destined to be our home.[1]

The next day Fathers Vimont and Le Jeune, along with the other priests, took us to the village of the natives, our beloved brothers. There our joy was great as we listened to them singing the praises of God. We were delighted to find ourselves in the midst of our dear converts who, on their part, were delighted to see us. The leading Christian put his daughter in our hands and within a few days a good number were entrusted to us, as well as all the French girls of suitable age.

We were given a small house for our residence until such time as a spot could be chosen for building our monastery. It had only two little

---

1. The Hospital Sisters were led to the upper town to a house built for them by order of their foundress, the Duchess of Aiguillon. The Ursulines fared less well. Madame de la Peltrie had rented a very small house only a few yards from the river. For the first few nights, however, both groups slept in a house belonging to the Company of One Hundred Associates, since neither of their houses was ready for occupancy.

rooms, yet we felt better lodged—having with us the treasure we had come to find, our beloved converts—than if we had possessed a kingdom. Our little house was soon to become a hospital because of an outbreak of smallpox which attacked the natives.[2] As we still had no furniture, we had to make up all the beds on the floor, and these were so numerous that we had to step over the beds of the sick. Three or four of our natives died. The Divine Majesty gave great devotion and courage to the sisters, who felt no revulsion at the sickness or the filth of the savages. Our foundress put herself in the vanguard and although of a very delicate constitution, she took upon herself the most menial tasks. How precious are the first fruits of a spirit impelled by the salvation of souls!

We had to study the language of the savages, and the urgent desire I had to teach them led me to be the first to embark on this. Father Le Jeune, who had just completed his charge as superior of the Missions, was commissioned by his successor, Father Vimont, to help us spiritually as well as in the study of the language. This he did with great charity, for which we will be forever in his debt. As it was more than twenty years since I had undertaken anything of a speculative nature, at first the study of a language so totally different from ours gave me a headache. It seemed to me that learning all these words by heart and memorizing the forms of the verbs—for we study according to the rules—was like rocks rolling around in my head.

All this, along with trying to put my thoughts into such a barbarous language, led me to believe that humanly speaking I would never succeed. I poured out all this lovingly to Our Lord who helped me so much that in a short time I had acquired considerable facility so that it no longer hindered or interrupted my interior absorption. My study became a prayer which made this language no longer barbarous but sweet to me. In a short time I knew enough to be able to instruct our beloved converts in everything necessary for their salvation.

There were a large number of savages at this time, and both men and women poured into our parlor. We instructed them and talked with them; and this was an indescribable consolation for me. For the next four or five years we were constantly exercising charity toward these poor Indians who came here from various tribes. We had many

---

2. One of the consequences of bringing the Indians in from the forest in order to "civilize and evangelize" them was that they became a prey to European diseases for which they had no immunity. The death toll from smallpox was enormous. Thus the Jesuit settlements were often associated with death, and the hospital begun by the Augustinians was called "la maison de la mort."

boarders, both permanent and transient, who were brought to us to prepare them for baptism and the other sacraments.

The Indians are very dirty and the fact that their bodies are permeated with smoke gives them a very bad odor—to say nothing of the fact that they do not use underclothes. Yet all of this never disgusted us; on the contrary, each one considered it a privilege to clean up the boarders who were brought to us. Our Lord has continued to give us this grace so that we have found our delights among these dear souls redeemed by the blood of Jesus Christ. Nothing else has seemed so pleasant to us. When their number decreased because of war and the violence of the Iroquois, this caused us a grief like the loss of something very precious.

L.

Now that I was in this country and able to observe it, I recognized that it was what Our Lord had shown me six years earlier. The huge mountains, the vast spaces, the location and shape of the land—all these were still marked on my spirit as though I had just seen them. Now I saw the very same thing except that there was less fog. This rekindled the fervor of my vocation and my desire—by a total abandonment of myself—to suffer everything and accomplish whatever Our Lord wanted of me in this new venture and in the kind of life one must live here—so different from that of our monasteries in France, yet no less regular and in its own way both poor and frugal.

From the beginning we marked off our cloister by thick cedar logs instead of walls. We had an entrance for the native girls and women as well as for the French girls—all for the purpose of instruction. Our house was so small that in a single room about sixteen feet square we had our choir, our parlor, our dormitory and our refectory; in the other, we had a classroom for both our French girls and our natives, as well as our kitchen. We had to construct a lean-to for the chapel and sacristy.

The filth of the savage children, who were not yet used to the cleanliness of the French, sometimes led us to find a shoe in a cooking pot. And every day we discovered hair and charcoal which, however, did not disgust us. People who came to visit and to whom we told these stories for amusement could not understand how we could adjust to this. Still less did they understand how we could embrace these little orphans, holding them on our laps, when their bodies were heavily smeared with grease and covered only by a small greasy rag, giving them a terrible odor. For us all this was an unimaginable happiness. Once they had grown accustomed to us, we tried to clean them up over a period of a few days, for this grease with its strong smell clung to their skin like glue. Then we gave them some underwear and a little tunic to protect them from the vermin which covered them when they first came to us.

Thanks to the goodness and mercy of God, our vocation and our love for the natives has never diminished. I carry them all in my heart and try very gently through my prayers to win them for heaven. There is always in my soul a constant desire to give my life for their salvation—should I be found worthy—and to offer myself as a continual holocaust to the Divine Majesty for the safety of these poor souls. It is this which strongly urged me to make a special vow into the hands of the Jesuit superior of the Mission: to do everything which God might ask of me, whatever I must do, and suffer in this vocation with which I have been honored.

In fact, this desire has deluged me with crosses. The most agonizing that I have ever suffered during the fifteen years I have lived in this new Church—or during my whole life—is that pertaining to our converts: Algonquins, Montagnais, Hurons—who for the last ten years have been the prey of their enemies. I could never express the anguish I have suffered on these occasions. Since this frightful persecution, we have not had so many boarders. Nevertheless, we have always had some except for a short period during our fire when our residence was destroyed, as I will explain later.[3] They soon returned, however, to our great consolation, along with the French girls of whom there are now a good number in this country.

We remained in our tiny residence for more than three years, with great bodily suffering and inconvenience, yet very happy in the way of the Spirit. For me personally, what gave me the greatest difficulty was still not having any lay sisters and having very few choir sisters. Since at this time there were only five of us, we had to undertake all the manual work as well. It was extremely difficult to fulfill our duties, and my poor sisters were terribly overworked. I did whatever I could to help them but this was very little compared to our great need.

During this time our monastery was being built in the most beautiful and convenient place in the country. We took up our residence there, finding it much easier to fulfill our duties now that we had space

---

3. For Marie's detailed account, see further, pp. 163–64.

for the recitation of the Office.[4] The number of religious increased through the Congregation of Paris as well as through our own Congregation since we had established a union—according to the desire of those involved—on which Our Lord has continued to bestow great blessings up to this present moment.[5]

LI.

Let me return now to my own particular dispositions and to God's guidance of me. Since our arrival here I have experienced in actual fact what the Divine Majesty had indicated would happen to me. This began at first by a change in the peace I had enjoyed during the voyage—a peace intense and profound although so subtle that it seemed distanced from me. Now it seemed very far away—a very painful and crucifying sensation for the human spirit. As I described in another state, the powers of the soul are no longer able to act, having been annihilated at their center by God when he took possession of the soul. It seemed that they were dead (although in fact they remained alive) and this, as I have remarked, is a very agonizing experience. Yet the soul consents even to this cross. Unable to wish for or to love anything but what the Spirit of God does and unconcerned about the sufferings of its lower powers, it pays no attention to anything but the divine darkness in which it is lost. In this state the lower powers experience what it is like to serve God at their own expense. It is here that one learns if one has solid virtue.

In all this Our Lord gave me the grace to continue to act as I had before. I discussed my attitude with Father Le Jeune who helped me in every way.[6] During the voyage I had been completely alone, with no ability to explain what was happening to me because of the subtlety of this action. I was able to speak only about what should be done in external matters. This was very painful because I had always had

---

4. The Ursulines moved into their new monastery situated in the upper town on November 21, 1642. Although it was, as Marie describes, beautiful and spacious, it was also desperately cold. They had not yet learned to build for the freezing Canadian winters. Marie later commented that one of the reasons why letter writing was so difficult in winter was that the ink froze in its bottle.

5. At the time of writing there were eight sisters from France in the Quebec mission.

6. Paul Le Jeune, although Marie's director until the arrival of Jérôme Lalemant in 1645, seems never to have inspired her confidence in the same way as Dom Raymond or Father Lalemant. The fact is that his many responsibilities often kept him absent when Marie needed him most.

facility in expressing myself and in saying enough to make my dispositions understood.

While in this state I entered into another yet more painful. I saw myself, it seemed to me, despoiled of all the gifts and graces God had given me, as well as of all my talents, both interior and exterior. I lost confidence in everybody; the holiest people and those from whom I had had the most support became my greatest crosses. God also permitted that they felt constant aversion toward me, as they later admitted. I saw myself as the lowest, most debased creature in the world, worthy of all contempt. In view of this I could only admire the goodness, sweetness, and humility of my sisters in accepting their complete dependence on me and in putting up with me.

I hardly dared raise my eyes because of the burden of this humiliation. In this humility of spirit I tried to do the lowest and most menial work, not considering myself worthy of doing anything else. At recreation I hardly spoke, feeling unworthy to do so. I listened with respect to my sisters, forcing myself to speak in order to avoid singularity. In my other duties I was able to act as usual and to continue to apply myself to the study of languages, since this was compatible with my inner state.

To my knowledge, nobody noticed what I was suffering, although it seemed clear to me that everyone would see me as wretched as I saw myself. I was so filled with this thought that I could find nothing good in myself, seeing only that I was far from God, deprived of all his graces and special mercies. I revealed a little of my feelings to Father Le Jeune, since I found myself powerless to do otherwise. He recognized enough to understand the problem and be compassionate. Sometimes a ray of light would illumine my soul and touch it with love, and this put it in a transport of happiness. It seemed to me then that I was in paradise and in the intimate enjoyment of God who held me in his embrace. But this soon passed and only served to increase my suffering, for I passed from an abyss of light and love into an abyss of obscurity and darkness.

I saw myself as though plunged into hell, full of sadness and bitterness arising from a temptation to despair which was born in a darkness I did not understand. I would have been lost had God not sustained me by a secret strength. Sometimes I was suddenly brought to a halt and it seemed to me that I actually saw myself on the brink of hell with flames pouring forth from the mouth of the abyss to engulf me. I felt impelled to let go and hurl myself down to displease God whom this impulse led me to hate.

Then in a moment his goodness and mercy, through a secret

outpouring of his spirit, aroused in the higher part of my soul a desire to be cast into hell, not in order to anger God but to satisfy his divine justice by my eternal punishment for having robbed him of my soul which Jesus Christ in his infinite mercy had redeemed by his blood. This was a simple act of faith which drew me away from the precipice. I saw that I deserved hell and that the justice of God would never be wrong in casting me into the abyss. I had a strong desire for this, although I would never want to be deprived of the friendship of God.[7]

LII.

Sometimes I was able to see the various reasons for this change of state in which I found myself. Then I was able to speak about it to the adorable Word Incarnate. While I spoke to him insistently, there appeared before me all the faults, the imperfections, the impurities which I had committed since being called by the Divine Majesty. What had formerly seemed like nothing to me now seemed horrible in light of the infinite purity of God who demanded exact reparation for all I had experienced. How could one ever express the ways of this divine purity and the demands on souls called to live purely a spiritual life? There is no way to express this or to describe how terrible this divine love can be, penetrating and unrelenting in regard to purity, that irreconcilable enemy of purely human nature.

Even when one feels that one's lower nature has been put to death and believes that one has risen above it so that all is the work of grace, still there remain those corners and turns and labyrinths of corrupt nature whose ways are incomprehensible, known only by the spirit of God. It is he who understands these paths and who can destroy them by his intense and penetrating fire and sovereign power. When he wishes, and is pleased to do so, this is a purgatory more penetrating than lightning—a sword which divides and cuts with subtle sharpness. In this purgatory one never loses sight of the Sacred Word Incarnate. He who had seemed to be only love and who formerly had consumed the soul by his divine embraces is now he who crucifies it and divides its spirit, except for the very center of the soul which is the dwelling

---

7. Strange theology, even for the seventeenth century! See the Bossuet-Fénelon controversy in which Bossuet argues that one cannot sacrifice salvation and Fénelon argues that one can, using this text of Marie's for evidence. Paul Dudon, "Lettre autographe et inédit de Fénelon à Bossuet sur le sacrifice absolu du salut," *Revue d'ascetique et de mystique,* XVIII (January 1937): 65–88.

place and throne of God which now appears like an abyss and like a place apart. I cannot express myself otherwise, for that is what this state leads to.

Thus the soul and spirit are honed by this cross and its penetrating thrusts; yet, as I have said, no matter how subtle these thrusts, they never reach the center of the soul which seems not to be in their power. (Although, of course, the soul is a single unity.) It sometimes happens that God, who is the master of this center, seems to hide and leave it for a while; and then it exists in a void—an intolerable state. From thence are born those despairs which would like to throw body and soul into hell.

One time as I was standing near the Blessed Sacrament, I saw a great flame near the window which I thought was the abyss of hell. In a sudden movement my whole being wanted to cast itself down, out of contempt for God. Suddenly his Divine Majesty with secret strength held me back and in a moment this terrifying vision ended. I think that if there had not been some panelling there which I could lean against I would have fallen, so violent was this experience.

I have already said that I carried my cross alone, for as far as creatures were concerned they only increased its weight and made it more oppressing. There was only this hidden vision of God to sustain me and help me consent to his divine commands and submit to the divine justice which I know to be fair except for the moment when I experience this complete emptiness. This brought only darkness, which excludes the sight of everything except the suffering one is enduring, a vision which is entirely contrary to God. Nor could I ask him to deliver me, for it seemed to me that my suffering was to be endless and I myself condemned for all eternity.

LIII.

What I wanted to explain at the beginning of the preceding section about the presence of the Sacred Word Incarnate as the cause of my suffering is that in my self-condemnation I was filled with an overwhelming compunction. This moved me to confess to him all my impurities by which I had blemished his gifts and harmed the spirit of grace by which he had led me. By my lack of correspondence, I had in some way given vigor and strength to the spirit of nature which injures and wrongs his blessed plans in an indescribable way. It is impossible to express how effective, how penetrating and painful to the human spirit are those insights issuing from him who has been appointed judge of the living and the dead—the more so since the soul not only recognizes her judge in the Sacred Word Incarnate, but her Spouse as well. Yet despite her impurities, he never denies her the role of spouse. Nonetheless, he wants to examine her relentlessly, by the secret fire of his divine justice, without telling her how long this scrutiny will last or what the results will be. This is what reduces the soul to an unspeakable humiliation.

Thus the soul is pierced by a painful love which makes it cry out like another Job on his dunghill, confessing his guilt and saying, "Who will give me tears of blood with which to weep for all the impurities I have committed against the purity of your divine Spirit? Oh, my heavenly Spouse! How could you endure that a soul whom you cherish so much has done you so much wrong? Why have you not cast it beneath the demons' feet? It deserves an even greater punishment: to be deprived of your divine countenance and your friendship. One could love you in hell but imagine the loss of seeing you and of being deprived of your good graces and friendship! Yet I deserve all this as my eternal punishment.

"Accept this confession of my sins and punish me according to your adorable judgments, I beg you, for I see that in justice your love must be satisfied. Oh, what punishments I should in justice bear! Then beyond what my own sins merit, my divine Spouse, you know of those two souls whom I have begged you not to leave in the world. I have offered to suffer the punishments for the faults they may have committed against your Divine Majesty and which could render them not only unworthy of your calling and friendship but also of the grace of being dedicated to your holy service. This, added to my own sins, means that I should be doubly punished. I have innumerable sins and hidden faults but here, in detail, are some which seem to me to have especially displeased you.

"You know well, my chaste Spouse, that in the beginning the divine goodness called me in an extraordinary way to follow you in true purity. This was when I was just nineteen. You showed me how mistaken I was to believe that I was in a state of perfection and after you had washed me in your Precious Blood and, through a showering of your infinite mercy, you revealed to me the price of purity. At that time I was reflecting, in the light of certain opportunities given me, if I should return to the way of the world and back into that state from which you had delivered me. This temptation arose under a specious reason which made it seem necessary because of the business which N. had left in my hands and from which, humanly speaking, I could not extricate myself.

"It upset me and would have confounded me had you not, in your boundless goodness, caused the Holy Spirit to speak by the mouth of a young woman who knew nothing of my affairs. During the course of a personal conversation (although I don't think she had any knowledge of the matter in question), she said to me, "One must belong entirely to God." These words struck me and enlightened my spirit, confirming me in your ways. Without this, O my divine Spouse, my spirit would have yielded through faithlessness and I would have left the path of your divine plans for me.

"Yet all of this has never stopped the torrent of your mercies. O my life! You know that on two occasions while I was still in the world, I spent my time in certain indulgences which came from the spirit of nature and in which, under the guise of good, I idled away my time. Finally, had your goodness not withdrawn me, I would have stifled the spirit of grace by which you led me so lovingly. What suffering this has caused me and how I have deserved hell in punishment for my infidelities! Yes, it is just, O Divine Love, that you receive satisfaction.

"Even as a religious I once committed what seemed to me to be an act of hypocrisy. I had false pretensions to humility which led me to beg my superior to humiliate me; yet had she taken me at my word, I think I would have been deeply mortified, for my intention, it seems to me, was not pure. I had a hidden pride which made me act in this way. This is why I deserve all kinds of humiliations from your divine justice. Mercilessly do away with this nothingness and dust. There is no punishment which would not be too light for me.

"One time, under the cloak of justice, I went to give my opinion to my superior. This was masked as virtue but in reality it was pride which led me beyond my duty. Consequently, I committed an act of imprudence—the result of my pretended justice and my brashness. O my divine Spouse, you have endured all this without stopping the flow of your mercy. It is only just that now you take your revenge. Behold me bowed down! Punish me according to the laws that your love has established for chastising my infidelities. Brought, as I am, to the very feet of the demons, I ask your pardon, my divine spouse.

"During conversations I sometimes had with spiritual people, I let myself waste time in what were frivolities and spiritual childishness, considering the purity and candor with which you have directed me. I abandoned this integrity, letting myself take pleasure in conversations in which I poured myself out too freely, revealing what I was experiencing spiritually. This is a grave fault even though it is concerned with spiritual things. Your Spirit, which acts as my censor, made me see the gravity of this. Had this not happened, I would have fallen into even more serious faults regarding the purity and detachment that you wanted of me—but for which you did not then punish me. It is only just that now you assert your rights and punish my folly and vanity which was only the outward manifestation of my secret hunger for my own excellence. Oh, infinite purity! For this I humbly beg your pardon.

"How true it is that you want no distortion in the ways of pure love. And now I have come to sully your new Church with my impurities. I myself have dug those broken cisterns which have infected my entire being so that their poisonous emanations are capable of ruining everything, for they carry with them all sorts of evils which excite the passions to revolt. It seems that you have let the devil take part in all this, to lead me to anger, then to hatred and aversion, and then on to despair so that had your divine hand not protected me, I would be helplessly lost.

"Besides this, I am like someone bound and restrained by means hitherto unknown to me and from which no one knows how to free me but you. It is, then, from you alone that I await help. My bonds hinder me from doing the good that I want and my passions incite me to commit the evil that I hate and want to hate. O God of mercy! Extend your hand, for without it I cannot go on. Forgive all my foolishness, my imprudence, my resentments into which I have fallen through my infidelities. What humiliates me even more is that despite this humility of heart which acknowledges that I am worthy of every rebuff, every disdain and abandonment, when any of these touch me I react like a mere novice, so that if you did not sustain me by your abundant mercy and hidden strength, the infection I carry in myself would make itself felt everywhere.

"My sins are also the reason why I am kept in a charge which prevents me from teaching our converts as I wish.[8] Alas, my chaste Spouse, you know very well my powerful attraction for this great vocation you have given me. Among all the crosses which I bear, that was what consoled me most: to teach them to know and love you. But you see the cause which denies me this happiness. I must let myself be despoiled of this one consolation which still remained to me and humble myself beneath your just punishments. Visit upon me every imaginable torment rather than diminish my love for these dear souls; for it is for their salvation that I have dedicated myself to do good, with

---

8. As superior she is kept busy with other work.

your help, my whole life long—if any good can come from this lowest and most sinful creature under heaven."

LIV.

I can find no way to express the way my soul sighed and cried to the Incarnate Word during this period of interior suffering which followed the first three difficult years of my superiorship.

A little while after, my disposition changed somewhat. The revolt of my passions continued but otherwise I had a free and clear-sighted spirit, delivered from that extreme anguish I had suffered earlier. In this state, however, since I was more free, I was more capable of sin. Ah! What graces God gave me during these countless occasions of sin! It was not that I did not slip and forget myself many times, but had his all-powerful hand not upheld me, I would have been entirely lost in the violence of this revolt. This was especially true in that state of habitual bitterness which aroused feelings of aversion toward my neighbor concerning our disagreements. Nevertheless, Our Lord sustained me so that I never said a single disrespectful word against the person who for various reasons bore the brunt of my aversion.

All this indicated to me a great lapse in perfection, and the interior humiliation I underwent was indescribable. I saw myself so impoverished and deprived of all virtue that I could barely endure it and, in fact, putting up with myself was in itself a great practice of virtue.

In the midst of these brutal attacks of passion I was kept very busy both with establishing our house and with the union of our Congregations.[9] Our Lord gave me the grace to solve the problems, no matter how thorny they were. Our seminary and all our works were going as well as one could have wished.[10] It was said that I was gentle and patient but I who bore my wretchedness found myself very imperfect; and when a trustworthy person came to visit me I could find no other topic of conversation except my imperfections. Although God had confirmed me in his holy intimacy, this simply humiliated me more, for I was unable to understand how such an easy approach to his Divine Majesty could be compatible with the revolt of my passions.

---

9. See the introduction, pp. 28–29.

10. Indian boarders are referred to as "séminaristes" and French boarders as "pensionnaires." In 1643, according to Marie's letters, the seminary numbered 48 pupils. Jamet, II, p. 398, n.e.

This feeling was very painful because it convinced me that I had seriously regressed in virtue. This weight was so heavy that I could hardly endure it. I saw nothing comparable to myself anywhere.

One time, on entering our cell I had a sudden insight which confirmed me in this feeling that I was even poorer and more worthless than I had thought. At that moment I put on a hairshirt which I wore for several days and nights without ever taking it off. My heart was broken with contrition. When Father Le Jeune came to see me, I described my disposition to him. He mortified me severely because I had done this on a whim without taking into account that I did not have his permission for it. To punish me, he ordered me to take it off. Then I threw myself at his feet, begging him to listen to me: that I wanted to confess all the sins and imperfections I had committed in my whole life and that through this he would see what a wicked person I was. I begged him so persistently that he let me do this; and, on the spot, I made a general confession without any examination except that which the Spirit provided, which was more clear and detailed than if I had spent several days examining myself.

In this circumstance it seemed to me that these words were verified in my soul: "I will examine her with lanterns." This critical and jealous spirit of pure love is inexorable and makes itself obeyed without compromise, for it forces the soul to recognize and experience that this spirit of love is the enemy of both compromise and relapse. Acts of contrition and compunction, all directed in this same spirit, are addressed to the Sacred Word Incarnate through the strength of this spirit which possessed the soul: "Pardon, my chaste Love; pardon, my chaste and divine Spouse. I have not wished to offend you. Mercy! my divine Love." Thus this loving action ceaselessly redoubles its sighing, unable to stop. "Pardon! I cannot wish to offend you. My dear Love, let me die a million times rather than ever willingly offend you. I know that I am only dust and imperfection but I want to be yours. O Love! destroy all this! Love is strong as death and jealousy is hard. You know very well what you have to do to make use of your divine mastery and your sovereign power on a soul who belongs to you but transgresses your laws. At them, then! Be pitiless and inexorable; destroy everything which is opposed to your exacting purity."

LV.

It is this purity of God which spurs the soul and drives it headlong, finally leading it to abandon everything by a total annihilation. Loss of honor or reputation means nothing to it. All that matters is that purity triumph. It sees, more clearly than daylight, the great importance of purity in order to be in harmony with the spirit of God. What is asked of the soul who is kept in an intimate, habitual union with God is unutterable. Yes, this is inexpressible. It stems from the great holiness of God which is incompatible with anything contrary to it. I have experienced that in this center of the soul (which is the dwelling place of God and in some way his heaven) nothing impure can exist. The devil himself, although he is a spirit, can find no access here.

There are, nevertheless, certain distillations of spiritual impurity having their source in the spirit of nature (little mischiefs, distortions, disguises) which want to blend with the spirit of God and try to slip into this dwelling place. They seem to have more facility at this than the demons themselves, for they try to masquerade as a kind of sanctity—under the guise of charity, zeal, piety, and even the glory of God—in order to put themselves on a level with that purity and integrity and thus to enter into intimate communion with God and come close to him. But all this is in vain because in this state of intimate and habitual union nothing counterfeit or impure can find entrance.

One might ask, what is this revolt of the passions of which I have spoken? After the terrible suffering of the first three years, I continued to suffer for another four from a bitterness aimed at some good and holy people. Is this compatible with that intimate union of which I have also spoken? I have already answered yes, and this is the explanation. It must be noted that the passions in such a revolt as I have mentioned are not like those easily aroused by natural causes. Nor do they resemble those of persons who, just beginning the spiritual life, learn how to mortify and tame themselves in order to advance in perfection, and try to acquire peace of heart by their own efforts with the help of grace. Ordinarily these have great difficulties to surmount according to their temperaments. They must make use of the examen, study, fidelity; and even after all this, one has for a long time attachments to this or that and to oneself, even more than to anything else, etc.

In this other case, however, far from being hindered or trapped in holding or pursuing what the aroused passions suggest, one endures everything like a punishment, more painful than can be described. None of the evil which occurs is voluntary; on the contrary, it serves for the humility and abnegation of the person; or it is like a burden which leads to great self-contempt. If such a person falls through word or thought, it is through distraction. If subjected to some injustice, one feels keenly a movement of anger or aversion but without any evil consequences. For at the bottom of one's soul there is a fear of God which makes one hate revenge or a spirit of vindication; and this overrides the passion.

Nevertheless, as I have said, one sometimes fails through weakness, complaining to some trustworthy person of someone who has done this or that. But these words cause the soul such embarrassment for its negligence that this is in itself a severe humiliation. What afflicts it in this is that it considers itself to be frivolous, without stability. Yet all this is compatible with an intimate peace in the very center of the soul—a place which seems quite set apart.

What redoubles its suffering is this bitterness in the sensitive part of the soul which is aroused whenever anything arises capable of stirring antipathy or aversion. I shall never grow weary of repeating that this is the most painful thing in the world for a soul who fears God and sin and who loves purity of heart. I sometimes wonder whether this soul is fearful, burdened with so many weaknesses and imperfections. This state is beyond explanation, nor can one understand the extent of the humiliation. The soul is desperately afraid of being deluded. It believes it has never had any solid virtue and that its passions were simply lying dormant from the time it was called to the interior life until its sufferings began. Whatever it thought to have received interiorly, it now feels has not come from God. It now appears that it has no stability or solid virtue, that all its peace has been a delusion, or that if there had been favors and graces, as people had judged them to be, it has now lost them through its own fault and lack of correspondence.

These, then, are the recurrent thoughts which torment the poor soul. One time, the fear that these imperfect feelings and emotions were ingrained in my spirit and my nature and sprang from my blood caused me to bleed myself so profusely that had God not come to my assistance, my health would have been seriously affected, for this occurred in the winter when it is very cold in this country.[11] I turned to God, speaking to him in love and with that familiar access which his goodness permitted in the center of my soul, begging him to deliver me from this disposition so contrary to the divine maxims of his well-beloved Son and so opposed to that pure love he wished of me and for which he had granted me so many mercies.

I had other crosses from which I could not ask to be freed; but the

---

11. Jamet points out that Claude omits this sentence. Undoubtedly he considered it an "imprudence" and therefore unfavorable to the image of holiness he wished to project. Jamet, II, p. 404, n.a.

Spirit who guided me drove me to beg to be delivered from this one, always with a view to true purity, so infrequently found and possessed in the spiritual life and in the paths of pure love of the Sacred Word Incarnate. After all my pleas it seemed to me that I was still bound and held captive in a way I cannot describe and that the Sacred Word Incarnate took pleasure in my bonds. I then abandoned myself to these ways which were so mysterious to me, to suffer and endure whatever would be pleasing to him.

LVI.

Following this state, Our Lord gave me the grace to deal with my neighbor and with the affairs of the community without manifesting anything of what was happening to me interiorly. It was not, as I have said, that I didn't commit faults through distraction, but it was easy to see that these were trivial things and that there was nothing evil in my heart. And, in fact, through the mercy of God, I was never attached to anything which had even the shadow of evil.

The devil tried to make me scrupulous about my imperfections —about which I had never been scrupulous—thus pushing me into fresh difficulties. But the goodness of God saved me by giving me a clarity in the depth of my soul which enabled me instinctively to distinguish between true and false.[12] The people I dealt with considered me prudent, candid, sincere, and of great patience—along with other qualities which I could not believe I possessed. On the contrary, the sight of my wretchedness acted as a counterbalance to the little good I saw in myself so that I was far from having any thoughts of vanity. If I saw that God had given me abilities for various tasks according to the state to which he had called me, I was convinced that, like another prodigal child, I had lost everything through my own fault and that I had abused all the graces and favors I had been given. All of this served to humble me completely.

During the six years that I was superior, we learned what we could and could not do and how to adjust the rules of our institute to this country. During this time we used a little rule we had drawn up under the guidance of Father Vimont, superior of the mission, as well as with the advice of Fathers de Brébeuf, Le Jeune and de Quen, who all

---

12. At first glance it does seem that Marie's bitter denunciation of her imperfections is a kind of scrupulosity; in fact, she clearly distinguishes "sin" from those acts contrary to that purity of heart to which she feels called by the Spirit.

helped us very generously in this and all other matters concerning our establishment and our spiritual growth. In 1645, six years after our arrival, Mother Marguerite de St. Athanase, a religious of solid virtue and one of those sent to us by the Ursulines of the Faubourg St. Jacques in the second year of our establishment, was elected superior in my place.

That same year Father Jérôme Lalemant, superior of the Huron mission, came to Quebec to be in charge of the missions of New France, replacing Father Vimont. Our Lord indicated to me very strongly that this was the person to whom I should speak and who would guide me personally in the paths of God, as well as guiding our community concerning our adaptation, our union, our Constitutions, etc., which we had been experimenting with since our first year.

We wrote to several people in France who were responsible for sending us sisters in order to have their advice and consent to draw up such constitutions as we must have for this country, in conformity with what our experience dictates can be done here. Their consent and approval was sent to us the following year. We were greatly heartened to see the union between our nuns from both Congregations. Following this we handed over all our papers into the hands of the said Father—who also held the place of our ecclesiastical superior, being the principal ecclesiastic in the country—asking him in his charity to undertake to draw up constitutions and rules in conformity with our union and adapted to this country and to our experience.

He did this with profound charity and with such deference to our feelings that there was not a single chapter which each sister did not read three times and did not discuss with him. Afterwards it was presented to the Community for a secret vote, and there was not a single item which was not accepted by all the sisters. Although according to the deliberations of our chapter we had decided that we would receive from Father's hand all he had done without all these formalities, in order to ensure our greatest freedom he preferred everything to be done by ballot. Each one had made a copy for her use but these were all burned in our fire, except the one Father had with him, which we used as the original from which to make copies.[13] It would be hard to find anything better or more appropriate for our purpose and for our Institute in this country. We are still benefitting from this, for the goodness and mercy of God has blessed us abundantly. We are deeply

---

13. For a new edition see the introduction, p. 27, n. 29.

indebted to this good father for having given us so rich a treasure, so filled with the spirit of God and the counsels of the Gospel.

LVII.

Let me return to my own particular dispositions. From the very beginning I found great freedom of spirit and openness of heart in communicating my state to this priest; and he, on his part, took very special care of my direction. It is true that he tested me in various ways because of the condition of which I have spoken and from which I was not yet freed. However, my pains were not so extreme as I have described before except for my continuing temptation to aversion and bitterness.

On the octave of Christmas, I had a strong feeling that if I were to commit myself by vow to seek always the greatest glory of God in everything conducive to my sanctification, his Divine Majesty would help me. I felt strongly moved to discuss this with Father who, having listened to me and recommended the matter to God, gave me permission to do this in the following way: to do, to suffer, to think, and speak whatever I knew to be most perfect and which seemed to me for the greatest glory of God. Likewise, to forgo doing, suffering, thinking, or speaking whenever I saw that this would be for my perfection or for the greater glory of God. All this referred only to those actions in which I was free. I felt myself powerfully strengthened by this vow, and through this Our Lord filled me with great grace which united me in a new way to the holy and divine precepts, although I continued to bear my cross. This vow included that of obedience to my director so as to be guided by him.[14] The whole matter was placed under the protection of the most holy Mother of God.

Let me say in passing that one of the greatest graces his Divine Majesty has ever given me in the course of the spiritual life has been to bring me to prompt obedience to his movements and inspirations. Unable to endure delay, I would go at once to find my director. It sometimes happened that these things were very mortifying to nature but the spirit of grace which directed me made me surmount all my difficulties. In addition, let me say that a soul whom God calls to a

---

14. This vow is reminiscent of the vow of obedience made to Dom Raymond while she was still in the world and a further indication of Marie's belief in the importance of spiritual direction and obedience.

continual life of the spirit must pass through many deaths before reaching its goal. This is beyond imagination, and anyone who has not experienced it would find it hard to believe how the soul must abandon itself and let itself be led in everything to where God directs it.

It is said, and in a way it is true, that contemplation is an idle life. Yet it has great work to accomplish which permits no leisure night or day along the roads and paths in which the spirit of grace leads it. No matter how submissive the spirit is, poor human nature feels this more deeply than I can express.

Let me resume my discourse. I have already said that Father Lalemant tested me and told me the truth about myself. Among other things, he told me one day—and proved it very reasonably—that in the light of my grave imperfections, I was not worthy to converse with God with such intimacy. He was right and my spirit was convinced of this, seeing myself even more wretched than he saw me. "What!" he said, "To converse with this exalted Majesty in this way! To wish to kiss him with your lips! Put yourself beneath his feet! Beneath his feet! This is too much for the likes of you!"

I saw this very clearly, and the zeal and ardor with which he said this annihilated me and would have incited me to go through fire to atone to the divine justice for my boldness. I disciplined myself severely in order to treat with my divine Spouse in another way, but I could not act otherwise. I begged him with loving respect to give me the grace of obeying him who held his place, but even as I asked this of him I found myself in a tender and intimate exchange with him. Then, forcing myself, I said to him, "My chaste Love, I must obey him who holds your place. This is what he wants. Pardon me, I beg you, you know that I want to obey." Then I forced myself insofar as I had the power to do so. Following this I saw myself in his divine presence like someone bound and made captive by obedience, and his loving goodness was pleased to see me thus. His gaze was in me and on me and mine on him and in my bonds I possessed an indescribable peace.

I spent some time in this condition and although I experienced that the Sacred Word Incarnate was pleased with my obedience when he gave me the freedom to obey, nevertheless outside of this I found myself in a very tender exchange with him. It was this which caused Father to leave me free to obey the spirit of God. In this state of union with God it is impossible to continue in any act contrary to his operation. Such acts might be possible when the understanding must act, reflect, etc., on bodily and material things and even on spiritual things which are on a different level from those by which God engages the soul. Sometimes even these acts are completely impossible because the powers of the soul have been rendered incapable of making choices, as I have said elsewhere.

I do not mean to include in this the mysteries of our faith, for although the soul is unable to meditate while in the condition of which I have just spoken, just the same, whenever God draws it to these it does have a way of contemplating them and speaking of them with great tenderness and affection. The least thought of these divine mysteries pertaining to the adorable Word Incarnate inflames the soul, which sees in them truth, certitude, and holiness. There is no need to reason or reflect in order to learn more because, united to the sacred Person of the Word, it is buried in the source which impresses all truth upon it so that it lives under its influence. This is the pasture Our Lord refers to when he says, "I am the Good Shepherd. If anyone enters by me who am the door, he will enter and leave and find pasture" (Jn 10:9). Thus the soul has life in him and from him in a manner so captivating that it can experience it far better than it can describe it.

THIRTEENTH STATE OF PRAYER

LVIII.

I continued to suffer from the revolt of my passions and my temptations to aversion until the Feast of the Assumption of the most holy Virgin 1647, when I had a strong inspiration to turn to this divine Mother to see if she would obtain my deliverance if this were for the glory of her beloved Son, my adorable Spouse. She was well aware of my weakness and that what I was suffering was contrary to the state that his divine Majesty maintained at the center of my soul. Finally, she knew that thus his holy will would be accomplished, for I longed to be a victim of his love in whatever way he wished. I felt, then, that it was the spirit of grace which induced me to speak to this divine Mother. I was at that time before the Blessed Sacrament, and in an instant I felt myself heard and my temptation was lifted from me like a garment.

Following this there was an outpouring of peace throughout the sensitive part of my soul. My aversion was changed into a cordial love for all the people toward whom I had felt hostility and against whom my nature had experienced such bitterness, and I rendered them as many services as my state permitted. Since no one knew what had happened to me or what motives or reasons made me act thus (except those to whom I gave an account of my soul), they could not understand it. Various judgments were made but they completely missed the point.

About this time something happened which, in its effect and its cause, had the power to humiliate me deeply; and, in fact, it did. This humiliation was much more painful because, humanly speaking, it came from virtuous people whom I had frequently helped. Finally, God permitted a combination of circumstances capable of humiliating me even more than anything that had happened before. I was aware of everything that was happening but I did not say a word to excuse myself; and Our Lord gave me the grace to have no imperfect feelings toward any of these people. I reflected on their conduct in a humble spirit before God, acknowledging that they were justified in their opinion because of my imperfections which could have given them a valid reason for their low opinions.

Before any of this occurred Our Lord had indicated to me what he wanted concerning this matter, to which there was some opposition. I said nothing to anyone, remaining in peace and tranquillity just as though I were enjoying every imaginable satisfaction. I never doubted the will of God or that in his own time it would be accomplished—which, in fact, happened, just as the Divine Majesty had indicated. After this I reported everything to Father Lalemant, my superior.

I must mention in passing that, to the glory of Our Lord, he has always given me the grace never to be attached to my lights or knowledge—either natural or supernatural—always feeling drawn to submit my judgment. Just as I practice this in my own case, I would like to see it practiced by all whom God calls to his service. Opposition mortifies me but I bear with it patiently except where the glory of God is at stake and orders me to maintain my opinion in the cause of justice. This is how I proceed in my free actions. As for extraordinary lights, I might be given an understanding that the Divine Majesty wants certain things from me. I tell this to my director and then I leave it to him to judge, keeping myself at peace whether he approves or not. If he tells me to act, I act; if he says, "Don't do it," then I have no inclination to do it because the spirit of grace impresses on me the truth that he holds the place of God and that it would be a mistake not to follow his guidance. I have always been like this since God called me to the interior life and since I have had a director.

One might ask if I have relinquished my imperfections every time he has spoken to me about them and if I have practiced the opposite virtues which he has counseled me. I answer that I have always had the determination to do so; but I am always weak and very imperfect. Even at the time of my greatest temptations, when my director said: "There is some fault or imperfection in this or that," at that very moment I felt my spirit abased under his feet and I would kneel to ask his pardon and beg him to give me a penance. Once when he mortified me in an extraordinary way (I was at this time in the anguish of my temptations), believing that I was beyond the boundary of every imaginable temptation, I was seized with terror that I might be suffering from possession or obsession. Immediately I begged N. to exorcise me if he thought this was the case because I could no longer bear these grave faults; but he sent me away without answering me. At bottom, it was not that my temptations gave me such trouble but rather it was to see the incompatibility between my imperfection and the perfection God demands of souls who belong to him that made me focus all my attention on my impurities and imperfections.

Finally, the effect of the grace God had given me through the merits of the most holy Virgin on the day of the Assumption made me experience more clearly than ever before the grandeur of this grace and also let me better understand those great interior crosses and temptations which I had borne for eight years. Consequently, I was able to assess my grave obligation to the Divine Majesty for his powerful help and protection in all the various incidents which had occurred during this time, as well as the details of his grace and favors (too numerous to mention) despite my lack of correspondence. Alas, as often as I reflect on this I am filled with shame, discovering new reasons for abasing myself and of singing the mercies of so good a God toward this mere nothingness and dust of the earth. May he be blessed forever!

LIX.

It is impossible to describe the peace and tranquillity which the soul possesses in seeing itself completely freed from its bonds and reinstated in everything it believed itself to have lost. Not only does it realize and experience that it had lost nothing, but that it has amassed indescribable treasures. The soul now sees that the blessings enjoyed in this intimate union with its Spouse which had been hidden from it had only been covered (as fire is covered by ash) for its own good and progress in those basic virtues which until then it did not possess in the measure the Divine Majesty desired.

The insights and experiences which have wrought this change are not the simple lights that come with reflection but come rather from the adorable Word Incarnate who dwells in the soul and are clearer than any light. These are impressions which bring with them effects worthy of their subject so that everything conforms to the precepts of the holy Gospel and nothing can be done except by his spirit and direction. Contemplating this condition, I could not stop blessing God who had me pass through so much distress and along such difficult paths. I asked his pardon for not having been sufficiently faithful during my temptations which caused me to be ashamed and humiliated in his divine presence. This was the heaviest part of my humiliation which since has served as subject for that spirit of loving compunction, along with so many other signal blessings, which Our Lord has given me.

I praise and bless this sacred Savior who has been pleased to humble me in various ways along these paths. I say to him with the prophet: "Ah, how good it is that you have humbled me" (Ps 118:71). I can truly say that not for all the treasures of the world would I have avoided this state of humiliation which I recognized as more precious than I can express. It seems to me that I have passed through the dens of lions and leopards of which the spouse in the Canticle speaks; yet instead of being injured by their teeth, I was saved by the power and riches of my heavenly Spouse which are nothing else but the precepts of the Gospel, flowing like a stream from his divine mouth. Were he to say to me, "Do good to those who do evil to you" (Mt 5:44), this is a law imprinted on my heart with the total power of love. There is no need for me to mortify myself on these occasions, for I am carried along by the impression that my divine Spouse's precept has made on me.

I have had various business affairs to settle since coming to Canada and, therefore, have had to deal with different kinds of people, which has led to many difficult situations. These divine precepts have been my strength and support. My conduct has often been judged as part of my natural disposition which it was thought made it easy for me to shake off and forget the annoyances which came from my neighbor. They were not aware that my spirit, possessed by this spirit of the Gospel, acted only according to this principle. What I am saying in general was only true of particular cases. It is not, as I have said before, that I never fell into imperfections through distraction or surprise, either within the convent or at the grille—since I have always had the responsibility of dealing with the neighbor. This country is full of upsets, above all in a new foundation where materials are very scarce and where various difficulties necessitate a variety of tasks on the part of those dealing with the neighbor—either as superior or procurator, the two tasks I have always been engaged in.[1]

LX.

In all these positions my spirit was always united to this spirit who had me work and act according to the precepts of the adorable Word Incarnate. It will seem that I do nothing but repeat over and over again these divine precepts which, as I have said, I was constantly pondering. It must be noted that in the way Our Lord has guided me, the Spirit— from the very beginning until this moment—has given me the precepts of the Gospel as my guiding principle. Without my either studying or reasoning or reflecting on them voluntarily, they came to my spirit spontaneously without my having read about them previously. Even when I did read, my memory was faulty so that what

---

1. As superior, Marie had been responsible for the building of the original monastery which had been completed in 1642. Following the fire in December of 1650, she assumed the responsibility of rebuilding.

came from the Spirit wiped out memories of other things, even holy ones. The precept proposed to my spirit provided whatever was useful for my spiritual development, and all kinds of blessings and graces came to me through my union with the sacred Word Incarnate.

With the passing of time and a change of state, the action of the Spirit also changes according to the state the soul is entering. Thus a passage from Holy Scripture will mean one thing at one time and have a completely different sense at another, but always with a greater perfection—not pertaining to God who is unchangeable but pertaining to the soul which matures in holiness to the end of its life. Whatever degree of union with God the soul has experienced in this life, there is always more, for God is infinite in his gifts. Here is an example of this. Before I became a religious—even before his Divine Majesty had given me the understanding and graces I have spoken of concerning the most Holy Trinity—the lights which I enjoyed from Holy Scripture produced such a lively faith that I thought I would go through fire for these truths, which were so transparent that they bore their own certitude and efficacy.

They gave me hope, not only that I would possess and enjoy those fruits and blessings which were shown to me, both in God and outside of him, but that I would possess God himself so that everything would be for God and his glory. This hope made me forget myself in order to bless my divine Spouse, impelling me to perform actions and take risks which surpassed anything a person of my sex could do. Those passages of St. Paul which dealt with the actions and effects produced in souls by these lights consumed me with love. At the time of my religious vocation, those passages dealing with the Gospel counsels were like suns for me which, while manifesting their exalted holiness, at the same time inflamed the soul with a yearning to possess them. This produced what God wanted of me in accordance with my state, guiding me in the practice of the divine precepts of the adorable Word Incarnate.

None of these insights and graces arose from any study on my part but rather as lightning succeeds thunder. Everything came from the center of my soul, from him who had taken possession of it and consumed it in his love, causing sparks to leap up and guide me.

Since the time of my vocation to Canada, all the maxims and passages dealing with the dominion and spread of the kingdom of Jesus Christ and the importance of the salvation of souls for whom he had shed his blood were like arrows piercing my heart with a loving anguish. I yearned for the Eternal Father to do justice to the cause of his well-beloved Son against those demons who were snatching from him what had cost him so dear.

Moreover, the manifestations and intimate actions of my divine Spouse on my soul, who in his close union and divine outpouring gave me a share in his divine glory, created in me very confident ground for all these truths. Had I written an account of all the graces and favors that the Divine Majesty has granted me in his great mercy since calling me to religious life, both concerning Holy Scripture and his intimate actions in my soul (always leading to higher perfection and spiritual growth, as I have already said), there would be a very large volume. But I have not written this, held back by my unworthiness and the lowliness of my sex. Nor would I say anything now except that I cannot do otherwise. When I recognize that these are lights that God has given me concerning Holy Scripture and that I must write them down, I am covered with shame. Yet another reason for my hesitation is that I have always believed that God has given me these graces for my spiritual development and sanctification but that I have spoiled these gifts. This makes me fear that I will be placed among the hypocrites for having given others reason to believe that I was something when at bottom I am nothing and am worth nothing because of my lack of correspondence. All this makes me very fearful of being chided and troubled at the moment of death.

LXI.

After all my temptations I was finally established in peace. My union with my divine Spouse effected in me those basic virtues dictated by the Gospel precepts, but in so spiritual a manner that they were apparent only through their effects. This continued for about a year before our fire. These effects were a remarkable gentleness and a profound detachment so that what I had formerly possessed of these virtues now seemed to be nothing. As for the virtues of religion, here I felt that I was a completely different person and that God possessed me through the precepts of his adorable Son, moving me in all that my state demanded by the power of this passage of Scripture: "Learn of me for I am meek and humble of heart" (Mt 11:29). "The Spirit of God gives witness to our spirit that we are truly children of God" (Rom 8:16). When I gave an account of myself to Father Lalemant, he told me that I should never refuse any duty concerning temporal affairs, since he saw that they never distracted me from the intimacy with which the Divine Majesty honored me.

During this year [1649] I had a very heavy cross to bear because of the Iroquois persecution. Since I shared in the concerns of my divine Spouse, the harm wreaked on our Church was an inner crucifixion, although I was entirely conformed to what God ordained or permitted. It was during this time that Fathers de Brébeuf, Garnier, and Lalemant were burned and massacred with all their flock, and that all the fathers of the Huron Mission, with the remnant of their poor Christians, were forced to leave their mission and seek refuge here. This was a fearful blow, the most terrible thing that had ever happened in this new Church. The fathers who survived suffered even more than those who had died. It was evident that these were people consumed by divine love, people in whom Jesus Christ lived more than they lived in themselves. Their holiness was so visible that everyone was struck by it.[2]

Thus they and their little flock, numbering about four to five hundred Christians, came here to Quebec. In my affliction at the sight of these poor refugees, my only consolation was that we would be near them and that they would let us have their children. Our Lord inspired me to study their Huron language, which I had not yet applied myself to, for from the beginning I had left this to Mother St. Joseph while I studied Algonquin and Montagnais, in which we had more work than in Huron. I learned enough to be able to teach the prayers and catechism to the girls and women. Mother St. Joseph and I did this on alternate weeks in our little shed.

In addition to this we had a fairly large family which we all helped to feed. Although many devoted people helped these poor exiles as much as they could, it was the religious houses and Madame de la Peltrie who did the most. The priests alone fed and instructed three to four hundred. Their profound charity led them to make extraordinary efforts to save those who had cost them so much sweat and fatigue in leading them to Jesus Christ and snatching them from the flames and rage of their enemies. As procurator, it was I who distributed each week the basic necessities to those in our care. It gave me great consolation to render this little service.

---

2. The Iroquois persecution was most violent in 1649. The Jesuits had at first devoted themselves largely to the evangelization of the Huron tribes, establishing a number of missions north and west of Quebec. Contact with the French, however, brought diseases which severely weakened the Huron tribes, making them vulnerable to the attacks of their Iroquois enemies. By 1649, most of the Jesuit missions had been destroyed and their heroic leaders tortured and killed. The priests who were left as a last resort brought the remnant of their flocks to Quebec.

Our Lord was soon to change all that by another of his visitations. This was our fire which occurred at the end of 1650. This was how it happened. A lay sister novice who had charge of making the bread, fearing that the dough might freeze, had put lighted coals in the bread trough and then carefully covered it. Since this was not customary, no one was aware of what she had done. This poor girl who had intended to remove the charcoal forgot about it so that at midnight, the fire having kindled the wood in the trough, which was made of pine, a highly inflammable substance, spread everywhere, even into the cellars which in this country are not vaulted.

The bakery was in one of these and our offices were just above it. Our provisions for the whole year were down there, both those which had come from France—lard, oil, butter, brandy for our servants— and domestic products such as fish, etc. When the fire had consumed everything down there, it rose to the ceilings which were double with earth packed between them. Had not one of the mistresses of the children been sleeping in this area and heard the crackling and noise of the fire, we would all have been destroyed by fire within half an hour. The fire had already broken through and the place was collapsing and about to fall. She woke the children—there was a sizeable number of them—then came to the sisters' dormitory, then ran back to the children whom she and some other sisters had difficulty in saving. The sisters saved themselves for the most part only half-dressed, not having had time to take along their footwear.

I was only able to throw out the window some community papers that had been in my keeping along with some little boxes I found at hand. The few minutes it took me to do this saved my life. I was already on my way upstairs to my office to throw a bolt of fabric out that window, sure that my sisters had left their habits in their cells in order to save themselves, when I thought better of it. Had I gone up there I would surely have perished, for in less time than it takes to say a *Miserere* all the corridors were aflame. I was the last one to leave the house, caught between two fires. I had hardly left my room which was situated right under the convent bell, when the bell crashed. As I tried to save myself, the fire swept after me. I escaped, as had some others who preceded me, through the grille which, fortunately, being constructed of wood, had been broken. Our parlor was at the end of our dormitory. As I emerged, I was bewildered to see the danger we had run—another sister and I. The whole length of the roof was on fire, for in this country all the boards are made of pine while the framework is constructed of dry wood and gum.

I found our poor community in the snow, as quiet and controlled as though nothing had happened, gazing at this pitiful sight as they prayed. Some were standing in the snow in bare feet. Those who had shoes or slippers insisted on giving them to their companions. It was a moving sight. Someone who was watching the sisters said aloud that either they must be crazy or they must have a profound love of God to be so detached in losing everything, seeing ourselves within a few minutes reduced to nothing in the snow. This good man did not understand the strength of the grace with which our good Jesus filled our hearts. All our good friends cried with compassion as they watched us.[3]

Because of the flames the night was as bright as day, so that everyone could see the state we were in. All our friends did their best to help us control the fire, but it had been discovered too late to be put out. The Father Superior as well as all the fathers and brothers risked their lives for this. A brother taking something from the sacristy at the end of the house thought he would be trapped. In the end we were reduced to begging and relying on the mercy of our friends who showed us the charity of their hearts by what they did to help us. This was especially true of the Jesuit Fathers who deprived themselves of everything they could to assist us in our necessity. The very night of the accident they brought us to the Hospital Sisters who received us with profound charity. We stayed with them for close to a month, living as though we were a single community. They dealt with us as liberally as with their own sisters, treating us in all our needs with the greatest possible charity.[4]

LXII.

Concerning our fire, as soon as I saw that the evil could not be remedied, I felt that my sins were the sole cause. So strong was my conviction about this that it would have been very difficult to convince

---

3. Additional details of the fire can be found in several of Marie's letters. See Oury, *Correspondance,* pp. 412, 421, 425. It is also described in the *Jesuit Relation* for 1651 and in Martin, *Vie,* pp. 556–58.

Dom Oury identifies the unfortunate novice as Françoise Capelle, who left the community the following May 1651. Oury, *Marie,* II, p. 438, n. 35.

4. In her letters, written closer to the event, Marie notes that they spent the night in the Jesuit parlor and went to the Hôtel-Dieu only the next day. There are various other slight discrepancies among the accounts. About three weeks later, they returned to their own property and crowded into Madame de la Peltrie's small house (built in 1644) which, sufficiently distanced from the monastery, had not been touched by the fire.

me otherwise. At that moment my soul accepted this punishment in great tranquillity while begging God to have mercy on all that my sisters would suffer. I would have dearly wished that I alone would suffer, since I recognized that it was I who had aroused his divine justice.

Nevertheless, I acknowledged this blow as the chastisement of a kind Father and a Spouse who, in visiting us in this way, wished to put us in a state of utter deprivation within the Octave of the Nativity— thus conforming us in some manner to the One in the crib. Never had my soul known such great peace as I experienced at this time. I sensed no pain, no sadness or ingratitude but felt myself intimately united to the Spirit and in the hands of one who had permitted and arranged this circumcision for us. Thus I was at one with his holy will, so that being in God and in total accord with this present act, I was powerless to do anything unless motivated and moved by his divine Spirit who guided my steps and my actions.

I had this thought: that my sisters and I were to accept this total loss of our monastery with everything in it in the spirit of the saints. Thus I had an inner vision of those of both Old and New Testament who through a spirit of compunction accused themselves and in bearing the temporal suffering God sent them, blessed him and sang his praises. Being thus impelled by a loving activity and in possession of a peace I cannot describe, my spirit and my heart cried endlessly: "It is you who have done this, my chaste Spouse. May you be blessed. You have done all. All you have done is well done. I am happy that you are satisfied with what you have done."

The praises which my soul showered on God kept pace with my breathing, and I was unable to stop this loving activity and this union of my entire soul with his divine will. The depths of my soul were bathed in a loving conformity to this holy will of God. I analyzed nothing, simply taking pleasure in the fact that his plan had been accomplished by our destruction and especially in my regard, for I had been instrumental in having this house built and had worked hard to bring it to its present state. In all of this I had suffered great opposition.

Realizing that I had committed many imperfections, I now took the side of divine justice, offering my gratitude and my submission for whatever satisfaction my destruction would provide. In a way my loving praise never ceased, and although all these acts were made in a very intimate familiarity with this adorable Majesty, nevertheless it was done in a spirit lovingly humiliated. I was convinced that everything directed me to God and that his Divine Majesty had a special design in everything that had happened to us in our accident.

I don't want to omit what happened to two very devout persons who had strong premonitions of what was going to happen to us. One of them had, as it were, an intimation of what we would suffer if our monastery burned. This good woman figured out where she might lodge us and do everything possible for us. This person lived two leagues distant from us so that she could not have known what was only discussed the day following our accident.

The other person lived close to our monastery. She saw in spirit a circle of light surrounding our house and voices in this light crying plaintively, "Alas, alas! Is there no way to avert this accident? Is there no remedy?" Then someone answered, "No, there is none!" It seemed that this was an angel executing the will of divine justice who made this reply: "It must be done; the writ has been issued." Then she saw something like a hand make a sign over our monastery. A very little while later the fire appeared and this person, hearing the tocsin and the cries for help, saw the vision come true. When I learned what had happened to this devout soul, it was a fresh blow to my heart, stirring up love and a willingness to be totally consumed and annihilated according to the good pleasure of divine justice.[5]

LXIII.

After our tragedy many of our friends believed that we would be discouraged and would inevitably return to France, for we did not have the means to rebuild or recover so significant a loss, since our loss included everything. For myself, I had never thought of rebuilding but of humbly using the little residence of our foundress which she had given us for our seminary. This had remained intact since it was about one hundred paces from our monastery. I thought that by means of some additions we could try to carry out our duties here. Personally, I was set against a return to France unless this should be the manifest will of God. I loved my vocation more than ever. Each of us was concerned only with following the divine will; it was inspiring to watch the peace and sweetness with which each one bore the cross it had pleased Our Lord and Master to send us. During this time one could

---

5. Such episodes seem to have been accepted without question. Dom Oury identifies the second narrator as probably Catherine de St. Augustin of the Hôtel-Dieu, a woman of extraordinary gifts, whom Marie would have met during her stay with the Hospital Sisters following the fire. Oury, *Marie,* II, p. 444.

witness the work of grace which was even more profound interiorly than appeared on the surface.

Although I have said that I never considered rebuilding or establishing a new monastery, I always had a premonition that this task would befall me and that I must begin this work over again. This filled me with a natural apprehension which I dared not manifest for fear of running counter to God's will. At this time I was coming to the end of my three-year term as procurator. All our friends, above all Father Ragueneau, superior of the mission—as well as the other fathers—and Monsieur d'Ailleboust, governor of the country, were deeply involved in our affairs. After having done all they could to sympathize and help us, they advised us that we must determine what was best for us to do in order to extricate ourselves from the wretched condition to which we were reduced. The affair was debated at length, and all were of the opinion that they should help us rebuild since otherwise it was impossible to continue in this country and perform our duties.

They decided to lend us money to get us started and promised us their help and good will. They told us their opinions and asked us to consult among ourselves to see if our opinions agreed with theirs. The affair was then presented to our community by our Reverend Mother and we all had the same feeling: to try, with the help of our friends, to rebuild our monastery on the same foundation which, having been examined by experts, was found capable of sustaining a building, having been built on solid rock.

The ruined walls would have to be brought level with the ground as soon as one could get near them, for the fire continued to smolder in the ruins for three weeks. I was given charge of all this both through obedience and by an inner inspiration of God. The governor himself wished to draw up our plans and, in his role as temporal father of the community, to oversee the whole enterprise and help us by his advice. Just a month before our accident, his wife's sister had made her profession in our house.[6] I was strongly inspired to ask the Father Superior of the mission to let us have Father François Le Mercier to help us.[7]

---

6. Philippine de Boullongue had entered the Ursuline monastery on December 2, 1648, and made her profession on December 9, 1650. Her sister, Marie-Barbe, wife of Louis d'Ailleboust, entered the Ursulines with her husband's reluctant consent in 1653. Despite her inability to adjust to religious life, she tried again in 1664, but without success. Governor d'Ailleboust, a trained engineer and a devout Christian, was a valuable friend of the Ursulines.

7. A skilled missionary who had spent most of his time on the Huron missions, he returned to Quebec in 1649. He was invaluable in helping the Ursulines with the Huron language as well as with their building.

This kind of work is very difficult in this country, especially because of our poverty. We had to rely on Divine Providence for everything. Our Reverend Mother was in accord with me and the Father Superior, who had done everything to help us, agreed to this with great charity. Father Le Mercier himself was filled with a strong feeling that God wished him to do this for us, and he has continued until the present time so that we will be eternally in his debt. He is presently Superior of the Mission and, therefore, our superior as well.

LXIV.

Once I understood the divine will and how God wished to use me in rebuilding our monastery, all the aversion I had had toward this plan disappeared and I felt strong and full of courage to spend myself day and night for this work which I considered to belong especially to the most Blessed Virgin, our mother and superior. I call her "our superior" because a little while before our fire, Reverend Mother St. Athanase felt strongly inspired to put the office of superior into her hands and ask her to be our first and principal superior. We did this with great solemnity, paying our homage to her and acknowledging her as our first and perpetual superior. I regarded her, then, in this project as my guide and my all under God. I no sooner began than I felt her help in an extraordinary way so that she was continually present to me. I did not see her with my bodily eyes nor with my imagination but in the same way that the adorable Word Incarnate in his mercy communicated himself to me: through union, love, and a constant communication which I had never before experienced with the most holy Virgin, Mother of God, although I had always had great devotion to her.

Now, beyond this interior union I enjoyed with her which led me to speak lovingly with her, very simply, intensely, in the core of my soul, as I did with her beloved Son—I also felt her with me, yet without ever seeing her. She accompanied me everywhere in all the comings and goings that were necessary for me from the beginning of raising the walls until the very end of the work. As I made my way around I spoke with her, saying, "Let us go, my divine Mother, to see the workmen." According to circumstances, I would be climbing up or down, along the scaffolding, without any fear, always talking to her in this way. Sometimes I was inspired to honor her by singing hymns or some of the antiphons of the Church. I followed these inspirations, often saying to her, "My divine Mother, please keep our workmen safe." And it's a fact that in the whole work of construction she took care of us so well that no one was injured. My weakness needed this assistance to endure all the fatigue I underwent even before the masonry was begun. Three buildings, under ordinary conditions, would not have given me any more difficulty. Nevertheless, I experienced what Our Lord said of his yoke—that it is sweet and light—and I felt the companionship of his holy Mother.

Since then I have learned in speaking with someone who has received great graces from God that some time after our fire the Blessed Virgin, appearing to her in an intellectual vision, made known that she herself would rebuild our house and undertake its care. She also revealed other secrets which it is not my intention to speak of here but which I will discuss later if I survive her. This holy soul told me everything that the Divine Majesty revealed to her. Concerning these things the Divine Majesty asked her, "Do you not believe this, my daughter?" She answered, "Yes." Three times he asked the same thing and she, to prove that she did believe this divine Mother, affirmed it with her blood. I did not know this until about two years afterwards nor did she know what happened to me in that loving conversation with which this divine Mother has in her goodness honored me.

LXV.

In the month of June 1651, following our fire, I resumed the office of superior which involved me in new responsibilities and laid on me a very heavy cross concerning certain occasions and situations very painful for me. I found comfort in the help of our divine Mother, our mediatrix with her Son. For many reasons I cannot go into detail; suffice it to say that it was not because of the difficulties of our new buildings nor from the debts accompanying the reconstruction of our monastery, for the Divine Goodness has showered us with such blessings that people who watched the state of our affairs, comparing what they first saw with what they see now, feel there has been a miracle. All honor and praise to God and to his beloved Son and to the most holy Virgin, for if many devout souls have helped us, it has been through their holy inspirations. They will know how to recompense them a hundredfold in this life and in glory in the next.

Since beginning my second term as superior, the inner state in which Our Lord has led me has been that of victim in a more subtle and intense manner than usual, consuming me in various ways through his Holy Spirit. Although it will be difficult, I will try to provide some details as best I can. Obedience exacts this of me, and I will do my best through the help of the divine Spirit who never ceases to overwhelm me with his mercy.

To begin, I dare to say that the goodness and generosity of my divine Spouse have communicated to me the effects of those divine words uttered in the holy sermon of the eight beatitudes. I do not presume, however, that this has been done in the same way as for the great saints who are worthily disposed to receive these profound graces; but it has pleased him to expand and prepare my soul as I await everything from him and hold everything in him. As for myself, I acknowledge that I am nothing and sheer powerlessness, capable of putting millions of hindrances to his extraordinary favors. The sense that I have of myself as I experience his divine intimacy and his wonderful generosity keeps me far beyond astonishment; for, in truth, I am a great sinner, guilty of endless lapses, of indescribable childishness and weakness. It is a cause for great admiration that a God who has thousands of millions of loving souls would cast his eyes upon the lowliest of his creatures and grant her such a share in his love and in his heart.

I have experienced that there are various degrees in true poverty of spirit. When Our Lord bestowed on me a religious vocation, his mercy taught me the value of this poverty in a way that I have described in some detail. My whole soul was inclined toward this sublime virtue which I saw held first place in the life of the Son of God. In it I saw all other virtues affirmed, and I understood that its goal was nothing but pure and unadorned love which, in its simplicity, has only God in mind.

I had not yet realized, however, what the Spirit of God wanted to accomplish in my soul in order that it experience the validity of this spiritual poverty. Since then he has done this again and again in the change of states in which it has pleased his Divine Majesty to lead me. In order to unify everything, he brought me to a true state of victim and of constant immolation which is so appalling to nature because of its subtlety. One would have to experience this to believe how the creature is reduced even in its noblest faculties. Perhaps I am speaking obscurely. Nevertheless, I understand very clearly what I am saying, but it is not possible to express the thousandth part of the divine impressions and action which the Divine Spirit has produced in my soul. Besides, the constant distractions to which I am prey do not permit me to explain myself at any length. I must be satisfied with describing the substance of what the Spirit who guides me permits me to say. In the next chapter, however, I am going to make a little discourse to explain the despoilment of the soul, the state of victim, and true and substantial spiritual poverty.

LXVI.

I. Let me say, then, that God has created the rational soul free, endowing it with the power to effect its salvation through grace, and with those other helps implanted in the Church founded by the Precious Blood of Jesus Christ. As the soul becomes aware of its dignity through the working of grace which reveals its vocation and its capacity, if it is faithful, it wishes to try to correspond by constantly reaching toward its highest and unique good. If this longing is pure, the Divine Goodness, who alone knows his creature and can see into the most secret parts of the spirit, bestows on this soul streams of light and fire; and, in short, gives it the key of knowledge and love and puts it in possession of his treasures.

The soul, finding itself overwhelmed in this way, wants to wander in those rich and fertile pastures, in these gardens and rooms made accessible to it. There its powers delight in a taste of wisdom impossible to describe. The divine pleasures, the nourishment and rest it receives, the holy intoxication it enjoys move it to sing a loving wedding hymn. This continues until through rapture Love itself puts an end to it in the streams of divine delights. Then he causes it to swoon in him, bringing it to participate in these holy raptures.

Awakening from this ecstasy, it begins its song again, speaking to and by the one who moves it so powerfully: "Let us exult and rejoice, remembering your breasts as better than wine. Thus the just and the right of heart love you" (Song 1:4). All this occurs spontaneously, effected by the fullness of the Spirit, bearing a meaning that makes the soul, as it were, dissolve with love. From this is born that exultation leading to torrents of tears which form a paradise in the soul because it delights in God in inexpressible intimacy. This condition spreads to the senses. The sensitive part of the soul is completely penetrated so that it can say, "My spirit and my flesh rejoice in the living God" (Ps 84:3).

So far there is no limit in this interior life. It seems to the soul that there is nothing beyond the joy it possesses in this life, and that it has been permanently established in this state where it is overwhelmed by the immense riches of its Spouse. Concerning the holy mysteries of faith, it possesses them through an infused knowledge from the Spirit who directs it with such certitude and so little obscurity that it cries,

"O my God, I no longer have faith; it is as though you had drawn back the curtain." In this experience it is "leaning on her beloved, surfeited with delights" (Song 8:5). It neither sees nor tastes nor desires anything but him. Thus engulfed and lost in delights, it does not see what is going to happen or where the Spirit will lead it.

This divine Spirit who is infinitely jealous and pitiless where interior purity is concerned, wanting sole possession of its domain, begins to assault the sensitive and lower part of the soul, causing it to suffer various privations which are excruciating. Nature, however, which has its own ruses and skills, wishes to have its own say; it does not want to surrender its citadel or its portion of spiritual goods which it has found more completely to its taste than all the other satisfactions it had formerly enjoyed with creatures. These now seem like nothing but subjects of mortification and distaste. Thus, unable to draw close to the joys of the spirit and finding nothing in those other joys, it does not know what to latch on to. It takes the offensive. It does its best to hold onto those good things of the spirit to which it had grown accustomed, and from which it draws its life and its sustenance in order to bear cheerfully all the difficulties and weariness to which the Spirit has reduced it in order to make it flexible and obedient. It feels everything is denied it, that all its efforts are useless, and that its lot is the captivity where it finds itself.

I have said that this sensitive part was without support and that it had a strong distaste for creatures because it had been allured by the sweetness of spiritual things. Nevertheless, it would very quickly have returned to these had it not been restrained by a hidden virtue, "by the laws of the Spirit which carnal man does not understand" (1 Cor 2:14). This virtue places the soul, as it were, among the dead, although it does not completely die. It is very deeply wounded, however, so as to let the highest part of the soul enjoy in peace all those blessings which it possesses exclusively. In this state which I call death with regard to spiritual goods, there are several degrees because in corrupt human nature there are numerous nooks and crannies and a store of deviousness and shrewdness always ready to spring into action. The spirit of grace, however, cuts this short and acts so that this rabble is deprived of eating the food from this table which has not been laid out for it. It is on this point that the true distinction between the lower and higher parts can be discerned. But this is not all. We are only at the first step in the state of victim and the acquisition of poverty of spirit.

II. Nature being thus brought to naught, first by penance and second by the deprivation of what sustained it, and thus made amenable to the Spirit's guidance—nature is now humbled beyond telling.

Meanwhile, the higher part of the soul experiences true satisfaction in seeing itself freed from what harmed it the most and in enjoying in true purity its sovereign and unique good. The understanding and the will now possess light and love in a way far beyond anything I have so inadequately tried to describe.

The Spirit of God, however, who wants everything for himself, seeing that the understanding, no matter how pure it may be, always mingles an element of its own with the divine actions—something which in this spiritual state is a grave impurity—suddenly puts an end to this through his divine power. Thus the understanding is suspended and rendered utterly incapable of the most ordinary acts which it does not even recognize as being acts, because in their simplicity they are almost imperceptible. The will, having been ravished by God and enjoying his embraces, has no further need for the understanding to provide it with material to stir up its fire. On the contrary, the understanding would only injure the will because it is so active. The will is like a queen who enjoys her divine Spouse in an intimacy of which the seraphim (with their fiery language) could speak better than a creature who has at her disposal only a language of flesh, incapable of expressing such high and exalted things.

Years pass in this way; but this divine Spirit, who is the inexhaustible source of all purity, still wants to conquer the will. Even though it was the Spirit who stirred these divine movements and made it sing a constant wedding hymn, nevertheless the will remained enmeshed in its own action. This the Spirit could not endure since it wished, like a jealous person, to be absolute master. In this sense, as it is he who is love, it is true to say that "love is strong as death and jealousy hard as hell" and that no one is exempt. "Its lamps are fire and flame" so that they must consume everything without exception (Song 7:6).

III. Then this loving activity, although very delicate, sweeter than all sweetness in the embrace of the divine Spouse, like an endless chain binding and centering the will in its sovereign and unique God, comes to a halt and is suspended as are also the memory and the understanding. These two powers are so connected in what concerns the spiritual life that on this point I am going to treat them in a single article. Behold, then, the victim, in that state to which the Spirit of God, loving infinitely the purity of souls espoused to the Son of God, reduces them in order to bring them to that condition where he wishes to take his pleasure in them. This bed is narrow and one must make room for him so that he will be its only Master and Spouse and its free and peaceful possessor.

IV. After this action—so painful for these ennobled powers—

what will happen? Could one think that they might remain thus, fixed and immovable, like the dead? It is unbelievable how painful this deprivation is for them, above all during the solemn feasts of the Church in which are represented the mysteries of our redemption. Formerly, these had been their delightful nourishment—a pleasing nourishment, rich in faith through the lights the Holy Spirit communicated on each of the holy mysteries. Now it is impossible for them to reflect on them. Sometimes the person who is led in this way is in fear, unable to understand that she is in the true way since she cannot rest quietly in what is most holy and most solemn in the Church. She does violence to herself, wanting to draw her understanding from the laziness into which she thinks it has fallen. But in vain! All this effort is due to lack of understanding of the divine action and to the natural urge to act.

After repeated and rigorous efforts, she realizes that the power of the soul, having lost its natural function through a supernatural way, there is nothing to be gained by so much effort. However, this natural appetite of the soul to act by means of its own highest powers does not die until the Spirit of God who guides it interiorly makes it die once again, being merciless in the matter of purity. This is done, as I have said, in order to prepare a dwelling, free of all noise, for the divine Spirit who delights in peace and silence.

V. Now that the will has been deprived of its loving activity, the soul in its unity and in its center remains in the embrace of its spouse, the adorable Word Incarnate. This state is a sweet and loving breath which never ends. It is an exchange of spirit to Spirit and from spirit into Spirit. I cannot express it in any other way, except by the words of St. Paul which verifies it when he says: "Jesus Christ is my life and my life is Jesus Christ. It is not I who live but Jesus Christ who lives in me" (Gal 2:19).

It seems that one should be silent in this simple communication. But, no! Divine love, that spiritual monitor, "has lamps of fire and flame" (Song 7:6). He wishes to purify even further. Even in this breath there is still something imperfect in the loving power of the will. He consumes this—and here at last is the sacrifice of the victim and here, finally, that true, pure, and essential purity of spirit.

It must be noted that in proportion to what occurs in the spirit in order to bring to an end anything impure along this spiritual way, God permits several external crosses in order that his will be accomplished in everything, as St. Paul says, "that they may be conformed to the image of his Son" (Rom 8:29). I repeat, one must endure great interior and exterior trials which would have terrified the soul had it seen them ahead of time, and which would even have made it abandon every-thing rather than endure more than it had already experienced had not a secret strength sustained it. For it seems that the waters of tribulation through which the soul has passed by so many spiritual deprivations have extinguished the fire which gently consumed its noblest part so that, deprived of all its powers, God alone was its only enjoyment. In fact, the poor soul does not itself recognize where it is. A cloud has formed, a kind of spiritual obscurity which has clouded its vision, and it seems that what it had possessed in its sovereign and unique good, the adorable Word Incarnate, has been taken from it. Finally, in his compassion he dispels the cloud, and the soul experiences, though very late, the sense of this passage: "Behold, my ditch has become a flowing stream and my river a sea" (Sir 24:31). It possesses more abundantly than ever the blessings of the adorable Word Incarnate who inundates and engulfs it in himself in a manner worthy of his largesse.

I have had to make this little discourse of my own experiences in order to explain in some fashion what I mean concerning that essential poverty of spirit and the state of victim.

LXVII.

The state I now experience—in conjunction with the passage cited above—is an extraordinary light in the ways of the spirit of the adorable Word Incarnate, realizing with great purity and certitude that he is love itself, intimately uniting my spirit to his so that "all his words are spirit and life in me" (Jn 6:64). Above all, my soul realizes that being in this intimate union with him, it is at the same time in union with the Eternal Father and the Holy Spirit, understanding the truth and certitude of what this adorable Lord and Master said to his disci-ples in his last exchange with them and in his prayer to God his Father. First, his reply to St. Philip who had asked to see the Father, saying, "Philip, he who sees me sees my Father" (Jn 16:8).

This kind of union is very pure and exalted and although I speak of "the Sacred Word Incarnate" I do not experience anything in the imagination. It is in spiritual purity and simplicity that the soul real-izes that the Father and the Word Incarnate are but one with the adorable Spirit, although there is no mingling of persons. It is through the spirit of the adorable Word that the soul experiences the divine operations. And it is by these motions, impressions, and operations that this same Spirit moves me to speak at one time to the Eternal Father, then to the Son, and then to the Spirit itself. Spontaneously I find myself saying to the Father: "O Father, in the name of your dearly beloved Son, I am speaking to you." And then to the Son: "My Beloved, my very dear Spouse, I beg that your will be done in me," and other things which the divine Spirit inspires in me. And I realize that it is the Holy Spirit who binds me to the Father and the Son.

I often find myself saying to him, "O Divine Spirit, lead me in the paths of my divine Spouse." I am constantly in this divine exchange in a way that is so delicate, so simple, and so intense that it cannot be expressed. It is not an action or even a breath. It is rather a pleasant atmosphere in the center of the soul where God has his dwelling which, as I have said before, I can find no words to describe. My glances toward this adorable Majesty carry whatever the Spirit wants me to say, for it is by him that I speak. In the language which the Spirit uses in these exchanges, by which his Divine Majesty honors my lowliness, I can do nothing at all except by his impulse. Since this is so very simple, how can my tongue express what my spirit cannot discern because of its increasing simplicity and purity?

The whole time of my spiritual exercises (from which I have just come) is spent in this way. Today it was these words of Our Lord which were imprinted on my spirit: "I am the true vine and my Father is the gardener. Every barren branch he cuts away; and every fruitful branch he cleans to make it more fruitful still" (Jn 15:1–2). This passage indicated to me the reason for those various states of purification I have just described and the importance of being united to our divine vine, the adorable Word Incarnate, in order to have no life except by his life, which is the divine Spirit. This is the highest point of the spiritual life and the consummation of the saints: to have life only in him, according to the words of St. Paul.

LXVIII.

There is still another disposition in which I sometimes find myself which is the result of that which I spoke of in the preceding chapter. This happens most often when I am alone in my room, having come from some exercise in choir, especially from Holy Communion more than at any other time. I experience an impression in my soul. Not that I imagine at the time that it is an impression. I speak thus in order to explain myself. It is something so captivating, so divine, so simple, and falls so completely beyond human language that I cannot express myself except to say that I am in God, possessed by God, and that God would soon consume me by his loving action were I not sustained by another impression which tempers the former. Had this first impression, which is always linked to the adorable Word Incarnate, my beloved Spouse, not been tempered, I would not be able to exist, for my soul lives only in him, loving him constantly, day and night, and at every moment.

The effects of this state are always an abasement and a true and fundamental acknowledgement that one is nothing but sheer weakness, along with a low esteem of oneself and one's acts which one sees as always corrupted by imperfection. The soul, convinced of this, remains in profound humility no matter how exalted it might be. There is also a fear—free from anxiety, however—that it might be deceived in the ways of the spirit, mistaking false for true. This fear leads to abnegation and a spirit of compunction. This fear also causes peace, a peace which comes from accepting pains, sufferings, the cross which has fallen upon the soul, receiving them from the hand of God as punishment from a good father who lovingly corrects his child who, following this punishment, throws itself into its father's arms. This state produces unwearying patience in suffering and a total inclination to peace and kindness to everyone as well as a gentle willingness to welcome those who have offended one. One skillfully looks for ways —without appearing to do so—of treating them as friends, either by words or services or a pleasant expression or anything else capable of winning their hearts and showing them that one holds nothing against them.

In short, the soul has a complete aversion to that spirit which clings to the insults and injuries it has received from the neighbor. The faults and imperfections which one commits now result from forgetfulness and distraction and steadily diminish, for nature has lost its strength, thanks to these divine actions. The effects of this state are to accept sufferings in love and union with the adorable Word Incarnate by a loving absorption in him, as well as a profound love for the vocation and state to which God has called the soul, and a willingness to do and undertake everything for love of him and to remain faithful; an ever greater love for everything done in the Church of God in which one sees only purity and holiness; finally, a whole-hearted inclination to let oneself be guided and to submit one's judgment to those who hold the place of God.

It must be noted that the Spirit who has guided me so lovingly has always tended to the same goal, leading me to the practice of the virtues I have mentioned above as well as to many others which I have not cited. This has always been in order to have me follow the spirit of the Gospel for which, from the beginning, my soul has had a constant attraction, aspiring always to that perfect possession of the spirit of Jesus Christ. He has bestowed on me that degree of perfection which has pleased him. This was accomplished by his holy actions in those successive states through which he had led me in overwhelming mercy, and to which, had I corresponded, my progress in holiness would have been very different. My lack of fidelity causes me—and rightly so— to fear.

I beg the God of goodness, my adorable Spouse, to cleanse all my faults in his precious blood and to have mercy on me. May he be blessed, praised, and glorified forever by his saints whom I implore to intercede for me before his divine justice.

FRAGMENTS FROM
THE RELATION OF 1633[1]

My longing for religious life grew daily; since the first year of my conversion it never left me.[2] If there was anything at all in the world which pleased me, it was the life of a religious and I followed this life and performed its acts as far as possible. Sometimes I feared that this was just a temptation to distract me and I protested to God, saying, "Alas my Beloved! Take this thought away from me. You know that I have made it impossible to reach this blessed state by giving up my own interests in order to serve my neighbor for love of you. Furthermore, I have a son whom I must take care of since this is your will and my obligation."[3]

Dear God! My complaint was followed by an inner reproach that I lacked trust and that this divine goodness was rich enough for both my son and me. Thus I abandoned myself, loving nothing but to follow the counsels Our Lord has taught us in the Gospels. I saw how the world longed for and insisted on riches, while for me it was impossible to want or ask for anything except to be poor. Whatever my sister gave me I gave to the poor, or else I used it to buy instruments of penance. I rejoiced in having nothing and in having to ask my sister as a charity for whatever I needed. She was so generous that she never let

---

1. Dom Jamet has divided the fragments of the *Relation of 1633* into five sections: La Préparation Divine, L'Itinéraire Mystique, La Vocation Religieuse, La Vie Religieuse, Supplément. The material I have used in this section is from "La Vocation Religieuse" and "La Vie Religieuse." See the introduction, pp. 32, 39.

* Bracketed numerals refer to the numbers assigned to the fragments by Dom Jamet

2. See *Relation of 1654*, pp. 49–51.

3. Having no resources of her own, it would have been impossible for her to bring the required dowry. In fact, when she enters the Ursulines in 1631, the archbishop dispenses her from this obligation. As for Claude, he is only six or seven at this time. See *Relation of 1654*, p. 94.

me want for anything but gave my son and me more than I would like to have had for our upkeep. After all, I considered myself the richest person in the world, hoping that despite my poverty, God's providence would never fail me and that I would become a religious, freed from all the cares I was presently involved in.

Although this desire to leave the world was constant, it never caused me any difficulty because my soul remained in peace, waiting for the moment Our Lord ordained, promising to be faithful to him when he opened this path to me. It was he who showed me the blessings of this religious state, so it must be he who would bring me to it. Once I was brought to a halt in the middle of the street, unable to sustain the power of the inspiration which bound me closely to God and gave me the unshakeable conviction that this is what he wished of me. Transfixed thus, I poured out my love for him, begging him to grant me this as soon as possible. As I urged him, I heard this loving word, "Wait, wait; have patience!" This strengthened and sustained me in his love, and I did not seek any further but waited on his holy will and the moment of its fulfillment.

The devil never stopped tempting me concerning poverty. He wanted to make me love riches. He filled my imagination so that I would leave so foolish a path as the one in which Our Lord led me and inspired me to remain. I have never had a temptation so insistent as this, for sometimes it was so violent that I found myself on the verge of consenting, like someone blind in the practice of virtue. My refuge was prayer in which I abandoned myself to Our Lord anew. Then I went to give an account to my confessor, who saw clearly that God wanted me in this state of despoilment.[4] Thus I remained at rest and the problems with my imagination ceased. As for my soul, it was always in peace, conformed to the will of God who was its satisfaction, its happiness, and its life.

[54]

Although I did my best to practice virtue on such occasions (and these were legion), I felt urged to leave the world with a clear recognition which indicated that I was not saving myself here because of the grave obstacles I had constantly to face. I did not know if Our Lord would continue to help me, and in this uncertainty I was enlightened to understand that I must avoid these circumstances. Were it not for the profound peace I enjoyed, these lights would have seemed like

---

4. Dom Raymond of St. Bernard. See *Relation of 1654*, p. 55, n. 8.

temptations because on the surface it seemed that I was more able to help my neighbor and grow in merit in my present state than I would be in religious life, where I did not see the opportunity of doing anything except for my own salvation. Besides, having no resources yet having the responsibility for a child, this attraction seemed almost beyond reason, and I resolved not to give it any more thought. But this was impossible, for my inspiration was constantly strengthened and I complained about this to Our Lord, telling him that since it was he who had put these thoughts in my head, he would have to accomplish it.

I suffered more than ever when I heard words which offended God, especially words contrary to purity. This tortured me, making me tremble when I was in situations I could not avoid. The more I heard this kind of talk, the more my heart clung to God, complaining to him. One time when I was in a situation where I had a great deal to bear, I felt myself interiorly moved to withdraw to another room to attend my Beloved, who seemed to want to give me some favor. However, I wasn't able to obey him as quickly as I would have liked and, finally, he made it clear that I was to leave those who detained me, giving me the grace to do so.

I withdrew immediately, and as soon as I set foot in my room I was seized with such a powerful attraction that I had to sit down immediately, unable to remain on my knees. It seemed that my soul longed to be freed from its body, no longer able to remain on earth amid such impurity—so horrible and appalling. My soul had been created for heaven, yet here below it saw only what could deflect it from this. I cried and sighed so deeply that I could easily have been heard, but I was alone on the top floor of the house, which was a great blessing; for those with whom I lived were incapable of understanding such spiritual things. This redoubled my plaints to Our Lord for leaving me in such danger and among so many people who did not really love him. I begged that if in his goodness he did not want to withdraw me from this world, he would at least put me with pure souls who would truly love him so that I would be able to express my love for him freely, for I could not continue to live in such intense suffering.

Meanwhile, this Divine Majesty looked upon me lovingly, enjoying my complaints; and the gaze of this divine Spouse brought me a calm which enabled me to go on. Although I don't know how, I felt myself completely changed and determined to contemplate him and listen to his divine words. He treated me with affection, assuring me that he would give me what I asked for so persistently and that he would satisfy my longing; but that he did not wish to do it quite yet. It is impossible to explain what I understood and enjoyed under this divine gaze. Feeling myself overcome with love and conformed to his divine grace, I said to him, "Do you not deserve that I give you everything? When I have the power and will to possess what I ask of you, I will put it at your feet, leaving there all my power and will for you to use according to your divine will. Is this not reasonable, my Beloved, my dear Love?"

Then all my acts came to a halt, for he united me so closely to himself that I cannot express it. This union lasted for a long time, leaving me in a tender peace, with trust and inner assurance that I would soon have what I longed for.

[55]

Oh, what an immense suffering not to be able to express spiritual things as they really are! One only stammers in speaking of them and, moreover, one must search for some comparisons in order to discuss them, for otherwise one must remain silent. The insights and graces Our Lord gave me are still as present as when they first occurred, yet I hardly know how to say anything about them, so removed are they from mere feeling and imagination. As for the gaze of Our Lord, of which I have already spoken, one might believe that I saw something imaginary; but nothing of the kind. I have never seen anything pertaining to God in this way since "God is spirit and he must be adored in spirit and truth" (Jn 4:24).[5]

This is such a delicate matter that the soul understands without seeing or hearing or tasting. She knows and recognizes God and whatever God wishes her to learn in a wonderful way and with indescribable certitude. He himself is the master of the soul that he leads in this way, ruling and guiding it through knowledge and love, letting himself be seen by it and uniting himself to it, hiding nothing of himself but rather showing himself for what he is in this life, by a knowledge and enjoyment which only he and his beloved understand. In a word, one can say that heart and soul are a paradise where there is nothing hidden between the Lover and his beloved.

[56]

At the beginning, I made no choice of this or that religious order, for I awaited everything from Our Lord without any preference—like

---

5. This firm avowal that the imagination plays no part in her extraordinary experiences of God is, as we have seen, a constant in her spirituality. See *Relation of 1654*, p. 49, n. 1.

a poor person who doesn't choose the alms she's given. I had, however, a strong inclination toward the Feuillantines. Yet Our Lord did not want this, for every time I passed close to the Ursuline monastery, I experienced such emotion that I thought my heart would stop in its desire to be there. I didn't want to become so devoted, however, because I dreaded becoming attached to something I could not achieve. Thus I tried to banish these feelings and this sense of esteem. Just the same, I often reflected on the thoughts Our Lord put in my heart concerning the effectiveness of this Order and of how it snatched souls from the hands of Satan. It was my opinion that I should value this more than all the austerities of the others. Furthermore, since it was amid the obstacles of the world that God's goodness had bestowed on me all the blessings I have recounted, this order would be more appropriate for me than any other; for here dealing with the neighbor was considered to be in conformity with what Our Lord did here below in teaching souls. I seriously weighed this consideration and found it to be of great importance. But then I turned back to my imperfect thoughts concerning those external penances that people make so much of, and I experienced some regret in being in a place where austerities were not so frequently practiced.[6]

Still Our Lord kept hidden from me the place where he wanted me—whether it would be the Feuillantines or the Ursulines. This is why I kept in mind the promise that the Reverend Father General of the Feuillantines had made me; for at that time I had not had access to or experience of the Ursulines. Even if I had had it, I would never have had the courage to ask for a place there. Such a request seemed unreasonable to me, for I had nothing that could lead these holy women to receive me simply for the love of God, since I could not be received anywhere except through charity.[7] Thus I constantly awaited the grace which had been promised me, and my thoughts always reverted to the Ursulines, experiencing, as I have already said, this interior attraction for the education of souls. I recalled that my very first thought of being a religious immediately after my conversion had been of being an Ursuline, although I had never seen them or even heard their functions spoken of. Still, this thought stayed with me.

Thus, lost in thought and struggling with both sides, ignorant of what God wanted of me, I waited in peace for signs of his will which I was completely determined to submit to when it was revealed to me, no matter what would happen to me.

---

6. Clear evidence of Marie's apostolic spirit which will find its flowering in Canada.
7. Another reference to her inability to bring a dowry. See also p. 184.

[57]

The more frequent the conversations, the more I was attracted, and she [Mother Françoise] was so gentle that once with her, I wished never to be separated. Although I had a deep intimacy with her, I never had the courage or even the inspiration to ask her to help me, for I always felt inwardly urged to leave everything in God's hands. I indicated to him very strongly at times during my colloquies the longing I had to leave the world and my powerlessness to bring this about, but everything continued just the way it was.

Then it happened that she was elected superior and the first time I had the honor of seeing her after her election, it crossed my mind as I was leaving our house that she was going to offer me a place. And, in fact, after I had greeted her she said very cordially, "I know what you're thinking; you're thinking that I am going to offer you a place here. Yes, you're right; I am offering it to you." I was completely surprised and full of admiration in witnessing such charity, so deeply touched that I can't express it. On the other hand, I pondered more than ever, for Our Lord still kept me in ignorance of whether this was what he wished or if he wanted me to turn to the Feuillantines.

Although I submitted everything to my confessor, resolved to do whatever he would order, nevertheless I begged him not to give an answer to Reverend Mother immediately, since I could not go ahead in this matter without some other interior sign. He, who wanted only to mortify me, told me he would let me know; and then to test my feelings he seemed to want to discourage me, no longer speaking to me about religious life except with coldness and indifference. I became so fearful that I hardly dared even see Reverend Mother, who also took pleasure in mortifying me in the same way.

Finally, the confidence I had in her led me to explain the perplexity I was in concerning the Feuillantines. This caused no coldness on her part, but rather she assured me that if Our Lord did not want me to be an Ursuline but called me somewhere else, she or her friends would help me as much as they could. I had never seen such great, disinterested charity. It was clear to me that all she did for me then and all she has done since was inspired by Our Lord, for there was nothing natural or human which would compel her to act thus. She did not know me and I had never done anything to obligate her to me, nor did she have anything to hope for from me. In a word, nothing could incite her to treat me so charitably except the pure love of God, who had reserved for her the grace of giving me the blessing I had awaited for so long a time.

Following this long perplexity in which God had kept me, one day when I was thinking about it least, the affection and desire I had for the Feuillantines was effectively dispelled and in its place I felt imprinted an affection and longing to be an Ursuline. And this with such an urgent inspiration to achieve this that I felt that everything in the world was threatening me with ruin if I did not save myself at once in this house of God. This, then, was resolved and my confessor consented to it.

[58]

Just as I was on the verge of accomplishing my plan, Our Lord sent me a very heavy cross, the most painful I have ever experienced in my life. Fifteen days before my entrance, I lost my son, who at that time was not quite twelve years old, and for three days I was without any news of him. I was sure that he was drowned or that some evil man had led him away with him. I was tormented by many thoughts like this, and I suffered much more than I let appear. Above all, I thought that God had let this happen to keep me in the world, for I didn't see how I could carry out my plan if my son were not found. I sent people into the countryside to search for him, but in vain. O God! I would never have believed that the loss of a child could be so painful for a mother. I had seen him mortally sick and I had willingly given him to Our Lord; but to lose him like this! I could not understand it. I never lost my inner peace with Our Lord, but this did not release me from the sharp pain of my loss or from the suffering of being deprived of the thing I loved most: that is, the blessing of religious life. Finally, I was forced to strip myself of every desire and, naked at the foot of the cross, resign myself with all my heart to whatever his goodness would ordain.

[59]

All during this loss I had graven on my soul the sorrow that the Blessed Virgin experienced when she lost the Child Jesus in the temple. Yet he was an exalted son while I, poor creature that I am, anguished over the loss of one who, by comparison, is hardly anything. This thought consoled me but there were many others which disturbed me, leading me to believe that all my inspirations to give myself to God and to leave the world were temptations rather than real inspirations.

Furthermore, those who knew I intended to leave my son to enter religion intensified my own fears by predicting something even worse. All this pierced me through so that I dared not say a word because my own mouth would condemn me. A religious person had predicted this torment some time earlier, saying to me: "Get ready to receive a great blessing from God but only after you have been prepared for it by a painful cross." By this great blessing he meant my entrance into religious life and by the painful cross, the loss of my son.

[60]

Finally, my Beloved did not find me worthy of suffering this loss any longer. He gave him back to me, and I began to hope that I would soon have what I thought I had lost. My brother and sister promised to take care of my child and to provide for whatever he would need just as though I myself were still in the world. Thus I resolved—being interiorly moved to do so—to leave him in the providence of Our Lord, under the protection of the Blessed Virgin and St. Joseph, with no other assurance than those informal words which I realized were very uncertain. In fact, my brother-in-law died a short time later.

Everyone blamed me for leaving a child who was not yet twelve years old, especially leaving him without any secure support, as well as leaving my father who was very old and who was deeply moved at not having me with him any more. All this hurt me deeply, but I had graven on my memory those words of Our Lord from the Gospel: "He who loves father and mother more than me is not worthy of me; and he who loves son and daughter more than me is not worthy of me" (Mt 10:37). This strengthened me so much that I grieved for no one, and holding Our Lord's will dear, I wanted only to obey it.

My confessor helped me a great deal, assuring me that Our Lord would take care of my son and that in the sight of God I was free to enter religious life. I left no material goods in entering religion, but I felt inwardly that in leaving my son whom I dearly loved I left more than all imaginable possessions—especially since I left him without support. For ten years I had disciplined him, not permitting him to caress me and on my part I acted the same, so that he would not cling to me when Our Lord commanded me to leave him. Yet all this did not stop him from feeling deeply resentful at my departure.[8]

For several days I was in such a profound union with Our Lord that even at night I could not rest, so powerful was this attraction. While conversing intimately with him and feeling myself in a state of great abnegation, I spoke to him of what he wanted me to do and of the child I was going to leave in his hands, being ready to abandon this whole plan if he wished. For in all this I wanted in no way to seek

---

8. See *Relation of 1654*, p. 95.

myself but only to obey him in everything, never fearing that he would leave me devoid of graces in this world where he had held me so dear.

I asked him not to let me commit a fault in leaving this child if he did not wish me to leave him; but that if it was his will I would rise above all human motives out of love for him. This Divine Goodness was pleased with my abandonment and treated me so tenderly that I don't know how to express it. During this union he prompted me to speak to him constantly and expressing my love for him in return, I tried to compel him to answer me, repeating ceaselessly, "What do you wish my love? Tell me: what do you wish, for I want only what will please you."

My inner peace constantly increased and I was urged to obey promptly. Thus I was so withdrawn from all reality that I was unable to pay attention to what was going on. If someone spoke to me I forgot immediately what he had said. I could eat only a very little and even this with difficulty so that it was feared I'd become sick. But this was all from that profound recollection and inner peace that could not interrupt my absorption in God.

[61]

As I left our house to enter the house of God, this child accompanied me, completely resigned. He dared not show me his grief, but I saw his tears which showed me very clearly what he was feeling. This filled me with such compassion that I felt my soul being wrenched out of me; but God was dearer to me than all. Leaving my son in his hands, smiling, I said goodbye to him.

Then receiving the blessing of my confessor, I knelt before Reverend Mother who in her generosity received me with love and affection. I was astonished afresh to be received as a choir sister, for I had hesitated to ask what she would do with me, wanting to leave myself entirely in Our Lord's providence. I thought I would be received as a lay sister, the other state being too exalted for me. But in the end, I remained as a choir sister, accepting without any choice on my part what was done for me.

[62]

At the very moment when I entered religion, I felt an extraordinary action in my soul. It seemed to me that all the interior dispositions I had experienced in the past were withdrawn and that I was filled with a completely new spirit. While in the world I avidly pursued all kinds of austerity, so filled with this spirit that I would have considered

I was disobeying God not to follow my impulse. In addition, I received Communion almost every day and involved myself in many activities of charity toward my neighbor. But upon entering religion, I felt myself despoiled of all this, no longer having any will or power over myself. I was like a child, yet without even missing the things I was deprived of. I was clothed with such great simplicity that I would have obeyed even a child. I felt I had become one, unable to convince myself of anything else. Actually, I could not bear the slightest fault to go uncorrected, for otherwise I would have felt like a hypocrite in front of people and as though I had not been sufficiently childlike toward God.

[63]

I enjoyed so perfect a peace in seeing myself freed from all the cares which had engaged me in the world that I found all the exercises of religion to be a paradise of delights and I was certain that no storm could ever attack me. What happiness to possess this great blessing after waiting ten or twelve years! I leave it to you to imagine how I expressed my love to Our Lord who granted me this enjoyment. Yet his goodness, which wanted me to live by his cross, did not leave me for long without trying me.

A number of people began to be scandalized at my withdrawal and advised my son that he should come to the monastery crying, so that I would be forced to leave. This threw him into such misery that he hardly budged from our grille, moaning and begging for me. On the other hand, the person who had most promised his help was now the most opposed, threatening not to do as he had promised.[9] Others said I was a cruel and heartless mother who had satisfied myself by cowardly abandoning my son. Others, finally, stirred up the rumor that the religious would soon dismiss me, unable to endure all this fuss so contrary to their peace.

All this was told to me, and many of my friends, believing it to be true, begged me to leave of my own accord before taking the veil rather than going through such embarrassment after receiving it.

[64]

I have never been so beleaguered. I thought I would be put out. Since I myself wasn't able to endure all this trouble, it seemed more

---

9. Undoubtedly Marie's brother-in-law, Paul Buisson, who had agreed grudgingly to undertake the responsibility for Claude's education.

reasonable still that Reverend Mother and the sisters could not endure it, for they had no obligation to do so. I found this just on their part, yet it was a heavy cross for me, for it would force me to return to the world. I was certain that this would happen and I abandoned myself into Our Lord's hands. Finally, however, he wanted to give me some consolation in my suffering and as I was walking up the steps of our novitiate, he gave me an inner assurance that I would be a religious in this house, a promise which strengthened me completely. On the other hand, Reverend Mother assured me that neither she nor any of the sisters had thought of making me leave.

Thus this squall blew over for a bit, but then it recommenced with even greater force. Before my entrance into the monastery, there had been no one more innocent than my son; but all the things that had been said to him embittered him and changed him so that he would not study or do anything else and it seemed he would be good for nothing. The devil assaulted me violently on this, convincing me that I was the cause of all this evil, that it was my responsibility to return to the world to establish some order there; that I had entered religion only to please myself; that it was not the spirit of God that had led me to leave the world but simply the inclination of my self-love; finally, that this child would be lost, that I would never find any happiness in all this and that I would be the cause of his damnation.

My understanding was so darkened by these thoughts that I really believed that all this would happen and that whatever certainty I had about my stability in religion was only a fantasy. Nevertheless, in all this my only fear was to offend God and I would have preferred a thousand times not to be a religious rather than displease him in the smallest thing. For notwithstanding all my sufferings and despite the fact that I believed that I was the cause of all the evil which temptation brought before my eyes, my intimacy with Our Lord was never interrupted.

One day when I was closely united to him, complaining about all my sufferings, he inspired me to ask him to suffer still more for the sake of my son. I spoke to him earnestly, "O my Love, let me suffer all the crosses you wish, provided that this child does not offend you, for I would rather die a thousand times than to see him offend you and not be among your children. I would prefer to be crucified, tortured in every way, provided that you would take care of him."

It was impossible for me not to pour out all these things; so there I was, surrounded by crosses on every side. It seemed that I had concluded a pact with Our Lord, that there was an agreement between us which I never would nor could retract.

[65]

I thought of all the means I could take to reach the depth of abasement and to deprive myself of everything I loved most. In fact, what I loved most were the duties of a choir sister, especially chanting the Office and teaching. This is why I decided to beg our Reverend Mother to make me a lay sister in order to be always humbled. I was impelled toward this for another reason, too—that is, that I did not see in myself any ability to perform the duties of a choir sister worthily. This other condition seemed more fitting for me and, furthermore, it would help to kill my deep-rooted pride which would finally be swept away with Our Lord's help—in whom I hoped to be hidden forever in the state I pursued. I would have liked to be able to humble myself even more, but my condition as a religious did not permit me to go beyond these limits in external activity.

I went, then, to see Reverend Mother, who questioned me about my reasons for asking to change my state. After I had replied to everything she asked, she did not want to consent to my proposal but wished to consider it more at leisure. For several days I entertained hope of receiving a favorable answer and I seriously reflected on whether this was for the greatest glory of God. I experienced great satisfaction in thinking how happy I would be in that state, humbled both interiorly and exteriorly; whereas in the state of choir sister I would aspire to many things which would satisfy me, even if it were only such a thing as conversation about spiritual things both with the sisters and with lay people. I saw in this, as in many other encounters, that one could commit imperfections and nourish the feelings of arrogant nature. In the state of lay sister I would be freed from this and would force these feelings to die. Once again, I went to Reverend Mother who referred me to persons who were competent to judge these things.

I submitted to this, offering everything to Our Lord who, while I was praying and speaking intimately to him, told me by means of a sudden and unexpected light to be on my guard against doing anything contrary to his will. To this I answered, "My dear Love, I want this only to please you more. I have made this proposal and I have great confidence that you will inspire your own desires in those from whom I will receive my answer. Will you not bring this about, my divine Spouse? For in this as in everything, I want only what you command. I will do my best to have my wish granted but I am sure that for your part, nothing will happen which will not be for your glory and my well-being. After this I will remain perfectly content with either a yes or a no—whichever will be said to me."

At the same time I felt without any will except to agree to what would be asked of me. There was almost a certitude in my soul that my request would not be granted and that I would remain in the state where Our Lord in his providence had put me. However, I did not stop pursuing this and using those who could help me in this plan until God's will was clearly manifested.

[66]

Although the assaults from my son were frequent, yet, as I have said, God never deprived me of my loving union nor of his sweet intimacy. One evening while I was praying and speaking to him confidently, I gave him my heart, although it was already all his and free from affection for everything else. It seemed that to make me suffer he wanted to leave me in doubt if he wanted it; and I left my prayer very uneasy yet without straying from the union where he kept me.

The next morning, as soon as I was in prayer and reunited to him, he said to me interiorly—as though he could not leave me suffer any longer—"Give me your heart." At these words I felt myself melt completely into him and it seemed to me that by this word, so sudden and so tender, he drew everything out of me, taking me for his own. This happened so quickly that the soul felt itself taken captive without being aware that it had consented, for in these consolations and others like them, it is so united to him that he no longer asks consent as he did at the beginning.[10] At such times he draws the soul to his Divine Majesty like a thing which has already been given to him long ago, so that there is no necessity of asking if it wishes to belong to its God. He knows that it is for him that it sighs and languishes and thus he lets it feel his loving caresses when it pleases him. And when it becomes aware that its Beloved has snatched it away rather than that it has acceded to his request, it calls him a charming abductor who by his gentle theft has stolen and carried away its heart.

As for the rest, it is a joy to see oneself thus ravished, for the divine Spouse takes nothing which he has not given. This is an inexpressible grace whose effects remain in the soul to encourage and strengthen it to be bolder and more familiar with him.

These favors provide a little truce to its crosses and sufferings, and it is here it finds a little refreshment and a fresh determination to suffer

---

10. For a later account of this grace, see *Relation of 1654*, pp. 115 n. 5, 116.

all anew. It is convinced that crosses await it everywhere and that it is in this that it can show that it loves its God.

[67]

This grace was followed by another even greater. On the feast of the Guardian Angels while I was in our cell, it occurred to me that our cells are like heaven, as St. Bernard said, and that the angels make their home here. As I was reflecting on this, I felt my spirit powerfully drawn by the Master of the angels, who united me to himself in a wonderful way, but with a strong sense of expectation—as if he were preparing me for a yet more eminent grace. This was brought about without my having any special understanding except that preparations were being made for something very rare. This feeling spread so that even my body was in pain and I experienced a strong impression that it was God who kept me thus.

I was in this state of agitation for three or four hours until I had to go to choir for prayer. As soon as I was in front of the Blessed Sacrament this agitation ceased and with a tenderness I cannot express, I felt myself completely changed. I had to sit down because little by little I felt my senses failing and I could not stay kneeling any longer. Instantly, my understanding was illumined with a vision of the most Holy Trinity which revived my knowledge of its grandeurs. Then by a profound love, this whole Divine Majesty united itself to my soul, giving itself to me with an outpouring I would never know how to explain. As at other times I felt myself captivated by the Person of the Word, but this time all three Persons of the Holy Trinity absorbed me in such a way that I could not see myself in one person without seeing myself in the others. Or to put it better, I saw myself in both their Unity and their Trinity simultaneously. What touched me most was that I saw myself in this Majesty like a pure nothing lost in the All. This was a loving revelation that although I was nothing, yet I was entirely apt for him who is my All.

Understanding that I was a nothing, apt for this ineffable All, gave me indescribable pleasure. I thought that this happiness was like that of the blessed. I understood once again that it was here I found real annihilation of my soul in God by a true union of love. This vision which I enjoyed and which enabled me to see that I, a nothing, was an appropriate object for this great All is beyond anything that can be said. The sight of my own nothingness which was given to me did not lessen my love but only increased it through the understanding that I was the appropriate object of this All. Not only was I lost in this Divine Majesty, but I acted tenderly to caress him and because this was appropriate, everything was permitted me. My actions never came from myself but were produced in me by him in whom I was totally lost. He gave himself completely to me and I let him take everything to himself. It seemed that this great God, being in me, made his home in me and my soul felt itself to be the paradise of God, remaining in him through an inexplicable love.[11]

At the end of this profound union, I was like someone drunk, unable to understand what was in front of me. Thus I remained for a long time, closed within myself, without the ability to pay attention to anything. This vision remained engraved in my spirit: that I was that very nothing which is the fit object for the All. This was a heavy burden, compelling the soul to accept for love of this All all kinds of pains and difficulties. It has much to suffer yet it wishes to suffer even more. In addition, it knows that this divine Spouse wants this love to be continuous, without interruption. For just as he gives himself to it, he wishes reciprocally that it look upon him, constant in its loving actions. He gives it the strength to act thus no matter what state it is in, even when pierced by a thousand crosses.

---

11. See *Relation of 1654*, pp. 98–100.

NOTES FROM
A TEN-DAY RETREAT (c. 1633)

GOD THE CREATOR

First Meditation: That God is your father according to nature.

"Your hands, Lord, have shaped me; you have given me life
and mercy; and your visit protects my spirit." (Jb 10:12)

My spirit reflected on the blessing of creation in general but it
could not be confined within the bounds of nature. Immediately it was
borne away to the blessings of redemption and justification; yet without an outpouring of my feelings—that is, without reflecting or enlarging on the circumstances of these wonderful blessings beyond
seeing that it is the Father who created me, the Son who redeemed me,
and the Spirit who justified me.

I understood that the Father while bestowing being on me has left
a multitude of creatures in their nothingness; that the Son while re-
deeming me has left an infinity of souls in their ruin, almost as though
they have not experienced his redemption; and that the Holy Spirit
while sanctifying me has left countless people in their sins.

Following this, my will completely overflowed in gratitude and
united itself in love to this most Holy Trinity, sometimes gazing upon
it in the unity of its essence and at other times in the distinction of
persons, confirming what the church teaches: that all the gifts that God
gives his creatures are common to the three divine Persons; and yet
one attributes creation to the Father, redemption to the Son, and
justification to the Holy Spirit when these are poured forth through the
infusion of grace. For since the three Persons have but a single power,
what one does the other two also do indivisibly.

My will, thus encompassed with love of him whom she knows to be so generous in her regard, felt itself moved to imitate him insofar as the weakness of her nature allows, going out of herself to communicate this in service to the neighbor.

I resolved to do this, asking the grace to be faithful on these occasions.

Second Meditation: That God is your father according to grace.

"He wills to bring us to birth with a word spoken in truth so
that we may be a kind of first fruits of his creation." (Jas 1:18)

In this passage I considered the choice God has made from all eternity of those he has called to Christianity; all these words put before me the circumstances of this incomparable blessing. He has given us life: he is, then, our father and we are his children. He has brought us forth freely and voluntarily: this divine birth is, then, an effect of his grace and of his pure liberality. He has brought us forth by the word of his truth—that is, by his Son; for thus his well-beloved Son accomplished in time what had been determined in the eternal council. He has brought us forth to be the first born of his new creatures, that is of whose who live according to the new law as his children through the grace of adoption.

All these circumstances so filled my heart that I thought I would faint from weakness in loving this Eternal Word to whom the Father had given me that I might be among the first of his creatures. I have never been able to find a way to correspond to such excess of graces and favors except to beg the same Word to receive me in his divine heart in order to consume me as a continual holocaust in the presence of the Father. Although in everything I am unfaithful to him, abusing his gifts, yet the fire of this divine altar will consume all my infidelities and sanctify my life, my thoughts, and my actions.

Third Meditation: That God has raised us to the order of grace in order to give us the means of overcoming the enemies of our soul.

"I will put enmity between you and the woman and between
your offspring and hers; he will strike at your head while you
strike at his heel." (Gn 3:15)

I thought that the woman who is spoken of here is the Church; and that the serpent is the devil; that the seed of the woman are those heavenly inspirations from whence are born the fruit of good works;

while the seed of the serpent are those poisonous suggestions which produce only the fruits of death and of works worthy of hell.

I lamented inwardly to see souls engaged in this struggle and in danger of being vanquished; but then my spirit was lifted at once thinking that all things turn to good for those who love God. The love that God bears his children shows them that it is he who permits their "enmities"—either to purify them, to prove their fidelity, to give them a chance to grow in merit, or to give them the opportunity of carrying off the crown of victory, and always to the confusion of their enemies if they are faithful to put to good use the strength which is given them by the sacrament of Confirmation which is instituted for this purpose.

Then it occurred to me that the foot of the soul is the humility on which it stands firm and unshakeable while it lives; and the head of the serpent is that pride which holds the highest place in the body of sin. The serpent thus casts snares for our feet as he tries to make us lose our humility, knowing very well that when the foundation is destroyed, everything of perfection in the soul will crumble into ruin. We crush the head of the serpent when we scorn and trample underfoot the glory of the world, the praises, the vanities, and all the other pomps of pride.

I have seen that the fiercest battle that I have to sustain is against thoughts of pride which sometimes attack me; from thence I have been powerfully moved to humiliate myself both interiorly and exteriorly in order to crush the feelings of proud nature which tend constantly to the elevation of self. I have resolved to work hard at this until the head of the serpent is entirely crushed in me.

SECOND DAY:
GOD THE LIBERATOR

First Meditation: That God has granted you his graces, without your having merited them.

"Before they call, I will answer; while they are yet speaking, I will hearken to them." (Is 65:24)

This sentence made me consider the means divine Providence has made use of to win me over to the love and infinite mercy by which he has prepared me so as to overwhelm me with them at a later time. For it is true that before I cried he heard me and before I spoke he listened to me. Before I sought him, I found him. How could I have cried had he not pricked my heart with compunction? How would I have been able to speak if he had not opened my mouth and given movement to my tongue and my lips? How could I have sought him if he had not anticipated me and if he had not let me find him, as he said through his prophet: I have been found by those who did not seek me?

My will has been deeply moved by this, not by a tender movement but by profound feelings of humble acknowledgement, confessing that I have everything from his infinite goodness. I felt myself drawn to give myself entirely to my liberator in a reciprocal love and by a total abandonment of my self. He has given himself completely to me and I give myself completely to him. What more can I do?

So that this love will be more pure, I resolved to give up the exaggerated care I have taken of myself and of the many things which do not really concern me and which he does not ask of me. Above all, I have seen the importance of being faithful in the way of grace and of love. For if I were so wretched as to turn aside from this way, who would cry for me since without him I would be unable to cry? And who would speak for me since without him I would be unable to speak? Who would seek him and find him for me since without him I could not seek him?

Second Meditation: That although God is infinitely glorious in himself, nevertheless, he wishes that you glorify him; and it is in glorifying him that you must find your own glory.

"All my being shall say, 'O Lord, who is like you?' "
(Ps 35:10)

I saw everything beneath God as narrow and limited. Blinded by the sight of this infinite being, I was happy and took pleasure in the fact that nothing can penetrate the depths of this abyss of majesty. I saw the beauty of the sun and the grandeur of the world, but all this appeared to me like mud and nothingness compared to the beauty and grandeur of God. I thought of the splendor and pomp of the kings of this world which is the best image we can form of God; but all their glory appeared less than a shadow compared to this supreme and incomprehensible majesty. I even contemplated the heavenly court, this resting place of the blessed, with all the happiness that scripture tells us is enjoyed there. Yet without God all this happiness seemed only misery and affliction of heart.

In all this my heart rejoiced that nothing can be compared to this infinite God and I said over and over: Lord, who is like to you? My spirit, impassioned by all these sights, sang praises appropriate to what it saw. In the vision of beauty, it sang of beauty; in the sight of grandeur, it sang of grandeur; in the sight of power, it sang of power, ending everything with these words: Lord, who is like to you?

I ardently desired to be deprived of whatever praise was given me and of that which might be given me, recognizing that it is only this infinite being who is worthy of praise and that all my glory is to glorify him. In order not to appropriate anything to myself, I resolved to give everything to him and to bear in my heart forever these words: Lord, who is like to you? To you alone be all honor and glory.

Third Meditation: That just as you could not go to God without God, so you cannot remain in him without him.

"For from him and through him and for him all things are."
(Rom 11:36)

All during my prayer, my understanding, incapable of reasoning, contemplated by a simple gaze the divine perfections; and my will conversed lovingly with the divine majesty. From time to time this simple gaze brought me especially to that sovereign power "of whom, by whom, and in whom are all things." Here my love redoubled, seeing that God exists independently of everything and that everything exists only through him.

Over and above this sentence, this other passage from the Apocalypse came to mind: "You have made all things and it is through your will that they have been created." My affection was caught up in this love and power which had not only given me life according to nature, but even more had drawn me into the paths of grace—and without which I could not exist for a moment in either of these states. Recognizing my fundamental dependence on this power and love, I abandoned myself to his control in order to be unreservedly and forever the slave of him who created me in this world and who drew me into the ways of grace by his pure will.

Since everything has been created by this love and this power, I earnestly desired that all reasoning creatures recognize and love their author. I asked for the conversion of Christian sinners who have so completely forgotten his love, as well as for that of infidels who have not yet known him. Then I remained in a peaceful union which lasted for the remainder of my prayer.

THIRD DAY:
GOD THE SANCTIFIER

First Meditation: How God loves you, detaching you from the vanity of creatures in order that you walk in his ways.

"Your decrees are my inheritance forever; they are the joy of my heart." (Ps 119:111)

This subject brought a fresh burst of love to my heart as I recalled the favors which this divine goodness had so generously distributed to me. The blessings he has given me as the portion of my inheritance are scorn of the world—of its pleasures, its riches, its honors; and love of the cross, of poverty, of humility; as well as the honor of his constant presence, of familiarity and intimacy with him, and above all the love of his love.

These are the evidences and the ways which have fallen to me forever through the grace of this wonderful liberator. I saw their excellence and their inestimable value; by comparison all the gifts, all the honors, all the grandeurs which the world grants and which men so esteem seemed to me less than a shadow compared to this reality. My soul in a sudden loving desire was lifted up to God whom she saw as infinite love, and thus she rested in him in a very close union. During this union, however, I remembered the greatness, the beauty, the holiness and justice of the ways of this divine majesty. This increased my admiration, my love, my desire to persevere in these same paths which were effectively "the joy and delights of my heart." They are my joy and my delights because they have emanated from him whom I love with a love I cannot express; and because they are the precepts for that holy life which he came to establish through the law of the Gospel.

Reflecting on the love I felt for "the ways which had fallen to me as my inheritance," I offered it all to him who had given it to me; and finding this still not enough, I yielded myself to his judgment by a simple gentle gaze which continued until the end of my prayer.

Second Meditation: That your true sanctification consists in being united to Jesus Christ and in living his life.

"Live on in me, as I do in you. No more than a branch can
bear fruit of itself apart from the vine, can you bear fruit
apart from me." (Jn 15:4)

At my first glance at this passage my will was drawn to God by a
yearning of love, saying to him: "It is true, my Beloved, it is true. May I
remain in you and you in me." In the union which I experienced with
the divine majesty, there was a light which let me see what it is to be
grafted into God through Jesus Christ and also what it is to be separated from him. I saw that to be grafted onto God through Jesus Christ
is to believe that Jesus Christ is God and to be united to him by faith in
order to live by his spirit through grace; just as St. Paul says, a wild
olive tree is grafted onto a cultivated one so as to make it share its life
and sap. To be separated from Jesus Christ is to have no faith; or if one
does have it, not to live by his spirit or his grace so as to be like dead,
withered members, still attached to the body but as if they were not
because they do not participate in the spirit of life which animates
the body.

These lights moved my will to plunge deeper and deeper into its
divine object, asking that these words become effective: "Remain in
me and I in you." I begged that they would have the same effect in my
soul as they had had in the Apostles, who would have been able to do
nothing without his spirit and the strengthening power of his love. I
said to the Eternal Father: "O divine Father, please give me this faith
which will unite me to your Son and make me one body with him; still
more, give me the grace necessary to live with his life and his spirit.
And because it is a useless thing for a branch to be united to the vine
and be filled with its life if it produces no fruit, give me those daily
graces necessary for me to be fruitful in virtue and good works."

This union lasted for the whole time of my prayer during which I
was almost always incapable of formulating specific acts. I did make
them, nevertheless, but only from time to time, when I felt in myself a
certain impulse which strongly urged me to do this.

Third Meditation: That God dwells in you as in his house which
he sanctifies by his presence.

"Christ was faithful as the Son placed over God's house. It is
we who are that house if we hold fast to our confidence and
the hope of which we boast." (Heb 3:6)

Jesus Christ as Son is in the house; and we ourselves are this
house, provided that we hold fast to a firm trust in him unto the end

and that we await with joy the blessing which we hope for. At the first moment of my prayer, I spoke to the Eternal Father in the name of his Son whose dwelling I am. Then, suddenly, without seeing how this happened, I found myself adoring the incomprehensibility of my guest with a burning desire that he sanctify this house and that he be praised and glorified forever.

All this occurred passively in my soul, for these acts did not come from me, nor were they of my choosing. In this condition, when the understanding is completely suspended and beyond all reasoning and reflection, the will, too, is beyond its own ability to act, undergoing these mysterious things in God who lets the soul experience first-hand that she is his dwelling.

In such prayer as this, I was unable to act; everything was passive.

FOURTH DAY:
GOD OUR BENEFACTOR

First Meditation: That since God's gifts to you have been far from ordinary, so your love and acknowledgement must also be extraordinary.

> "He looks with favor upon their hearts and shows them his
> glorious works. . . . His majestic glory their eyes behold; his
> glorious voice their ears heard." (Sir 17:7,11)

Two of God's wonders, contained in this sentence, were shown to me: one concerns the particular and the other the general, and I have been affected by both of them.

Concerning the general: I saw the wonder of those works mentioned in the first chapter of St. John who describes the incomprehensible union of the divine nature with the human nature and I saw the marvel of these acts, truly the very marvel of marvels. For how can God do anything more wonderful than to make a God-Man as great, as good, as wise, as powerful as himself? This wonder is available to everyone, for it is written: "The Son is born for us," and the Eternal Father has given him to us. Yet I consider this as an inestimable blessing for me personally, looking upon this Son as if he were given for me alone and as if he were born solely for me. Thus he is mine, all mine, my single love. And truly "the Eternal Father has cast the eyes of his goodness upon our hearts so that we might see this wonder." For as the Beloved Disciple says in the same place: "We have seen his glory, the glory of the only Son of the Father, full of grace and truth." We have seen him; we see him still by faith. We have even seen him and heard him through the eyes and ears of the Apostles and especially of the one who says: "What we have seen, what we have heard, what we have touched of the Word of Life—this is what we announce to you."

This is the special aspect which engages me. I have seen as in a great light God's guidance on my soul in the three states it has pleased Providence for me to traverse and in which I have tangibly experienced the guidance of his love. In this knowledge my understanding remained as it were suspended, unable to make any act except to admire the divine abundance of his goodness. My will, transported by love, said over and over: O great abyss, how captivating are your charms! May you be blessed, O my great abyss, O abyss of goodness.

What touched me most was the wonderful resourcefulness which the Eternal Father used to win my heart by his extraordinary light—or to put it better, by his Word who himself lifted and directed me in the ways of grace with so tender and special a love that I can truly say that this was, in my opinion, the wonder of his works. Except for the mysteries of our faith, it seems to me that I see nothing more wonderful.

While still in this union with God, I resolved to renew my fidelity and correspondence to his love, praising him for so much mercy. Once again I wanted those who did not see the light to be enlightened in order to participate in these many blessings.

Second Meditation: That God, although an abyss of riches, wisdom, and knowledge, cannot enrich you more than to give you himself, filling you with himself.

"How deep are the riches and the wisdom and the knowledge of God! How inscrutable his judgments, how unsearchable his ways" (Rom 11:33)

At the very moment when I recalled the divine perfections, I found myself in a state of infinity where there were neither boundaries nor limits, and inwardly I cried in admiration: O Height! O Depths! O Greatness!

In this infinity, all thought was forgotten except that this immense infinity in which I am lost is my love, that he is in me and I in him, and that he alone is my riches and my treasure. At this, all the powers of the soul are abandoned, eternally lost in this vision. The will undergoes such divine things that I cannot express them.

This continued until the end of my prayer. I longed to speak of God, of his inscrutable ways and incomprehensible judgments; but my understanding, effaced during this process, withdrew into a state of passivity where it remained powerless for some time. Thus I am supported by his love and remain in great intimacy with him who has given himself to me so generously in order that he may be my riches and my treasure always.

Third Meditation: That however great the favors God has bestowed on you, you, on your part, must keep yourself in humility of heart and in a loving fear of losing them.

"This treasure we possess in earthen vessels to make it clear
that its surpassing power comes from God and not from us."
(2 Cor 4:7)

My spirit was filled and completely taken up with the lights from my first prayer of the day, concerning the grandeurs and wonders of God and especially of those which particularly concern me. This present passage, coming on top of all this, has brought me to an extreme humility and annihilation when I saw how precious the treasure of graces God has given me and how sublime the gifts he has bestowed on me—and all this confined in an earthen vessel, so weak, so easily broken, and its contents so readily lost.

Nevertheless, this humiliation was no obstacle to the union of my will but rather set it on fire even more, because in treating with God about human suffering and my own weakness I saw that this did not hinder him from communicating with souls, since he reveals himself only out of pure goodness and love.

I had a special light which showed me the frightening inclination our nature has toward sin; and in this light I was seized with fear and trembling, understanding that my soul, still in a mortal body, could sin and lose God. For this earthly vessel is easily broken and the treasure of grace which by his goodness it contains can be lost and wasted. This was a new source of fear and humiliation in the sight of him to whom I felt so intimately united. But in a moment my fears were gone and I began again to express my love, abandoning myself to his love and firmly believing that my soul would be safe in his hand.

I concluded by promising him to be faithful to him.

FIFTH DAY:
GOD THE SHEPHERD

First Meditation: That God gives you as nourishment for your soul the most priceless and delicious thing he has.

"For what wealth is theirs, and what beauty! Grain that makes youth flourish, and new wine the maidens!"
(Zec 9:17)

From the beginning of my prayer the sight of the goodness and beauty of God drew my will so powerfully that it was in an uninterrupted state of love, treating constantly with him about the wonderful effects he produces in souls through the communion they have with him in the most holy sacrament of the altar. I say that these effects are wonderful because, as St. Paul says, "Lust is found in ordinary wine" but virginity is found in this, for it is this which makes souls pure.

My soul was ecstatic to realize that her spouse is the goodness and beauty of the Eternal Father; that in comparison with this good all other goods are evil; and in comparison with this beauty all other beauty is ugly. Thus, what I should ask of this divine Father and what I should hope from his generosity is that good which is the wheat of the elect, and that beauty which is the wine which makes virgins. As goodness, he is the object of my affection; and as beauty he is the object of my glory and my delights.

I discovered many other special secrets in this divine mystery without my will being diverted from its union. I had a burning desire for the reception of the Divine Sacrament and I was completely filled with the spirit of Jesus Christ in order to resemble him by a conformity of life. I abandoned myself completely to his grace and his love so that he would prepare me for these gifts at his good pleasure.

Second Meditation: The dispositions with which you ought to eat the food that your Shepherd gives you.

"I myself am the living bread come down from heaven."
(Jn 6:51)

This sentence of Our Lord and the other which he spoke to his disciples before the Last Supper—"I have desired with an ardent desire to eat this Pasch with you before I suffer"—are linked together, and both have strongly impressed my spirit concerning Holy Communion.

This divine Shepherd, wishing to communicate his very self while giving communion to the Apostles, is filled with zeal—an ardent and burning zeal. "I have," he said, "desired with desire to eat this Pasch with you." This has shown me the disposition with which I should receive him. It is in a transport of love that he receives and eats himself sacramentally; it is by a like transport that I should approach him. Seeing this, my will was completely encompassed by love and transported with desire to be united and, if possible, identified with this Shepherd in the divine sacrament.

It seemed to me that he has left himself in the Holy Eucharist so that we would have under the veil of the sacred species what the saints have in full view and uncovered in heaven; and that as in heaven he is the paradise of the blessed, thus on earth he is also a paradise—but a hidden one—for pure souls who love him in truth. This word—paradise—strongly impelled my soul, along with all its powers, into a profound union with this loving savior. I recognized him as the center of my happiness and my good fortune—to the point of sacrificing my life (if need be), my honor and everything in the world. During this union I experienced a strong desire that the many souls who do not belong to the Church, and so many others who do belong but who are not in the state of grace would be sincerely converted. Thus would be satisfied the desire of him who gives himself to them with such love and who wishes to be their paradise and their happiness in this life in order to be so more fully and perfectly in heaven.

Third Meditation: The delights of the food God offers when it is eaten with the proper dispositions.

"He has satisfied the empty and filled the hungry with good things." (Ps 107:9)

My spirit imagined the feast described in the Song of Songs, which consists of myrrh, wine, milk, and a honeycomb with its honey. I saw in this mystic feast the delights found in this most holy Sacrament of the Altar where the soul is fed with the divinity of Jesus Christ—symbolized by honey—and the humanity—symbolized by the honeycomb. Along with this heavenly food one must drink both wine and milk. By wine I understood love and charity; and by milk the purity and innocence which are the essential dispositions for profitably eating the solid food of this divine banquet. Before all this, one must have gathered myrrh; that is, one must have performed many acts of mortification and penance symbolized by the bitterness of myrrh.

In connection with this subject I have noticed that the divine Jesus completely fills only empty souls—empty, that is, of themselves, of the demands of nature, of attachment to the world, of the smallest sins, and even of deliberate imperfections. He will satisfy with his blessings only those who are hungry for God and his gifts of grace and virtue.

While engaged in this feast of love with Our Lord, I was granted a light so clear and insistent that I cannot explain it. This light showed me distinctly that in order to be welcome at the banquet one must sustain a complete and perfect union with the divine presence, and that this union is the marriage garment demanded by the Spouse. Without this garment I would have been thrust out of the feast like the foolish man spoken of in the Gospel.

SIXTH DAY:

GOD OUR LIGHT

First Meditation: That Jesus Christ is the only light by which you can reach your final end.

"May the splendor of God Our Lord always be upon us to enlighten us. And may you, O Lord, prosper the work of our hands . . . prosper the work of our hands." (Ps 90:17)

My spirit no sooner glanced at this sentence than many other phrases crowded around it to strengthen it. The first was from the first chapter of St. John where he says that Our Lord is the "true light which enlightens everyone who comes into the world; the light which shines in darkness"—that is, which pushes it aside and dissipates it. Then came those four words of St. Paul: "Christ Jesus, splendor of the Father." That Jesus Christ is the splendor of the Father had a wonderful effect on me. Finally, these words from the Nicene Creed rose up in my soul like a sun which filled it with brightness: that the Second Person of the most holy Trinity is God of God and Light of Light.

All this knowledge was given to me in order that I might understand that the divine Jesus is the true and only light, without whom we are always in the darkness of sin and the shadow of imperfection. I was convinced of this and in this conviction my heart was flooded with desire to be constantly filled with this divine Word, this Word of light, this Word which shines like daylight in souls, so that "anyone who follows him will not walk in darkness but will have the light of life."

I saw all the benefits of the state of grace far beyond that of the law. "So many patriarchs, so many prophets, so many kings have desired to see it and possess it but they have neither seen nor possessed." We see and possess it in the state of grace. "He has been found by those who did not seek him." And it is for this reason that this state is properly called the state of grace. I consider myself especially happy to possess it and I see clearly that there is no happiness in the world equal to it. Without this possession, all happiness is only wretchedness.

It seems to me that there are two things which ordinarily hinder this divine light from enlightening the spirit as much as it could. Even when it does enlighten, it does not succeed in directing the "works of our hands" nor "the work of our salvation"—which is called our work par excellence because whatever else we do is only idleness by comparison. The first of these obstacles is the false light of our own spirit which wants to commingle with the light of God. The second is an unregulated affection for worldly things which rises like a cloud, hindering God's light from illumining and directing us.

In return for this grace I resolved to put nothing of myself into what he teaches me, in order that "the works of my hands" and above all "the work of my salvation" be accomplished with all the purity he desires.

Second Meditation: That Jesus Christ is especially the light of the humble.

"Father, Lord of heaven and earth, to you I offer praise; for what you have hidden from the learned and the clever you have revealed to the merest children." (Mt 11:25)

From the beginning my spirit, still absorbed in the knowledge and lights of my last prayer, was unable to make any specific acts; but reflecting on the subject in general I returned to the lights I had received this morning and this became an occasion to render thanks to God: "I will give you thanks, O Father, Lord of heaven and earth."

My understanding was in a state of deep humility, realizing that this sovereign and infinite majesty who hides "his secrets from the wise and learned of this world" deigns to reveal them to the simple and to little ones, and to me who am the last of the world and the outcast of creatures. This is why, full of gratitude, I repeated: "I give you thanks, O Father, Lord of heaven and earth, for you have hidden these things from the wise of the world and have revealed them to the humble and to little ones."

Following this, my will was lost in an extraordinary love—that is, a love completely passive. All that I was capable of doing of myself was to long to love eternally, after experiencing such abundant knowledge; to love, I repeat, with a love perfectly pure and free. My spirit went back over some imperfections contrary to this perfect detachment and especially to one thing which has often caused me distraction and weakened my attention to God. I resolved to correct myself of this in order that my understanding be solely consecrated to this light and my heart to his love.

Third Meditation: That your true glory consists in knowing God and loving him.

"Let not the wise man glory in his wisdom, nor the strong man glory in his strength, nor the rich man in his riches but let him glory in knowing me." (Jer 9:23)

At the first I was caught up in a great joy and an unparalleled happiness in having within me the source of my glory and in seeing that the true cause of my glory is to know God and to recognize him by faith. I considered how different this knowledge is from other kinds, for this occurs not only in the understanding, but even more fully in the will. This is the true wisdom of the saints which consists in knowing God and loving him: the knowledge of salvation which brings about the forgiveness of sins.

This deep-seated joy was followed by a completely new kind of love, resulting from the details of this heavenly knowledge of which the divine goodness has given me so wonderful a share. I abandoned myself anew to the guidance of his will; and glorying in knowing him, I said: Let the wise not glory in their wisdom, for the demons are wiser than they; let the strong not glory in their strength, animals are stronger than men; let not the rich glory in their riches, for sinners are generally richer than good people; but those who wish to glory, let them glory in the knowledge and recognition of God. There will be found my glory and my honor. The great of this world draw their greatness, as the prophet says, "from the grandeur of their array," but the knowledge of my great God and the confession of his holy name is my grandeur, my crown, and my glory.

I resolved to mortify myself by denying myself some little amusements and some curious thoughts which sometimes rob me of my sweet rest in prayer and of a part of the attention I owe to his love. Oh, how can I so forget myself as to put in competition with him what is so unworthy of him and so unworthy of a soul who wants to love without alloy? How is it possible for me to mingle my little vanities with the knowledge of God? Thus it is like a cloud of dust which covers my crown and obscures it.

SEVENTH DAY:
GOD OUR LOVE

First Meditation: That since God is love you will dwell in love if you are united to God; it is in this that you will find your perfection.

"Over all these virtues put on love which is the bond of perfection." (Col 3:14)

While reflecting on the divinity as a profound abyss of perfection, my understanding was brought briefly to a halt in the sight of my love—the person of the Eternal Word. Even before beginning my prayer, my will had been completely moved and was now plunged into an encompassing union which lasted until the end of my prayer. The subject of my meditation was that since God is love, I should also be all love in this union; that since he is fire, being in him I should burn and become fire like him; that since love is the bond of perfection, I should want no other bond or any other perfection except Him who is love.

Following these transports, I found myself in a state of great detachment from all creatures and in a perfect disposition to cling to this heavenly spouse everywhere and at all times in everything related to his commandments, so that if he wished me to go to the ends of the earth, this would become my country; for since he is everywhere, all places are the same for me. I had a strong desire to assist my neighbor and help him find God insofar as my condition and my weakness would permit.

Second Meditation: That in order to bring forth fruits of charity, one must remain in God who is charity.

"May charity be the root and foundation of your life." (Eph 3:17)

From the very beginning of my prayer, my understanding was lost in the depth of the mysteries it found hidden in this sentence, incapable of acting by itself. My will, realizing even more than my understanding, abandoned itself, saying, "O great Love, encompass me since I cannot encompass you."

A little while after this I was borne away by a powerful impulse, crying more with love than with words, "I love you, O Love; I love you, O great Love! And since my spirit cannot understand your incomprehensible grandeurs, I will know you by loving you and I will be filled with the fullness of your Spirit." I remained for a time in a state of weakness until by a fresh renewal I questioned him with humble courage, asking him, "What have your saints done, O Lord, that compelled you to fill them with your spirit and enabled them to bring forth fruits of charity—that is, those noble deeds which belong only to heroic souls? If all that was necessary was to shed one's blood, then here I am, ready to give all of mine. But no, it is not this; rather, it is 'that they were planted and rooted in love,' and thus they were filled with love like trees which, being planted and rooted in the earth, are filled with its strength. What I long for is to be eternally 'planted and rooted in you' because it is you who are true and perfect love. Thus I will be filled with your spirit; I will be filled with your love and with your gifts—that is to say, your grace which will produce in me those fruits you want of me."

Third Meditation: That as God proves his love for you by the gifts he has given you and by giving you himself, you must give witness to him by keeping his holy laws and by giving yourself to him completely.

"Those who love the Lord will keep his ways." (Sir 2:15)

A great number of passages from Holy Scripture came to mind, especially Psalm 118, which deals continually with the law of God. I contemplated these by a simple glance, without reasoning or reflection, content that they were the commandments of my great God which should be obeyed blindly and without analysis. My will was so completely taken up in this that in order to provide a little relief and give my heart a breath of fresh air, I repeated frequently the passages which had occurred to me.

Far from providing relief, the repetition of these passages only aroused me more so that they were like a current of air fanning. I felt moved to prostrate myself and renew the vows to keep the divine commandments which I had made at baptism. I did this but as I did so I felt a fresh fire in my heart which continued until the end of my prayer. I cannot explain what I understand of the ways of God, of his justice, his holiness, his judgments, his witness, his justification, his commandments. For beneath all these different names I understand one thing: the commandments of my great God.

These are his ways because it is through these divine precepts that we must go to him: this is his justice which is equitable and fair; this is his holiness through which we are sanctified and which is the basic rule for all creation; these are his judgments because they are the articles on which we will be judged; this is his testament which by keeping we prove that we understand its subject; these are his justifications because they will justify us in his presence when we observe them and they will justify God himself when he gives sentence against those who scorn him. These, finally, are his commandments because they put everything in harmony within us and beyond us and which when they are not kept throw everything into chaos and confusion.

During all this time the movements of my heart were so strong that I was not even able to speak to his Divine Majesty. Yet without speaking and by a simple loving gaze I indicated to him that he understands everything I want to say and that he could not ignore my heart's desire to carry out his divine precepts and his adorable will.

EIGHTH DAY:
GOD OUR SPOUSE

First Meditation: The thoughts which God has had for all eternity to make your soul his spouse.

"All that is mine is thine and what is thine is mine and I will be glorified in them." (Jn 17:10)

I saw in this passage the supreme degree of unity among the divine Persons and the perfect union of this sovereign Majesty in souls who consent to abandon themselves to the designs which God has had for them from all eternity and I exclaimed with the prophet, How good it is to cling to God!

After this first consideration everything took place in my will. I recognized the loving action of the divine goodness on my soul and the fulfillment of his designs for my sanctification. It is this goodness that placed me so high in his love and that planned all this for me while I was still nothingness and could neither act nor request or desire anything. Meanwhile, I was in close union with God, repeating over and over again: "Everything that is mine is thine and everything that is thine is mine. Glorify yourself in me and triumph over her who belongs to you because my glory consists in belonging to you and you to me. Everything you have is mine. You have given me a part of it and have led me to hope for the rest. And all that I have is yours, for I have nothing I have not received from you and I wish for nothing except for you.

"How is it possible for what you have not to be mine since you yourself are mine? And since your Father has given you to me, has he not given me everything else in you? And how could all that I have not be yours since I am yours, given to you as an irrevocable and perpetual holocaust?"

Almost all my prayer was spent in such reflections. I disavowed all the works of corrupt nature which is sometimes unwilling to abandon itself to the designs of God. I asked him for the grace to conquer this nature in everything for the sake of his love.

Second Meditation: That the condition of spouse demands that you belong completely to your spouse by a loving abandonment of yourself.

"I will call to mind the deeds of the Lord, for I remember
the wonders you have performed from the beginning."
(Ps 77:12)

This thought was linked to my memories of the great graces and extraordinary favors I have received from this most holy and adorable Trinity: to be a soul endowed with reason, to be ennobled by the grace of baptism and by the title and dignity of being a child of God, to be honored by the condition of spouse through the grace of an extraordinary union—and still more by his continual presence—, to be favored by intimacy and familiarity; to receive constantly such sublime graces that I could never forget them. "I shall always remember the marvels he has accomplished in me since the very beginning."

All these favors, especially that of being his spouse, were shown to me so vividly that I could do nothing but abandon myself into the arms of him whom I knew to be my God, my Father, my Spouse. What overwhelmed me was the thought that it was he who gave me the ability to recognize that I actually experienced those blessings which I have just recounted, and thus to see myself so exalted in his good graces.

Occasionally I offered to each of the divine Persons each of my powers: I sacrificed my memory to the Eternal Father so that I would forget all creatures and no longer think of anything but him; I sacrificed my understanding to the person of the Son so that he himself would be the word and end of all my thoughts; I offered my will to the Holy Spirit so that I would never place any other love before his nor be kindled by any other fire but his, which is the fire and love of Father and Son. Then, reflecting that my soul, having been created in the image of God, is one in itself as God is one in his nature, I renewed the sacrifice of my soul to the Divinity in order to be lost in its unity.

I wished to be lost in this way so that I would have no more life or movement except by his life and his movement, for I feared that living and acting of myself I might corrupt the high thoughts of a child of God and the inviolable fidelity which his spouses owed him. In a word, I had no other desire but to be entirely lost in him and to become his very self, if that were possible, in time and eternity.

Third Meditation: As the Divine Word has become your spouse by offering himself in sacrifice, thus you ought to be his spouse in sacrificing yourself and all that you are for him.

"And Abel offered the first-born of his flock, the fat portions of them, and the Lord received Abel with favor." (Gn 4:4)

From the moment that I wanted to begin my prayer, I was in a loving colloquy with God, loving him as the spouse of my soul. A short time after, I told the divine Majesty that in my preceding prayer I had given him all that I had, that there was nothing in myself nor of myself of which I did not want to make a complete sacrifice; and that during this hour I begged him simply to let me love him, since I could do nothing but keep myself in this divine union.

Nevertheless, this passage from the Apocalypse came to mind: "He has made us kings and priests to God and for the Father." Then I renewed the total oblation of myself, recognizing that the state of spouse is that of victim because a spouse does not belong to herself but to her spouse—just as the state of a husband is also a state of victim because he does not belong to himself but to his spouse.

I told him that he knew that I loved him without any pretense and that as a sign of my love I would repeat the sacrifice of those things I had immolated in my last prayer. I wanted to add to this the first-born affections of my heart; I did not wish to make a distinction between the first-born and all the others but rather wanted all to have the rights of the first-born so that all would belong to him. I saw that my soul existed in very fragile flesh, which gave me a great mistrust of myself. I asked him for his grace and that he would continue his divine mercies, recognizing myself to be no better than many great souls who have fallen from the heights.

Finally, I completed my prayer as I began it, by a loving colloquy with the heavenly spouse.

NINTH DAY:
GOD OUR CONSOLER

First Meditation: That God is the source of true consolations in this life.

"In that day they immolated many victims and rejoiced therein." (2 Esd 12:14)

I was hardly able to reflect on this subject, for my spirit was so totally absorbed in God that I could not be touched by any feelings except the impression of God himself. My will followed the direction of my spirit and was thus also completely absorbed. Finally, however, it was impelled to utter some loving words which could melt my heart in the sweetness of its holy love. Yet even though my will seemed melted, all the other powers of my soul were left untouched. By that I mean that what my will enjoyed or the feelings of love with which it was penetrated never radiated to any of the other powers.

Frequently the will renewed its sacrifice, wishing to cling to God in whatever state he wished, convinced that during this loving union only the purely spiritual part of the soul experienced the delights of his love. This taste of God, although not experienced by the senses, gave it a sure sense that everything beneath the sun is only "suffering, vanity, and affliction of spirit." This led the will to a fresh resolution to set aside all those little enjoyments which could, ever so slightly, divert it from its sovereign good in whom, it realized, were all true and substantial pleasures.

I saw and experienced once again that these holy joys are given only to souls who have entirely sacrificed the pleasures of creatures. Thus this sentence from the subject of my meditation seemed to me to be true: that those who "sacrifice a great number of victims" are on the eve of "great consolation."

Second Meditation: That God is the source of the joys of our future life.

"I remember God and the joys I have had. I meditate and my
spirit faints." (Ps 72:4)

My spirit no sooner glanced at this subject than my soul was
caught up in an extraordinary joy at the thought that God is the
inexhaustible source of the pleasures of our eternal happiness and that
nothing beneath him can ever satisfy it. At the same time my will was
filled with fervor and an ardent desire to possess God, certain that
nothing else could provide anything but false, vain joys.

In the ardor of its longing, my will said with the prophet: "My
soul is thirsting for the living God; when shall I go and appear before
the face of the Lord." "You are the fountain of life, Lord, and it is in
your light that we shall see the light of your glory." "When shall I be
inebriated with the delights of your house? When shall I drink of the
river which gladdens your holy city? Of the torrent of delight that you
give to your blessed?" In the sight of these eternal joys both my understanding and my will slipped into a trance, powerless either to act or to
desire: the first having reached the perfection of its knowledge; and the
latter the goal of its desires.

Nevertheless, during this period of passivity I longed to speak and
I managed to do so—but only half-words uttered in a broken voice.
What I wanted to show Our Lord was that I wanted neither joy nor
consolation nor happiness except in him, as he is in himself and in his
glory. Thus I said to him: "You understand, O Love, you understand."
Then words failed me completely and I remained in this silence.

My whole prayer passed thus except that toward the end I had the
freedom to utter some loving words, consistent with what I had experienced within myself.

Third Meditation: The effects of heavenly consolations.

"Sorrowful thoughts may fill my heart but thy presence is my
joy and consolation." (Ps 94:19)

From the beginning of my prayer a number of things concerning
the effect of these divine consolations came to mind. I saw that God
gives them as an enticement which detaches us from creatures, as a
bait to win us to his love, as a reward for our fidelity in his service, as a
heavenly ointment which makes the practice of virtue easier for us, as
an experience which shows us the difference between the consolations
of God and those of creatures, and as a remedy which gives us a taste
for the blessings of heaven and a distaste for those of earth. I saw all

this in a moment, as with a blink of the eye and then, immediately, my understanding was suspended.

My will was strongly impressed by the fact that the human heart, scorning heavenly consolations, is so urgently and impetuously carried off toward earthly pleasures. But then the will, too, was suspended and incapable of acting except from time to time by fresh movements of love which resulted from the union it enjoyed with God. Certain transports sprang from my heart which relieved it and gave it room to breathe.

During this union I begged Our Lord to make me worthy to serve him faithfully and to let me manifest the effects of his heavenly grace which he has bestowed on me with such generosity. I believe them to be as great as those he bestowed on the saints who have shed their blood for his love or those he has given to those who risk their very lives for the conversion of infidels. I abandoned myself without any choice of my own to the will of his grace and his love. This I did with complete submission of my spirit.

TENTH DAY:
GOD OUR GLORIFIER

First Meditation: Nothing can satisfy the human spirit but the unclouded knowledge of God.

"Now we see only puzzling reflections in a mirror but then we shall see face to face. My knowledge now is partial but then it will be whole like God's knowledge." (1 Cor 13:12)

The thought of what the clear and blessed vision of the divine essence is made me say to this same God these words of the prophet: "I shall be satisfied when your glory is made manifest to me." I saw that outside of God there was nothing capable of satisfying the human heart, for as the well-beloved disciple has said: "All that there is in the world is concerned with pleasures or riches or honors."

Pleasures are not riches, nor are riches honors; neither are honors pleasures. The heart can have one without the others and be grieved in the loss of what it does not have. Even when it would have them all together—pleasures, riches, and honors—the heart would not be satisfied because it would not have all pleasures, all riches, all honors, the pleasures, riches, and honors of one person not being the pleasures, riches, and honors of others. Even if he could have all these pleasures and riches, along with all the pleasures, riches, and honor of all the others, he would not be perfectly happy because all this being limited, he might still desire more.

What has detached me most from this life is the fact that God himself, the single object of my love and my desires, and the only portion of my inheritance, cannot satisfy me in the way I possess him in this world, because I see him in a mirror and obscurely and I long to see him face to face, completely revealed. I know him now only imperfectly and in part and I long to know him perfectly, in the way he knows me—with perfect clarity. Thus I repeated endlessly, "I will be satisfied, O my great God, when your glory is made manifest to me."

Unable to say anything else, I remained clinging to this sovereign good, receiving his loving impression in the darkness of faith, happy to possess him in the way he wishes in this life since this is his will. At times, however, I recalled that with God's mercy I will one day be eternally absorbed in this abyss of happiness with all his saints and that I will be freed not only from my darkness but even more from the corruption of nature which hinders my heart from being pure and perfect. That is the earthly suffering which most wearies my heart. This thought aroused my desire and I persisted in it while awaiting the moment of God's command.

Second Meditation: The purity and beauty of the city of God.

"Each gate was shaped from a single pearl and the streets of the city were of pure gold, like translucent glass." (Apoc 21:21)

I no sooner looked at these words than it came to me that the gate made of pearl is purity, because nothing unclean can enter the kingdom of heaven; and that the shining, glowing paths of God are the lights and love of the beatific state into which one can enter only through the gate and by the pearl of purity. It seemed to me that the soul destined to dwell in this holy city ought to resemble it and to have some link with this city; for the soul is the kingdom of God through the beautiful qualities with which the spouse of the heavenly Jerusalem— which also belongs to him—has wished to adorn it.

Its inner paths are all of gold because of its holiness, but of a gold both radiant and glowing—radiant by the light of his wisdom and glowing by the ardors of holy love. Yet the soul can enter into itself to walk in the ways of grace and holiness only through the pearl, that is the gate of purity. Only if the soul opens out onto these golden paths through substantial mortifications which cleanse it of the impurity of sins, vices, and voluntary imperfection will this goal be attained. Thus the soul must enter into the holy Jerusalem on this earth before entering into the heavenly Jerusalem.

Just as only the sovereign architect is able to build the holy city which is the dwelling place of the blessed, likewise only he can build this mystic and spiritual city. Thus it is written: "If the Lord does not build the house, in vain do the builders labor; and if he does not guard the city, in vain does the watchman guard it."

As all these truths presented themselves to my mind, my will was moved by an extraordinary ardor. Finally, both will and understanding, powerless to act, came to a halt. Thus I remained at rest, taking pleasure in God and receiving whatever he in his goodness was pleased to grant me.

Third Meditation: That God is the essential glory and ultimate end of man.

"His servants shall no longer need the light of lamp or sun,
for the Lord God will give them light and they shall reign
forever." (Apoc 22:5)

The understanding, by a simple glance, saw that the divinity is the eternal light which enlightens the blessed spirits in their abode of happiness and which will enlighten even their bodies through Jesus Christ—like a light shining through a lantern. Thus it is written that the city has no need of the sun or the moon to enlighten it, for the brightness of God will illumine it and the lamb will be its lamp. The understanding, as I say, by this simple glance found itself powerless; it remained in silence while the will was left in loving reverence.

My soul was united to this incomprehensible light which, nevertheless, seemed to me like darkness although I saw quite clearly that it was indeed light and a light at once incomprehensible, immense, and infinite. Then I said, "O my great God, thus it will be that I will see you eternally in the splendors of your majesty, that I shall be lost forever in the abyss of your lights; thus forever will I find you in yourself to enjoy the grandeurs of your glory and to 'reign with your servants forever and ever.' "

My whole prayer was spent in this way, except that at the end my heart felt its ardor increase and there arose in my understanding a light which illumined with extraordinary clarity the overwhelming love God has for his children. This gives me such an unquenchable hope that I will be with him forever that I cannot find any way to express it. This hope has brought about a renewed act of abandonment of my total self into his hands, asking him for the grace to put to good use the great favors that his divine majesty has bestowed on me and that he has the goodness to continue granting me.

At the same time that I spoke thus to Our Lord, I felt determined to be faithful to him. Thus remaining in silence, I affirmed this resolution by a simple loving glance.

SELECTIONS FROM
THE LETTERS 1639–1670

TO MOTHER FRANÇOISE DE ST. BERNARD,
URSULINE SUPERIOR AT TOURS [MAY 20, 1639[1]]

Dear Reverend Mother,
Your holy blessing, please!

I am sure that when you receive this letter, you will not be expecting news of your daughters until they reach Quebec; nor did we expect the comfort of sending you our news. Happily, some fishermen have followed us into the Channel and wished to do us the favor of taking the letters we wanted to write to our friends.

We have just passed along the coast of England and, thanks to our good Jesus, we have left the Channel in very good spirits—although not without having been in danger of capture by the Spanish and the men of Dunkirk. Just a few days ago we sighted one of their fleets numbering about twenty vessels. Our captain, to avoid a confrontation, prudently took the route close to England. We have sighted many other vessels from a distance without being able to see their colors or to distinguish where they were from.

At present, having left the Channel, we are out of danger from our enemies but God alone knows if we will be protected from storms and from the sea itself. Ever since we embarked we have tried daily to prepare ourselves for death, both because of our enemies and because of the violent turbulence of the sea. Yet our hearts have not been troubled by the disturbance of the elements because the One to whose providence we are abandoned has made us forget ourselves and all

---

1. This, unfortunately, is the only letter dealing with the crossing. The letter promised to Mother Françoise has been lost. Marie wrote briefly to her eldest brother on September 1, but does not provide any further details. See the detailed account of Cecile de Ste. Croix, Oury, *Correspondance,* pp. 951–59.

these things. It is impossible to imagine the peace one feels when one gives oneself to God once and for all.

We have all been seasick but this is nothing. We are presently in as good spirits as though we were in our monastery. It would be hard to find anything better ordered than the crew of this vessel. I will save you the details until we get to Quebec. I can't tell you the kindness and care Father Vimont has shown us.[2] No mother—no matter how concerned—could be more solicitous for her children with regard to our well-being, spiritual as well as material. Monsieur Bontemps, our captain, is equally kind, giving us every convenience so generously that it seems that he makes this voyage only with us in mind.

For the moment I will keep from you the deepest secret of my heart, for it is not the time to speak of it. We are already as used to the sea as though we had been brought up on it. A religious who does her duty everywhere is at ease everywhere. Please tell our news to all our friends. Adieu, Adieu, Adieu.

TO HER SON, NOVICE AT THE BENEDICTINE ABBEY AT VENDÔME [SEPTEMBER 4, 1641]

My dear and beloved son,

Your letter brought me so profound a consolation that it is very hard for me to describe it. All this year I have been in great torment, imagining the pitfalls where you might stumble. But finally our gracious God gave me peace in the belief that his loving and fatherly goodness would never lose what had been abandoned for his love.[3] Your letter has confirmed this, my dear son, letting me see all I had hoped for you—even beyond my dreams—for his goodness has put you in a very holy order, one I deeply honor and esteem. I have wanted this grace for you ever since the reformation of the monasteries of St. Julien and Marmoutier; but since vocations must spring from heaven, I said nothing to you, not wanting to interfere in what belongs to God alone.

You have been abandoned by your mother and your relatives, yet

---

2. See *Relation of 1654*, p. 133, n. 12.

3. Claude, after an unsuccessful effort to enter the Jesuits, was accepted into the Benedictine Congregation of St. Maur on January 15, 1641. Marie had had no word of him for almost two years. Hurt and angry, she wrote exhorting him in September, 1640, "It would be shameful for such a well-favored young man to be so lacking in courage" (Oury, *Correspondance,* p. 115). Now her joy and relief at this turn of events is boundless.

hasn't this abandonment been to your advantage? When I left you before you were twelve years old, I endured terrible agonies of spirit which were known to God alone. I had to obey his divine will and it was his will that things happened thus, leading me to the hope that he would take care of you. My heart was strengthened so that I was able to overcome what had delayed my entry into religious life for ten long years. Still, the necessity of this act had to be pointed out to me by Dom Raymond and by other means which I cannot commit to paper although I would gladly tell you in person. I foresaw that you would be abandoned by your relatives, which cost me a thousand pains; this, linked to human weakness, made me fear your ruin.

When I was passing through Paris it would have been easy for me to obtain a place for you. The queen, the Duchess of Aiguillon, and the Countess of Brienne, all of whom regarded me favorably—and who still honor me by their letters—would not have refused whatever I wanted for you. I thanked the Duchess of Aiguillon for the benefits she wanted to obtain for you, but it seemed to me that if you received worldly advancement your soul would be in danger of being lost. Still more, the thoughts which had formerly preoccupied me—to desire only poverty of spirit as our mutual inheritance—made me resolve to leave you a second time in the hands of the Mother of Goodness, trusting that since I was going to give my life for the service of her Son, she would take care of you. Had you not also taken her as your mother and your spouse when you entered the Congregation (on the day of the Purification)? You could, then, expect a blessing from her equal to the one you now possess. The advantages offered you in Paris would indeed have been great but they would have been infinitely lower than those you have now.

I believe, and your letter assures me of this, that you do not regret these things, such as the lowliness of your birth, about which you speak and which is of no importance. (I don't know who informed you about this, for I had carefully avoided speaking to you about it.)[4] I have never loved you except in the poverty of Jesus Christ in whom I have found all riches. . . .

You are now in the militia, my very dear son. In the name of God give consideration to the word of Jesus Christ and reflect that he says to you: "He who puts his hand to the plow and turns back is not worthy of the kingdom of heaven" (Lk 9:62). What he promises is so

---

4. A reference, perhaps, to the unfortunate state of his father's business at the time of the latter's death.

much greater than the favors you were offered that you must esteem everything "dirt and mire in order to possess Jesus Christ" (Phil 3:8). Your glorious patriarch St. Benedict has given you a wonderful example. Imitate him, in the name of God, that my heart may have this consolation with the mail that comes with the first ships, that my vows, offered to his Divine Majesty for twenty-one years without interruption, have been heard in heaven. I am aware of your holy resolutions which lead me to hope that God will give you perseverance. Not a day passes that I do not offer you to his love on the heart of his well-beloved Son. Thanks to his goodness may you be a true holocaust, wholly consumed on the divine altar.

It is true what you say, my very dear son. In Canada I have found something very different from what I had anticipated but in a different way from what you think. My labors here are very sweet and easy to bear so that I experience what Our Lord said: "My yoke is sweet and my burden light" (Mt 11:30). I did not squander any of the thorny vexation of learning a foreign language, but it is now sufficiently easy for me so that I have no trouble in teaching our holy mysteries to our neophytes. We have a large number this year: more than fifty pupils and more than seven hundred visits from the natives—both men and women—whom we have helped both spiritually and materially. The joy my heart experiences in this holy work which God has given me wipes away all the fatigue that I experience during the ordinary course of events. I am asking Reverend Mother Françoise de St. Bernard to send you a copy of the account I wrote concerning the progress of our seminary.[5] . . .

It is thought that there will be some martyrs in following the course we must take, for the devil, enraged that Jesus Christ is conquering his kingdom which the devil had dared to usurp so many years before, has aroused some wicked people to injure the preachers of the Gospel. I hope that you will see the *Relation.* I will try to have one sent to you when they are printed.[6]

The wish that you made for me—that I would be a martyr—was a very touching consolation. Alas, my dear son, my sins will deprive me of this blessing. So far I have done nothing which would make me able to win the heart of God; for, remember, one must have worked hard to be found worthy of shedding one's blood for Jesus Christ. I dare not set my hopes so high. I leave this to his immense goodness who has always

---

5. This account has been lost.
6. See the introduction, p. 5, n. 1.

given me so many favors, that if, without any merit on my part, he wants to do what I dare not aspire to, I beg him to do it. I give myself to him and I give you as well, begging him for that blessing which you have asked for me, that he will overwhelm you with those blessings he has granted so many brave soldiers who have kept an unshakable fidelity to him.

If one should come to me and say, "Your son is a martyr!" I think I would die of joy. Leave it up to him. He has his own time, this God so full of love. Be faithful and you can be certain that he will find occasions of making you a great saint, if you obey his divine movements, if you die to yourself and follow the example which those great saints of your Order give you. If Our Lord gives you the grace of making your profession, please let me know and tell me, too, some details of how his goodness has called you and the means you have taken to respond.

Finally, my very dear son, please keep me informed about your affairs. News from you gives me great joy, as you can imagine. I believe that Reverend Father Superior will permit you to do this. I am giving myself the honor of writing to him and thanking him for the honor of his affection and of his care for you. Pray for me to God. I visit you many times a day. I speak of you ceaselessly to Jesus, Mary, and Joseph. It is possible that one of our mothers from Tours will be coming to us with the first fleet. It is not yet certain, depending on certain circumstances which can be cleared only in France. She is Mother LeCoq de St. Joseph, whom you have met as my novice mistress. She is a great servant of God and is presently superior at Loches.[7] Nevertheless, it is from Tours that we have asked for her, for she was professed there. Monsieur de Bernières has written to me of your good fortune. He is delighted. Dom Raymond and all my relatives have also written, as well as our mothers at Tours who love you dearly.

Adieu, my very dear son. I will never tire of talking with you. Father Poncet wishes to be remembered. He, too, is delighted with your happiness. Mother Marie de St. Joseph, also, to whom God gives many graces and great ability for winning souls. Pray for her and for me who am, my very dear and beloved son, your very humble and affectionate mother.

Pray for me on the feast day of the glorious apostle St. Paul. I was professed on that day.

---

7. No Ursulines came to Quebec in 1642.

TO MADEMOISELLE DE LUYNES[8] [SEPTEMBER 29, 1642]

Mademoiselle: I greet your heart in the loving heart of our divine Jesus!
I have no doubt that this divine Savior possesses you since you wish to be hidden in him. It is why I look for you there, I find you there, I see you there, there I love and cherish you. What more shall I say? I wish that I could enclose my heart in my letter to assure you of the love I bear you. This protestation is still too weak to express the reality. Our dear Lord must tell you himself since only he can do so. Every day I make my humble thanksgiving to him for the blessings he has given you and of which your letter informs me. Father de la Haye, who is deeply touched by this, confirms my feelings; and the tender sentiment that God stirs up in me when I speak of you to him assures me so powerfully that I cannot doubt the love he bears you.

This is a letter from my heart; my other one which relates what has happened in this new Church of God can be made public and communicated to others.[9] . . .

We have received your alms through M. de Bernières, and I give you my most humble thanks. Without this help I think it would have been necessary to send our Indian boarders away this year, as it may be necessary to do in the future, as M. de Bernières has notified us for reasons that I will tell you. This would be a very painful privation for us to which, nevertheless, we must resign ourselves if our good Jesus wishes it. We are his servants who should bow our necks before his judgment.

You know the great affection our good foundress had for us, bringing us into Canada with more than heroic generosity, as everyone is aware. She lived with us for a year in those same sentiments and with a completely maternal heart, toward us as well as toward our boarders. Then she began to want to visit the savages from time to time—a very laudable desire. A short time later she left us completely, coming to visit us only rarely. One judged from this that she disliked the cloister and, not being a religious, it was only reasonable to give her her freedom. On our part we felt that provided she helped us financially,

---

8. Dom Oury conjectures that Marie had met Mademoiselle de Luynes when she was passing through Paris. The former was then living with the Ursulines of St. Denis and contemplating a vocation to New France. Although this never materialized, she remained a faithful and generous friend until her death in 1646. Oury, *Correspondance,* p. 178, n. 1.

9. Once again, this letter has been lost.

which she was verbally committed to do (and for which both we and our friends trusted her), her withdrawal would not do any harm to the seminary.

However, time passed and her willingness to help our foundation diminished day by day. What was an even greater setback was that the nobleman and lady who came here last year from France to establish a house in Montreal had no sooner arrived than she went off with them. Then she took back her furniture and several other things she had given us and which were being used both in the church and in the boarding school. We let everything be carried away without showing the least displeasure, rather—to tell the truth—I felt a great joy in giving them back, imagining that God was treating me like St. Francis who, when his father abandoned him, returned everything, even his clothes. I gladly despoiled myself of everything, leaving the seminary in great poverty. For since this woman had joined us, all her things were used in common and we were able to get along with what she had, along with the furnishings that our mothers in France had given us, since her endowment was so small that there wasn't enough to provide furnishings for us and also for our boarders.[10]

By her withdrawal, however, she left us only enough to sleep three boarders, although we sometimes have more than fourteen. We make them sleep on planks, putting under them whatever we can to soften the hardness and we borrow from the store some skins to cover them, our poverty not enabling us to do anything else. Under God, I cannot say that our foundress is wrong. For on one hand I see that she does not have the means to assist us once she is separated from us, her means being insufficient to maintain her on the travels she undertakes. On the other hand, since she is returning to the world, it is fitting that she be provided in a way suitable to her social position. Thus we have no cause to complain if she takes her furnishings. Finally, she has so much piety and fear of God that I cannot doubt that her intentions are good and holy.

What has caused me the most suffering is her establishment at

---

10. Marie has not included this painful episode in the *Relation of 1654*—charity, perhaps, discouraging her from leaving any permanent record. "The nobleman and lady" Marie refers to are Paul Chomedy de Maisonneuve and Jeanne Mance, who had come to work for the future colony of Montreal. Jeanne Mance, clearly a woman of charismatic gifts, began the first hospital at Montreal. Madame de la Peltrie's shift in allegiance was a source of great hardship for the struggling community. It is to their credit that when she returned in 1644 she was cordially welcomed. In 1646 she entered the Ursuline cloister, but this was not her gift and a few months later she returned to her small house at the side of the property, where she lived until her death in 1671.

Montreal where she is in manifest danger of her life because of the incursions of the Iroquois, since there are no other savages in that area. And what is most upsetting is that she is staying there against the advice of the Fathers as well as the governor who has done everything possible to make her return. They are making one more try to persuade her to come back. We are now awaiting her answer, although one hardly hopes that it will please us.

This great change has put our affairs in a very bad state. M. de Bernières, who takes care of me, tells me that he cannot manage with the small funds that we have—only nine hundred pounds.[11] The Hospital Sisters have three thousand pounds and their foundress, the Duchess of Aiguillon, helps them generously. Even so, they have trouble surviving. This is why M. de Bernières tells me that unless God come to assist us, we must resolve to send away our boarders and our workmen as well, since we have not enough to pay them. Just for the freight of the things he sends us he has to find nine hundred pounds, which is the whole sum of our foundation. Moreover, he says, if your foundress leaves you, as it appears to me she will, you will have to return to France unless God raises up somebody else to support you.

At these words, Mademoiselle, would you not say that all is lost? In fact, one would have to believe so if there were not a loving providence which takes care of even the smallest earthworms. This news has deeply afflicted our friends who understand its importance; yet, nevertheless, my heart is in peace through the mercy of our good Jesus for whom we labor. In the trust I have in his love, I have resolved to keep our boarders and to help our poor savages up to the end. I have still retained our workmen to build the seminary, trusting that God has not led us here to destroy us and make us turn back.

If, however, his goodness or his loving justice wants to punish my sins, then I am ready to accept the shame before the whole world. It doesn't matter what happens, provided he is glorified. At the moment that I am writing to you, my heart is enjoying a peace so complete that I cannot express it. I feel a deep satisfaction in telling this to you, as to someone whom I love and honor more than anyone in the world. Yes, Mademoiselle, since your humility brings you so far as to wish to honor me with your affection and kindness, you have so won my heart that it cannot keep from telling you both the good things and the evil things that happen.

---

11. Jean de Bernières remained in charge of the Ursulines' finances until his death in 1659. It is unfortunate that none of the correspondence between him and Marie remains. See *Relation of 1654*, p. 117, n. 8.

After what M. de Bernières has written to me, he will, no doubt, be upset in seeing that I am asking for food as usual and even more that I am sending the accounts for the six thousand pounds which have been used to pay the wages of our workmen and purchase material for our building—without mentioning our freight expenses. In all this we have nothing but the providence of God. They say that all is lost; yet I feel impelled to pursue what Our Lord has given us the grace to begin in this new Church. The arrival of the vessels will give us new instructions and perhaps new courage to work more than ever in the service of our Master.

After the common afflictions of which I speak in my other letter and which we suffer in respect to this new Church persecuted both by demons and by the Iroquois, you see here my private crosses. You have them, too, Mademoiselle. Let us join yours and ours together in order to make only one to be offered to Our Lord. For myself, I offer mine very freely with yours and with the greatest affection I can have in this life. I think you believe me and that you do not doubt the complete sincerity of your servant. This does not hinder me from having a very heartfelt consolation at the great blessing which God gives your affairs. I bless him for it with all my heart, for it is a sign that justice is on your side. I dare to repeat this to you: God is waiting for great things from you if you will let him govern your heart and if your soul follows his inclination in whatever direction he turns it.

You complain that I ask nothing from you. You do so much for us that I dare not put myself forward for fear of taking advantage of your affection which continually anticipates our every need. Moreover, we are in need of everything, as you can see, especially of building material; that is what prevented me from telling you last year of our need for cloth. By not telling you, I wronged the boarders for whom you have such great affection. Nevertheless, while I was preoccupied only with lodging them, God inspired a man in France to send me two strong pieces of serge and ready-made shoes to clothe them. Without these they would have had to suffer the rigors of the winter. Is it not wise to count on the providence of so good a Father? Assuredly it is.

Another effect of this loving providence is that which inspired you to command me to tell you what would be most useful for us. In order to obey you I have the courage to tell you that it is strong red and gray cloth and linens for everyday use which are very rare and very necessary in this country. It is in order to obey you that I express myself in this way, but if our Divine Master should turn your heart in another direction, please do all that he will tell you, for that is all that I want.

Ah! Mademoiselle, how great a despoilment God desires in souls whom he calls to this new Church. He wants from them, I repeat, such great dependence on his pure providence that in order to enjoy perfect peace they must be disposed to accept from moment to moment the dispositions of his plans for them. Do, then, all that this mover of hearts wants you to do; no more. That will be our pleasure. . . .

As I was finishing this letter, a bark arrived from Montreal informing us that this good lady is determined to spend the winter in the midst of those dangers. I have told you that her intentions are good and holy, for she writes to me with great cordiality and tells me that the reason she stays at Montreal is that she is looking for the means of making a second establishment of our Order, in case she is again able to dispose of her fortune. I see no appearance of this, however, and the danger she is in afflicts me more than all the promises she has made.

The vessel is about to raise anchor so I must finish and offer you once again my very humble thanks for all your benefactions. As for the affection my heart has for you, words are too weak to express it. May the infinite love of our adorable Jesus tell it to you since he alone knows that I am entirely yours. Yes, without reserve, I am your very humble . . .

TO HER SON [AUGUST 2, 1644]

My dearest and beloved son:

Blessed be our good Jesus who has brought the ships safely back to us with our Reverend Fathers and our two dear sisters, along with all the help sent to us from Old France. I have also received your letters and the things you have sent.[12] . . .

Now that I know the times of your religious exercises, I shall be with you in them all, praising our divine Master with you. With the Spirit as your guide, you have sufficient work to do in order to become holy. My dear son, be a worthy follower of those who have gone before you and do not fear to expend your life in the service of him who has been so prodigal with his for your sake. When I will hear that this is true, my joy will be complete. You are among so many saints who will help you on your way to heaven. I cannot tell you how I feel at God's mercy in letting me participate in all the blessings of such a holy

---

12. These are two sisters from Tours: Anne Compain de Ste. Cécile and Anne Le Boutz de Notre Dame. Claude at this time was continuing his studies at the Benedictine monastery at Jumièges.

Congregation. It is the cure he has given for my poverty and, truly, I experience its effects.

Let me tell you something of the Church of the Son of God. The Iroquois persecutions have been intense, motivated more out of desire to kill and rob than anything else. This is their main reason. Nevertheless, if they capture a Christian, they torture him because of his prayers, which they think are a kind of magic bringing all sorts of evils upon them so that they want to rid the world of those who make use of these things. Father Jogues has suffered several martyrdoms throughout his whole body; but God has delivered him alive, bearing the marks of his Son's livery.

Just recently, these barbarians have killed six of our French, of whom two have been struck with an axe, then burned and forced to eat their own flesh. In addition, they have captured a large number of Hurons and Algonquins. Last Easter they captured one of our Fathers, a Roman by birth, a truly apostolic man, of whom somebody in France had prophesied what was to happen to him here. We still do not know what these barbarians have done with him or with a young Frenchman whom he was taking with him to the Hurons.[13] Three Iroquois who have been captured alive have told us different things concerning this priest. This makes us fear that he has been treated like the others, especially since at that time Father Jogues, for whom they had great esteem but whom they were going to burn nevertheless, had been rescued. This priest yearned for this happiness in order to win martyrdom, but the Dutch, to whom the French had appealed, took him while he was being forced to travel with these barbarians and made him get into their boat secretly; not that they loved this priest— they are heretics—but because the queen of France asked this of them. My other letters will tell you more about this.

Now these barbarians are in possession of all the approaches to the river, from about four leagues below Quebec to about sixty leagues beyond in order to lie in wait for the French and the savages. Our governor has just left with a number of soldiers in order to provide a way for these poor Hurons and Algonquins to pass—and most especially for the Fathers of the mission who are going up to the Hurons and the Nipissiriniens—and for whom the Iroquois wait persistently to seize them along with all their possessions and take them away into their own country.

---

13. The other Jesuit is Francesco Giuseppe Bressani who, like Jogues, regains his freedom through the Dutch.

Among the soldiers just come from France is a young man of good family, about twenty-two years old, who has been touched by God to serve him in this country in the salvation of souls. You would be charmed to hear him speak and to see a young man who has been in command of armies in France with only contempt toward himself. He will be in charge of the soldiers who are going to spend the winter with the Hurons, accompanied by the Fathers of the Mission. He would like to go everywhere to win souls for Jesus Christ among these nations that have just been discovered and where our Fathers have still not been. He is going to study their language for this purpose. Pray for him, my dear son.

Despite the persecutions, Christianity is spreading widely and faith is becoming more esteemed among the Hurons as well as here. Our Christians from Sillery have spent the winter in distant lands where they encountered many savages who had never heard God or faith spoken of and had never seen any Frenchmen. They catechized them and prepared them for baptism. Father de Quen, who has been at Tadoussac where a number of tribes are to be found, in the spring baptized a large number who are living a very exemplary life. Madame our Foundress, after hearing reports of this, went to visit them, undaunted by fatigue, in her efforts to advance the glory of God. She has been for some time with a companion living in a little bark cabin with these converts. This winter we had living close to us the tribes of the Iroquois and Algonquins of the Isle. They have been instructed in our chapel where many have been baptized, Our Lord thereby giving us a chance to render some small service in our field of work.

God has kept us in good health. One of our boarders, convinced of the articles of our holy faith, died in the forest. We had thought she might become a religious, for she would have been capable of it.[14] But now she is dead, her book in her hands, praying to God. We have several other courageous young girls. Offer them to our God; they pray for you, my dear son.

Please offer my humble greeting to your Reverend Prior and to all the Reverend Fathers whom I dare ask to pray for this Church and for our establishment in this country and for my unworthy self. My dearest son, let us love and serve our Master, our Exemplar, and our All. I see you in him. Look for me there and we will find ourselves together in order to render our obedience, while waiting to see him revealed

14. Later Marie, like the Jesuits, reaches the conclusion that the Indians cannot be trained to religious life. See letter of August 30, 1650, to her son in this volume, p. 242.

and thus to enjoy him in a purer fashion than is possible in this life. Adieu.

TO HER SON [SEPTEMBER 15, 1644]

My dear and beloved son,

I cannot let this opportunity to write to you pass and so I am giving myself the satisfaction of doing so. One of our best men, lieutenant to the governor of New France, and one of our best friends, is here. He has promised me to see you, for he tries to please me in every way he can. He may appear to you like a courtier but in fact he is a man of great prayer and virtue. His house, which is close to ours, is regulated like a house of religious people. His two daughters are our boarders. They are young women who have imbibed virtue with their mother's milk, for she is one of the purest souls I have ever known.

I tell you all this, my dear son, so that you will honor this gentleman, as well as to show you that there are devout souls in Canada. He is going to France for the concerns of the country and of the French colony. He will tell you everything that is happening here. Since he once gave us advice concerning our business affairs, he has had permission from the Father Superior of the mission to enter our monastery; he will tell you all the news if you would like him to.

My very dear son, the ships are about to weigh anchor so I cannot open my heart to you as I would like. I am extremely tired because of the number of letters I have written. I think I have written more than two hundred. One must do all this, along with all our other duties, while the ships are here. I have written four letters to you; I think you should have received one in the month of September and the other two in December.[15] This one is simply to renew my affection and my strong desires for your sanctity. I am edified by all you have told me of your holy Order. I cannot stop blessing God for having called you there. Don't stop praying for me and recommending me to the prayers and sacrifices of all the Fathers. I consider them my own since they are yours. I am giving myself the happiness of writing to the Reverend Prior of your house and that of Tiron. All my sisters and Madame our Foundress send you greetings. Please offer all these to God and myself

---

15. This provides an indication of the extent of Marie's correspondence. The "four letters" are a necessary means of insuring that at least one or two will make the crossing safely and reach their destination.

as well, who am, my dear and beloved son, your very humble and affectionate mother.

TO HER SON [OCTOBER 3, 1645]

My very dear and beloved son,
The love and life of Jesus be your sanctification and salvation!

I have received your two letters with your kind present which I accept with affection and devotion, as did those with whom I shared it. When I want to give my spirit a little relaxation I imagine the triumph of the Holy Virgin and those saints who have sung about this.[16] But now let me answer your first letter. . . .

You are right in what you tell me about the union of our Congregations in France. If this is to be accomplished, it must be with the consent and through the means of all the bishops of the dioceses in which there are monasteries, for we are subject to them. And what is annoying is that, since each is free to draw up its own constitutions and customaries, there is great difference in customs even in the same Congregation. Add to this the fact that each Congregation's original constitution has been changed and overthrown through all the changes made by the bishops. Today all these are so weakened that in order to bring unity it would be necessary to have a union of bishops with the consent of the Holy See draw up a constitution approved by His Holiness.[17]

I have just received a letter from France which tells me that in the Assembly General of Prelates which was to have been held at Paris last May, this affair was to be discussed. I don't know what has been done but I put this into the hands of God. The Congregation of Paris and our own Congregation are the most important and also the most alike. Yet, nevertheless, I have no doubt that there would be difficulties to resolve because of the large number of houses of which they are comprised, as well as the different dioceses where they are located.

As for our Union here in Canada, that is not the same thing. The prelates and superiors who sent us here know very well that since we would comprise only a single house, it would be essential to adjust our customs; for it would not be possible to remain in peace were we all different from each other—especially in the midst of people entirely

---

16. Oury conjectures that this was a sermon on Our Lady since there is evidence that Claude often sent sermons, etc., to his mother. Oury, *Correspondance,* p. 272, n. 1.
17. Gueudré, I, p. 258.

contrary to us in morals, in disposition, in customs. Thus it is much easier to abandon these original customs through necessity rather than to do so by force or even through a loving adjustment.

It is true that there is an important difference which must be adjusted by common consent. The mothers of the Congregation of Paris make a fourth solemn vow: to teach young girls. We do not do this in our Congregation of Tours. We are only required through a papal bull to do this after ten years of religious life or at the age of twenty-five. In order to adjust to this, we are making this vow without, however, any obligation to do so solemnly if we do not wish, and only for the period of time we will be in Canada. For who can predict the events of providence? It could happen that reversals would force us to return to France although I foresee no trend toward that. In order to compensate for our adjustment, the mothers of the Congregation of Paris have adopted our habit, which is different from theirs, under the same conditions in which we have taken the vow. These are the most outstanding difficulties of our Union which, nevertheless, have been peacefully resolved.[18]

Who can have told you that I have had difficulties in our establishment? Yes, I have had, and unless one has experienced this it is hard to believe how many problems one encounters in an establishment made in a new and completely barbarous country. One depends so completely on France that without its help one would not know what to do. In addition, no matter how urgent and important things are, one must wait a year in order to have them resolved; and if this cannot be done during the period when the ships are in France, then one must wait for two years. When the ships return, those to whom some concern has been entrusted are apt to think only of their own affairs; thus one can hardly ever have a clear solution to any problem. Even more, most of our plans are not understood; thus quite often things are resolved differently from what we had wished. This is what obliges the Fathers to sometimes send one of their own men for their affairs, just as there are deputies for the affairs of the country.

I don't mention the innumerable thorny problems with which we are constantly faced by this country. In a word: nature has no hold on what could comfort it nor any claims which could flatter or satisfy it. I must admit to you that I have suffered so many crosses that except for an extraordinarily strong grace of God, I would have fallen under their weight. But after all, the divine Goodness has always brought success

---

18. See the Introduction, pp. 25–29.

to our little affairs, both spiritual and material—even to those which, according to human appearance, ought to remain imperfect.

Above all, we suffer because of our Bull of Union which we thought to receive from Rome but which the pope does not wish to give us until there is a bishop here to receive it. We are trying another expedient in the hope that the present pope will be more obliging than his predecessor. With this in mind I am writing to several influential people to beg them to work at this as something essential for us. If you had had a bull from Rome confirming the union of your Congregation of Saint Maur with that of Cluny, the latter would not have let it be so easily broken. I cannot see, however, what could trouble ours, here at the end of the world, except my sins.

We experience here a profound grace which unites us powerfully to Our Lord and, just between us, here is a sign of it. This year we have had the election of a superior, for I had been in charge for six years and our rules do not permit any further time without an interruption. We have elected one of the mothers of Paris who is a wise and virtuous daughter, in order to show that we make no distinction of Congregations.[19] Besides, we felt that in acting thus our union would become stronger and more firmly cemented. Yet the fact that our union foundered for lack of a bull makes me concerned and leads me to make every effort to obtain from Rome what we still lack to ensure our Union. I hope for this grace from Our Lord, for there have been so many extraordinary circumstances in our vocation and in our mission to Canada that I would have to suffer great difficulty before I could convince myself that his divine Majesty would leave this work unfinished. All our pains and crosses have never let me lose heart. I expect still more than I say, even were I to see a complete reversal of plans; this is due to the profound experience I have had of his divine mercies toward me. If you realized this, my very dear son, your heart would melt with love toward my Benefactor. But enough on this subject; I must answer your other letter.

If what I write to you touches you, it is our God who makes up for the lack in my words. It is true, though, that it is my heart which speaks to you. If my little labors please God, they belong to you as well as to me; and if you accompany me in my duties, then I accompany you in yours. The Sacred Heart of Jesus controls the center between us, and his divine Spirit is the link of our conversation. For it is with him that I

---

19. Marguerite de Flécelles de St. Athanase, who until her death in 1695 frequently held the office of superior.

speak of everything which touches you and everything which concerns me. I make only a single subject of yours and mine. Or to express it better: I make only a single host to be consumed in the fire burning on this divine altar.

No, I have no difficulty in believing that God is giving you zeal and devotion for the salvation of souls. This vocation may be a general one, however. If I may express my thoughts, I would advise you not to repulse it. (I never even knew there was a Canada and when I heard this word spoken, I thought it was invented to frighten children.) It is not only the place which can improve a vocation. God often begins with a general thought, then brings the heart to a halt in the place where he wants it to be—either by being actually present there or simply by praying for the souls in that place or working for their good in some other way.

My vocation has been of this kind and there are many others like this. I spent many years without knowing where my spirit should rest: this was a general vocation. Then very clearly God let me understand that it was Canada where he wished me to serve him. Then, finally, he accomplished this in a remarkable way. On my part, I have done nothing about this but submit to the divine will. Often I rejected the inspirations God gave me because I saw the great disproportion between what I was and what was being interiorly suggested to me. Then I was immediately admonished to follow God's orders which I awaited in peace, abandoning myself to his divine will. . . .

What will you do, powerless as you are, to follow God and imitate his perfection? For myself, when I see myself in this powerlessness, I try to lose myself in him. I do my best to forget myself in order to see only him and, if possible, I speak with him intimately. To put it naively, my whole life is constantly taken up with this exchange. I so dearly love this union of heart and will with God in the love of this same God that this is the reason for the requests I make of you.

I cannot understand how there can be a light in our spirit without our will being possessed. Is it not true that God is so lovable, so sweet and captivating, that one must submit to him unquestioningly at the very moment when he makes himself known? The same is true with regard to his virtues and his divine works. It is through an excess of his goodness that he reveals himself to us and he even seems grateful when we throw ourselves into his arms to caress him lovingly.

This is why he will be all and we will be nothing; for thus we will be more easily lost in him. My dear son, let us come together in this loss of ourselves—or better, in this infinite abyss where all our failures will be obliterated, for charity covers everything. I am much more imperfect than you, but why should we hesitate to lose ourselves in him who wishes to purify us and who will do so if only we will lose ourselves in him by a bold and loving trust?

Small children give small gifts; but God divinizes his children, bestowing on them qualities conformable to their high dignity. This is why I am more pleased to love and express my love than to stop and think about my lowliness and unworthiness.

I am deeply indebted to all the Reverend Fathers who honor me by their charity and their remembrance of me. Assure them that I pray for them and that they have a share in my labors. . . .

TO MOTHER MARIE-GILLETTE ROLAND,
RELIGIOUS OF THE VISITATION OF TOURS [OCTOBER 10, 1648[20]]

. . . You speak to me about a hidden life. What shall I tell you, my very dear and beloved sister? Since it is hidden it is very difficult to talk about what does not appear. In this country and in the atmosphere of this new Church there reigns only a spirit of obscurity. All the events which happen to us are secrets hidden in Divine Providence who is pleased to blind everyone regardless of his condition or virtue. I have seen and talked with many people, all of whom have said: "I don't understand any of my affairs yet despite my blindness they go on without my being able to say how." This is true with regard to the country in general as well as of the state of individual families.

It is the same with spiritual matters. I see that those people whom one believed to have had some perfection when they were in France are now, in their own eyes and in the eyes of others, very imperfect. This causes them a kind of martyrdom. The more they work the more they discover imperfections in themselves. The reason is that the spirit of the new Church has such a profound purity that the slightest imperfection is incompatible with it, and one must be purified by dying constantly to oneself.

I see this primitive Christianity as a kind of purgatory in which, as these souls cherished by God are purified, they share in the communications of his divine Majesty. The very same thing, I say, happens here. This hidden spirit, which is none other than the spirit of Jesus Christ and of the Gospel, gives the purified soul a certain knowledge of itself,

---

20. Marie-Gillette Roland, like Marie, had been a penitent of Dom Raymond. She and Marie were friends before either of them entered religious life.

establishing it in an interior life that brings it closer to its resemblance of Christ. If you were to ask me what this life is, I could not tell you except to say that the soul loves and relishes only the imitation of Jesus Christ in his hidden life. She sees herself very small in her own eyes and imperfect in her actions, compared to the purity and holiness of our divine Exemplar.

I don't feel free to say any more to my dear sister because of the distance between us and for fear that letters may be intercepted; and what I have just said was only to comply with her wishes, being unable to refuse her anything. While waiting to see each other in another life where you will see me in all my poverty, I beg you to be satisfied with this and to pray for me who am all yours in Jesus.

TO HER SON[21] [MAY 17, 1650]

My dear son,
The fact that a frigate from Quebec is going to the fisheries at Isle Percée gives me the opportunity of writing this little note to you, for they will meet some fishing vessels there which will return to France sooner than the ones from here. In giving myself this happiness I think that I give it to you as well since you and I are only one in Our Lord.

Let me tell you that since the letters I wrote to you last October, the whole country has been at peace. We still don't know what happened among the Hurons except that in November our Fathers completed their fort, which has very strong walls. We learned this from a Huron who traveled three hundred leagues through underbrush and unblazed trails for fear of being apprehended. This fort is to be a refuge for the Hurons fleeing from their enemies as well as for the Fathers of the Mission. As for those who live in the countryside, God alone can protect them.[22]

As I have already said, we ourselves have been in peace, although fifteen days ago some Iroquois appeared. Some of them were captured and the others put to flight. Some of them, however, have done what they have never dared do before. Previously, they never came closer to us than about forty leagues, but this time they ventured to within three

---

21. Claude had completed his studies and been ordained to the priesthood the preceding year.
22. The years 1648–49 had been a difficult period for the missionaries. The Hurons, fleeing from the Iroquois, first took refuge on the Ile St. Joseph and when that became impossible, arrived in Quebec.

leagues of here, attacking the dwelling of one of our inhabitants, killing two of his servants, and putting his whole family to flight. They pillaged his house and all his possessions. From there they set fire to the house of a good gentleman which is a little farther off. These incursions have terrified all the inhabitants who are scattered here and there the better to carry on their business. It is rumored that the Iroquois are armed in great numbers to come to attack us, but don't worry about us, for our house, besides being very strong, is also protected by the cannon from the fort. But this is not the source of our confidence and our strength: it is our Jesus who is that.

Father Bressani, who left in September to go to the mission, returned after traveling only fifty leagues. He has spent the winter here with a group of Hurons whom he instructed. Our three houses of religious along with some charitable lay people are contributing to feed these poor exiles who have just left for their own country to look for the rest of their families to bring them here closer to us. These new inhabitants are forcing us to study the Huron language, which I had never attempted before, being satisfied to know that of the Algonquins and Montagnais, who are always with us.

Perhaps you will laugh that at the age of fifty I am beginning the study of a new language, but one must undertake everything for the service of God and the salvation of our neighbor. I began this study a week after the octave of All Saints. Father Bressani has very kindly been my teacher up to the present. Since we can study languages only in the winter I hope that someone else will come this autumn who will provide us with the same help. Pray to Our Lord that he will open my spirit for his glory so that I can render him this little service.

Let us do even better, my dearest son, let us study the action and language of the saints, and above all the Saint of Saints. I believe that you are doing it very well. For myself, I have the desire but I confess to you that I am not proceeding as quickly as I believe God wants me to. Please recommend this to him. It is time for me to think seriously about eternity, for although I have a strong constitution and good health, I think that when one reaches the age of fifty one must believe that life will not go on much longer.

This fills me with joy, but essentially I do not wish for either life or death. I think that as our soul tends naturally to its last end, mine, feeling it approach, rejoices at the thought. It is in the loving resting place of eternity that, having finished our course, we shall see each other, through God's mercy. What happiness! Who would not rejoice while waiting to possess it? These are the sweet thoughts which overwhelm my soul with a peace I cannot express. When I speak of eternity

I mean the enjoyment of the Eternal God whose goodness, never tired of showering us with his favors in this mortal life, will himself take pleasure in inundating us with them in eternity.

I will not risk writing to you more fully. I am entrusting this letter to chance, never having experimented with this way before. If you receive it, let me know so that we will not neglect any means of sending you our news. We are awaiting yours and that of all our friends. May it be good news through his grace! As I finish this letter, I learn that the young men have been mustered to go to fight the Iroquois, who are very close. People are very much afraid of them because they hide in the underbrush and pounce on people when one least expects them. They are real murderers who cannot be suppressed, for they mock even the most skillful.

TO HER SON [AUGUST 30, 1650]

My very dear and beloved son,
May the life and love of Jesus be your life and love for all eternity!

It is a wonderful witness of your affection for me that you wish for me the same destiny as that of our Fathers. Alas! I am not worthy of such an honor and such an exalted grace—although it seems very close to us. Since I wrote and told you something of the extraordinary persecution of the Iroquois, there has been another great clash between the French and the barbarians in an encounter which took place near Three Rivers when they were out looking for nine Frenchmen who had been captured and led away.[23] Today the Iroquois intend to take Three Rivers, and you will note that they have several Dutchmen to help them. These were recognized during the skirmish, and afterward a Huron who escaped confirmed this.

After they take Three Rivers they are determined, according to what we have been told, to attack us. Although on the surface there is not so much to fear since our houses are strong, yet nevertheless what has happened in the Huron villages which have been destroyed by fire and arms (for they are very powerful) ought to make the French fear a like disaster if speedy help doesn't reach us. This is the opinion of the wisest and most experienced, such as the Fathers who have come

---

23. Three Rivers was a small settlement west of Quebec, about halfway to Montreal.

down from the Hurons, having borne the weight of the force of these barbarians.

This help can only come from France because there is not enough strength in the whole country to resist them. If France fails us, then— in a word—we must either leave or die. But since all the French, who number about two thousand, will not be able to find means of withdrawing, they will be forced to die either through want or through the cruelty of their enemies. Furthermore, to leave all the goods they have acquired in this country and to see themselves deprived of all means of support in France—this will lead them to choose death in this country rather than want in another.[24]

We ourselves, through the mercy of Our Lord, have other motives. It is not possessions which keep us here but rather the remnant of our good Christians, esteeming ourselves a thousand times blessed to die with them if that were possible. These are our treasures, our brothers, our spiritual children whom we cherish more than our lives and more than anything under heaven. Rejoice, then, if we should die and if someone brings you the news that our blood and ashes are mingled with theirs. There is every appearance that this will happen if the thousand Iroquois who have divided to go to the Neutral Nation return to join those who are at our gates.

Father Daran to whom I am giving this letter is one of those who have just come from the Hurons.[25] He has suffered all that can be suffered without dying; thus he will be able to tell you at leisure all that has happened to this new Church in the last years, and I promise that you will be deeply edified by what you hear. He is going to make a tour of Europe while waiting to be recalled should the affairs of the country be restored, for he is deeply missed here. I miss having him just as the others do, but you must assuage my regret by receiving him as he deserves. Others, such as Fathers Ragueneau and Pijart are also going to France to ask for help from his Majesty. The former has the greater concern because he is the Superior of the mission to the Hurons. He is

---

24. There is a certain bitterness in Marie's comment. The mother country had never given its colony the help it needed. The Company of One Hundred Associates had shown little interest except in the profits to be reaped from the fur trade; thus, the economic and personal safety of the colonists had gone unattended.

25. Adrien Daran, S. J., had spent just four years in Canada; he did not return after 1650 nor did Pierre Pijart. With the destruction of the Huron missions, the Jesuits were forced to reorganize their work. A number of priests returned to France permanently at this time. Father Lalemant, as superior of the Mission, returned to France on business and so was absent during the destruction of the Ursuline monastery in December 1650.

one of the greatest and most zealous missionaries of New France, but I esteem him even more for his great sanctity than for all his natural abilities and graces. We hope to see him again next year.

When I finished speaking to you about Father Ragueneau just now, someone came to tell me that he was asking for me to say goodbye. He has promised to see you, and with this in mind he wrote down your name. He is one of the best friends of our seminary and one who has a deep knowledge of the graces that the divine goodness has bestowed there. He has told me again that in his experience of the strength and fury of the Iroquois, he feels that unless we receive prompt help from France, or unless it pleases God to assist the country in some extraordinary way, then all is lost. This is not an exaggeration. From my own small store of knowledge, I tell you the same thing.

You can tell by this that while we wait for help we remain in the pure providence of God. For myself, my very dear son, I am so happy in this state and my spirit and my heart so content that they could not be more so. Should it happen that next year someone brings you news of my death, bless God and offer the holy sacrifice of the Mass for me and also obtain for me the suffrages of your holy Congregation which has always been so dear to me. Should God call me to himself, and should he be pleased to grant me this mercy, your Congregation will be even dearer to me and I will be in a better state to beg his Divine Majesty and to win for it his holy blessing.

I am very happy that God has detached you from creatures and from the love or claim of love that you could expect from them. My dear son, the kingdom of peace is to be found in a heart devoid of all things and which, through a holy hatred of self, is pleased to destroy the remains of corrupt nature from which even the holiest suffer right up to the moment of their death and which is the true motive of their humiliation. . . .

I have answered in another letter the means you suggest for training some savages so that they would win their companions to the faith. In addition to what I am writing to you, you should speak about this with Father Daran. He will tell you that even should the country recover, it would always be necessary to depend on Europe for preachers of the Gospel, for the nature of the American savages, even of the most holy and spiritual, is not suited for ecclesiastical roles but rather to be taught and led gently into the path of heaven. It is this which makes one wonder in this collapse if perhaps God wishes to have here only a transient Church.

It is true that Father de Brébeuf had received that sacred gift I have spoken to you about. Father Garnier, one of those who won the crown this year, had it eminently. My dear son, you will never know this through study or through the power of speculation but only through humble prayer and in submission of soul before the feet of the crucifix. This adorable Word, incarnate and crucified, is the living source of this spirit. It is he who apportions it to chosen souls who are most dear to him so that they will follow and learn his divine maxims and by this practice, I repeat, consume themselves to the end in imitation of him.

This holy spirit, this union of which I have spoken, is not that of glory but only a foretaste. And do not think that it always makes work easy, for it does not always make itself felt in the senses. But it does give, in the depths of the soul, an invincible strength for bearing heavy and painful things. It would be necessary to have a very large book to describe the life of this Father, animated by this holy spirit. He was eminently humble, gentle, obedient, and filled with virtues acquired through great labor. It was gratifying to see the consequences of his virtues in practical affairs. He was in a continual colloquy and familiar conversation with God. Pierced with wounds he was still moved by charity making an effort to drag himself toward a poor woman who, having received a number of hatchet blows, was in a desperate plight and needed to be helped to die well.

Father Chabanel, one of those who was massacred this year, had the strongest possible aversion to living in the cabins of the savages. On this account one had often wished to exempt him and send him to other missions where he would not be engaged in this kind of life. But through an extraordinary generosity of spirit, he made a vow to persevere there and to die there if it pleased God to show him this mercy. Nevertheless, his superior, knowing that he was extremely tired with the work of the mission, recalled him; it was during this return voyage that he was taken and killed. No one knows who his murderers are or what they have done with his body. Whatever happened, he died in an act of obedience.

The other Fathers who have returned from far-off missions have suffered so excruciatingly that there is no human language to express it. I do not exaggerate; and if Father Daran does not conceal it through his profound humility, ask him for some of the details of his sufferings, for his experience has made him an authority. I give you these examples in order to convince you that our union is never stronger than in the works suffered in imitation of and for the love of Jesus Christ who at the moment of his suffering and especially at the point of death reached the highest degree of union with God, his Father, for the love of mankind. This sweet and loving union is beatitude already begun in mortal flesh and its merit is in acts of charity toward God and neighbor and the other theological virtues. But in the union of which I speak, which is a consequence of those acts of charity, there is a question of giving one's life in a consummation of work which leads to a resemblance to Jesus Christ. Certainly one must give this first place while waiting for another life to understand its merit and excellence, for at present our language is unable to describe it properly.

I bless God for the desire he has given you to suffer martyrdom. You are still young, my dear son, and if you wish to be faithful to grace you will suffer a long one, even though you remain in your solitude. This desire ought to be for you a powerful goad to lead a life penitential, mortified, and regular. This is the martyrdom you must suffer and which God asks of you while waiting, perhaps, for some opportunity that his Divine Majesty keeps for you and which you can neither expect nor foresee. You must arm yourself, however, with the virtues required for such an elevated grace; yet after all your good dispositions, you must still acknowledge yourself as unworthy.

I agree with you that the lack of money may well hinder the expedition of our bull at Rome. Besides, I see that the affairs of the country will keep things in suspense. There are three things one must consider in our circumstances. The first is that neither we nor all Canada can exist for two more years without help. The second—according to the most knowledgeable people—is that if help fails we must either die or return to France. Nevertheless, I feel that if our enemy goes to war with the Neutral Nation and the Andastoue this will provide a diversion which will enable us to subsist a little longer. But if they continue their conquests and victories, there will be nothing more for the French to do here. Trade will not be able to be carried on; if there is no trade, no more ships will come. If the ships no longer come, everything necessary for living will be lacking—such as cloth, linens, the greatest part of our food, bacon and flour, which the garrison and the religious houses cannot do without. It is not that people do not work hard and that food is not produced, but the country still does not produce what is necessary to subsist.

The third thing which slows our affairs is that if trade decreases because of the constant warfare, the savages who only stop here in order to trade will slip off into the woods. Thus we will not need a bull any longer since there will be nothing for us to do, we who are here only to attract the savages to the faith and win them for God. You can see from this that a bishop would never come here in a period so full of disaster. In addition, the Church being only transitory would have no need for a pastor. I am speaking according to the conjecture that God will permit the crisis that we fear. Since this Church is in such obvious danger, do me the kindness of performing some devotion before a statue of the most holy Virgin so that she will be pleased to take it under her protection. Pray for me, too, and for our election which we will have during Pentecost week.

This danger and these fears do not in any way diminish the worship which the French and the savages are accustomed to offer to God. You would have been deeply touched to see the procession at Quebec on the day of the Assumption of the Mother of Goodness. Two Fathers of the Company of Jesus carried her picture raised on a litter, nicely decorated to the three religious houses designated as stations. As the places are a good distance from one another, two other Fathers were prepared to take their place and relieve them in their duty. Besides a large number of French, there were about six hundred savages walking in order. The devotion of these neophytes was so profound that it drew tears to the eyes of those who watched them. Out of curiosity I watched from a place where I could not be seen; and I assure you that I have never seen in France a procession so orderly and apparently so devout. With the savages this always strikes me anew, for I think of what they were before they knew God and of what they are now that they know him. This touches me more than I can tell you. From this you can imagine how much I suffer to see the power that the barbarous Iroquois exercise over them. My dearest son, how happy I would be, how content if all this persecution would fall on me. Present this desire to the Holy Virgin to whom I will gladly present yours.

I have written this letter in several stages and in the meantime there is always some news. The captive who escaped from the Iroquois reports that the warriors of the Andoouesteronon and the Neutral Nation have taken two hundred Iroquois prisoners. If this is true they will treat them horribly and this will be an added threat for us. This captive will be here for a fortnight before revealing all he knows, for it is the custom of the savages to say what they know only little by little over the course of several days. This makes the French impatient, for they are quick in spirit and would like to know everything all at once, above all when it concerns important matters reported by a single messenger.

Since I wrote the above, two more Hurons have escaped from the captivity of the Iroquois. They are both good Christians in their hearts and catechumens in fact. Their desire for baptism led them to make strenuous efforts by long journey through the woods without any provisions. They reported that our two Algonquins from Sillery who were captured last June were burned alive manifesting profound sentiments of faith and religion. One of them, for the love of whom I write you this note, was particularly marked by zeal and fervor. He was about twenty-two years old and was my spiritual son who loved me as much or more than his own mother. He was three days and three nights in the most horrible torture in ridicule of the faith which he confessed with his last breath. These savages said to him in mockery, "Where is your god? He doesn't help you." Then they would begin to torture him again, mocking him, saying, "Pray to your god and see if he will help you."

This courageous servant of God redoubled his prayers and his praise of him for whose love he suffered. He sang naturally very well and this enraged these savages. He was named Joseph and had been raised in the faith by Father Le Jeune almost from his infancy. In your opinion don't I have a good son? He is, rather, my father and my advocate with God. I am overcome in my love for him at the exalted grace he has received in persevering with such generosity. He was a young man, perfectly formed and extremely modest, but I praise only his fidelity. If one came to tell me the same news of you, my dearest son, who could express the joy that I would feel! But it is not within our power to choose these signal graces; they are among the treasures of God who gives them to chosen souls.

I must end this letter with this final wish which is one of the greatest evidences of my affection for the person who is dearest to me in the world.

TO HER SON [SEPTEMBER 9, 1652]

My very dear son,

This is in answer to your letter of April 13. . . . .

I find everything you say concerning our remaining in this country or our withdrawal to France as reasonable as prudence could suggest. I share your feelings but the outcome rarely conforms to our thoughts, as those indicate who are familiar with God's conduct in these regions where it seems that his providence plays games with human prudence.

I, too, am certain that his Divine Majesty wants our reestablishment and that the vocation I have to labor here comes from him, just as certain as I am that I will die one day. Yet notwithstanding this certitude and the energy we have expended, we do not know what this country will become. There is, nonetheless, a stronger appearance that it will endure than otherwise and I myself feel as strong in my vocation as ever; yet ready, just the same, for a withdrawal to France whenever it will please God to give me a sign to that effect through those who hold his place on earth.[26]

Our foundress shares this disposition concerning her vocation but not the return to France. God has not yet given her this grace of detachment; on the contrary, she has such a strong determination to build a church here that the incursions of the Iroquois do not hinder her from gathering the necessary materials for her project. People are earnestly trying to persuade her not to consider this, but she insists that her greatest desire is to build a house for God; and that following this (these are her words) she will build living temples. She means that she will gather some poor French girls who have gone astray in order to train them in piety and give them a good education which they could not have in their estranged state. She has not been inspired to help us with our buildings, her heart being all drawn to her church, which she will have built little by little with her income, which is meager enough. This year M. de Bernières has sent her five barrels of flour which here are worth five hundred pounds. He has also sent us a clock along with a hundred pounds for our poor Hurons. What will you say to all this? As for me, my interior inclination is to let myself be led by such a loving providence and to accept all the events which his leading will bring to flower in me from moment to moment.

This morning I spoke to two people experienced in the affairs of this country concerning two young women whom we would like to bring from France as lay sisters. They found no difficulty with this; for myself, I find a great deal. First, because of the perils at sea; second, because of the difficulties in France; and, finally, because of the composition of our group.[27] This is why we still have not come to any decision. The hostility of the Iroquois is not what holds us back. There are some who consider this country to be lost, but I do not see that we have so much to fear on that score as, I am told from France, people of our sex and condition have to fear from French soldiers. I tremble at what I have been told. The Iroquois are barbarians, but they certainly do not deal with persons of our sex as I am told the French have done. Those who have lived among them have told me that they never resort

---

26. In a letter written the previous week Marie reviewed their reasons for staying in Canada. Now it has less to do with the conversion of the Indians than with the need of the French colonists. "The French children would be real brutes without the education we provide for them." Oury, *Correspondance*, p. 476.

27. A reference to the various congregations involved which made unity difficult.

to violence and that they leave free those who do not want to consent to them.

I would not trust them though, for they are barbarians and heathens. We would rather be killed than taken prisoner, for it is in this kind of rebellion that they kill; but thanks to Our Lord we have not reached that point. If we knew of the approach of the enemy, we would not wait for them and you would see us again this year. If I saw only seven or eight French families returning to France, I would consider it foolhardy to remain, and, even were I to have a revelation that there was nothing to fear, I would consider my vision suspect in order to hold to something more certain for my sisters and me. The Hospital Sisters are determined to do the same.

To speak to you frankly, the difficulty of getting the necessities of life and of clothing will be the reason for leaving—if we leave—rather than the Iroquois. But to tell the truth, the latter will always be the fundamental cause, for their incursions and the terror they spread everywhere bring trade in many of its aspects to a halt. It is for this reason that we clear as much land as possible for cultivation. The bread here has a better taste than that of France, but it is not so white nor so nourishing for the working people. Vegetables are also better here and more abundant. There we are, my dear son, concerning the Iroquois.

I agree wholeheartedly with your feelings concerning the necessity of providing for the observance of our rules in the future.[28] For now, I say to my shame, I do not see in me a single virtue capable of edifying my sisters. I cannot answer for the future but as far as I can see of those who have come from France, I would be as certain of the majority of them as I am of myself. And even should they wish to return—which they are very far from doing—those whom we have professed from this country, having been raised in our rules and never having tasted any other spirit, would be capable of maintaining it.[29]

This is why we are in no hurry to ask for more sisters to come. Further, the wound that the hand of God has inflicted on us is still too fresh and we still feel its inconvenience too keenly.[30] We are also afraid that they might send us subjects who are not suitable for us and who

---

28. They are still waiting for the canonical approbation of their constitutions.

29. Geneviève Bourdon, the first Canadian-born Ursuline, who had entered the novitiate just thirteen days before the writing of this letter.

30. A reference to the destruction of their monastery by fire, as well as to the death of Marie de St. Joseph who died in April of this year after a long and painful illness. Marie had written a very long letter to the Ursulines of Tours commemorating the life and virtues of her first companion. See Oury, *Correspondance,* pp. 436–68.

would have difficulty in adjusting to the food, the climate, and the people. What we fear even more is that they would not be docile and that they would not have a strong vocation. For since they have a spirit different from ours, if they do not have a spirit of submission and docility they would have difficulty in adjusting, as we would perhaps in putting up with them.[31]

This vexatious spirit has already caused two hospital sisters to return and having this example before my eyes arouses my fear. For what good is making a display of traveling a thousand or twelve hundred leagues to people of our sex and condition amid the dangers of the sea and of enemies if one is then to retrace those same steps? I would have difficulty in resolving this question unless there were an absolute necessity; for example, if a young woman were so determined to return to France that she could only be restrained with violence and perhaps with detriment to her salvation.

I had a strong desire to have my niece of the Incarnation come here who, I have often been told, is both wise and virtuous and has a stable vocation.[32] I would even like to prepare her for her duties and for everything concerning this country. But the fear I have that she might not be happy as well as that of exposing her to the risk of returning to France has held me back. Furthermore, I am getting old and when I die I would leave her in a solitude which might be too difficult for her. Finally, the hindrance that the Iroquois bring to Christianity does not permit us to have the savage girls as before. This would be a very sharp pain for her to see herself deprived of the very end for which she had come. For to tell you the truth, this is extremely painful and depressing. How would a young woman have the heart to learn these very difficult languages, seeing herself deprived of the very subjects with which she hoped to use them? If hostilities were to last for just a little time, the spirit would make an effort to overcome this repugnance. But death may come before peace does.

This is what prevented me from letting my niece come here in spite of my wish to please her and in spite of the consolation I could have hoped for from her. Since I am so far away from you and any opportunity of seeing you, she would have been for me another you,

---

31. In fact, two Ursulines who had come from France in 1642 and 1643 did return to France after a period of bitter controversy. See Marie's letters to Tours, Oury, *Correspondance,* pp. 559, 569–70.

32. Marie Buisson is the daughter of Claude and Paul Buisson. Left an orphan by the sudden death of her mother in 1643, she lived a tempestuous life for a short time until she was converted and entered the Ursuline monastery at Tours, taking the name of her aunt, "Marie of the Incarnation."

for you are the two people for whom my spirit most often wanders off to France. But it is rather in the heart of our lovable Jesus that I visit you both, offering my wishes for your sanctification and the complete immolation of yourselves. I offer the sacrifice of this satisfaction to my divine Jesus, leaving everything in his hands both for time and eternity. He knows what he wants to do with us; let us be glad to let him do it. If we are faithful to him, our reunion in heaven will be that much more perfect since we will have broken our ties in this world in order to obey the maxims of his Gospel.

But to come back to our subject. We are not in a hurry, then, to ask for choir sisters from France, for we feel it is necessary to wait a little and take measures so that neither we nor they will have any reason for discontent. Nevertheless, in spite of all the reasons I have listed, we simply have to ask for two lay sisters, perhaps even this year.

Well, my son, this is how life goes on. If our good Lord did not supply a shower of actual grace who could survive? I confess that I have no reason to complain but only reasons for singing his mercies. I assure you that I need a courage stronger than any man to carry the cross which is heaped up in our affairs as well as in the general affairs of the country where all is full of thorns, where one must walk in darkness, and where even the most clear-sighted are blind, and everything uncertain.

Yet with all this my spirit and my heart remain in tranquillity, awaiting order and events from providence, as they come, in order to submit to them. All the darkness I encounter makes me see into my vocation more clearly than ever and reveals to me lights which were only obscure and incomprehensible when God gave them to me before I came to Canada. I will speak to you of this in the writings I have promised you, so that you can understand and admire the guidance of the divine goodness on me and how he has wanted me to obey him beyond human reason, losing myself in his ways in a manner I cannot express.[33] . . .

When I speak to you concerning our poverty, don't think that I ask anything of you except your prayers, which I esteem as true riches. I leave all the rest to divine Providence which is abundantly rich to meet all our needs. I assure you that despite all our losses, he has never yet let me want for the necessities of life, nor even of clothing, and that he has provided for everything most paternally. Even during the long

---

33. The first draft of this account was burned in the fire; but despite the work of rebuilding and the dangers in which they lived, Marie clearly intends to comply with Claude's persistent request. See the introduction, pp. 35–36.

illness of Mother St. Joseph this Providence has so helped us that she could not have been better taken care of in France in the midst of her relatives, except for the inconvenience of her accommodation. I have already told you of her death; I will not say any more about it here. Her death is my loss but I console myself that God possesses her, for without this thought the loss of so valuable a subject would be extremely painful. Finally, may God be blessed for everything. He is my all and my life wherever I may be.

TO HER SON [SEPTEMBER 24, 1654]

My very dear son,
May Jesus be our life and our love for all eternity!

I cannot let the vessels leave without telling you something of what has happened in this new Church since last year. I have already told you what happened concerning the captivity of Father Poncet and of how he was brought back after many sufferings inflicted on him by the Iroquois. It seems since that time that God has been pleased with the offering made by this good priest to die as a victim in order to appease God and by his death to procure peace for the whole country. Since then the Iroquois have done nothing except come and go asking for peace. And what is most wonderful is that those neighboring nations who were not aware of what was happening have come to treat for peace with us at the very same time. . . .

Last July, the Iroquois came to see the governor of New France and the Fathers where, after many council meetings and exchange of presents in which both sides participated, it was agreed that one of the fathers go to visit their five nations in order to see if they all concurred in this desire for peace. Father Le Moyne, whom in their language they call "Ondeson," was appointed for this, along with a young Frenchman who offered to accompany him.[34] They left with the ambassadors, who promised to bring them back within fifty days. They were no more than half-way when messengers ran like deer through all the villages of the Five Nations crying: "Ondeson is coming! Ondeson is coming!" At this noise a group of people gathered and went out to meet him to pay him honor. Nothing like this had ever been seen among the savages. It was all feasts and festivities. Among the Hurons

---

34. Simon Le Moyne had been in Quebec since 1639. Having at first ministered in the Huron mission at St. Joseph, he was to act as ambassador to the Iroquois for the next few years.

and the other nations the Fathers hardly dared speak at the beginning. They had to endure extreme discomfort until they could tame them. But these people honored the Father from the very beginning, giving him the first place and begging him to preside in all their councils. . . .

In the village which was the capital of the Onondaga Nation, Father found among the slaves some Hurons who had formerly belonged to his flock at the village of St. Michel. These poor captives, seeing their Father, were like people raised from the dead; to make their joy complete he heard their confessions and administered the sacraments. Imagine, I beg you, the wonderful resources of divine Providence! God permitted these poor Christians to be taken captive by these barbarians for the salvation of these nations. For these it was who gave them the knowledge of God and who sowed among them the first seeds of the faith. It was through them that the Iroquois learned of the priests and of us, whom they call "Holy Daughters."

If this peace lasts, as there is reason to hope it will, this country will be in good condition and very suitable for the establishment of the French, who multiply abundantly and who are doing well through the cultivation of the land which has presently become quite productive now that the trees which made it so cold are being felled. After three or four years of work it is as good and in some parts even better than France. Cattle are raised both for food and for milk products. This peace will increase trade, particularly the beaver trade which is very heavy this year because there has been freedom to hunt everywhere without fear.

But trading in souls is the happiness of those who have crossed the seas to come to search for them in order to win them for Jesus Christ. We are hoping for a great harvest now that the way to the Iroquois is opened. Some savages from far off say that beyond this country there is a wide river leading to a vast sea, thought to be that of China. If, in time, this is verified, the way will be greatly shortened and there will be a means for the workers of the Gospel to go into these vast and populated kingdoms. Time will tell.

Here you have a short summary of the general affairs of the country. As for what concerns our community and our boarding school, everything is in good condition, thanks to Our Lord. We have some very good Indian boarders whom the Iroquois representatives have seen each time they have come on an embassy. Since the savages love singing they were charmed, as I have already said, to hear them sing so well in the French manner. As a sign of affection, they repaid them with a song of their own mode which does not have such a regular beat. We have some Huron pupils whom the Fathers have thought appropriate to raise in the French manner, for since all the Hurons are presently converted and dwell near the French, it is felt that in time it would be possible for the French to marry these Huron girls. This could not take place unless the girls were French not only in language but also in custom.[35]

In the peace treaty it was proposed to the Iroquois that they should bring us some of their girls and that Father Le Moyne, when he returned from their country, should bring with him five daughters of their women captains, but this time conditions were not favorable. These women captains are important women among the savages with a deliberative voice in their councils, reaching conclusions just like the men. It was even they who delegated the first ambassadors to make a peace treaty.

Finally, the harvest is going to be very great and I think we will have to look for workers. It has been proposed to us, and we are now being urged to establish ourselves at Montreal. But we cannot answer this call unless we find some available means, for one does not find anything ready-made in this country and nothing can be accomplished except at immense cost. Thus no matter how willing we are to comply with the wishes of those who invite us, prudence does not permit us to accept.[36] Help us to bless the goodness of God for his great mercy to us and for the fact that not only has he given us peace, but even more: he wants to make our worst enemies into his own children, so that these children may share with us the blessings of such a good Father.

TO HER SON [OCTOBER 15, 1657]

My very dear son,
May the life and love of Jesus be our life and our love!

I have received such good news from the Iroquois Missions that I have to tell you about it. I learned three days ago that the progress of the Gospel is very great there. Father Mesnard alone has baptized some four hundred people at Oneiout and Oiouen. The other missionaries have baptized proportionately as many in their own missions. . . .

---

35. This mixing of races seems to have had none of the stigma it later acquired. The "métis," children of such mixed marriages, were to be scorned by both French and Indians.

36. In fact, the Quebec Ursulines, although spreading to other parts of French Canada, never made a foundation in Montreal.

Concerning our monastery: I am writing to our mothers at Tours about two sisters of our Congregation who must be taken to Brittany so as to be sent to us by the next ship. I declined their offer to come this year because of some changes that have taken place in our house and especially because of the great losses we have suffered.[37] I agree strongly with the opinion you have given us concerning the passage of religious from France and that the young women of this country should be more suitable for our spirit than others who will bring an alien spirit. This is all very true and we experience this; yet there are still not sufficient subjects to be found in this country. Either they marry very young or they have no vocation or they cannot bring with them anything to support them; the dowry is absolutely indispensable since our community is very poor and can receive choir sisters only on this condition. As for lay sisters: we have received three or four of them without dowry.[38] This need compels us to have recourse to France. At present we need mature persons prepared to serve rather than novices. With novices we would have to wait a long time and even so we would still not be sure if they would have the talents required for the duties of our community.

Last year we asked for two sisters, one from each Congregation. The one from Paris was ready but the one from Tours is still missing. You can see from this that we cannot be held responsible for this unfair way of dealing with us and that our mothers of Tours cannot accuse us of a lack of affection for them. We have five professed sisters here, one from this country and four who have come from France in secular dress. We have presently two novices and two boarders who are asking to be admitted. We have four professed from the Congregation of Paris. Even though we are gathered from different places, we live together as if we were professed of the same Congregation and the same house, under the direction of Reverend Mother Athanase who has succeeded me in office.

But whatever union we have, should we find suitable subjects in this country, we would not ask for any at all from France, both for the good of our community and to avoid those very real inconveniences of which you spoke to me. Ultimately, God is the master of all; he is our true superior and for this reason it is he who will provide for the needs of the community and who will search where he wishes for fitting

---

37. Destructive summer storms inflicted substantial losses to their property. Oury, *Correspondance,* p. 592, n. 6.

38. All four of them were French-born but had entered the novitiate at Quebec.

subjects to serve him according to his plans for them in this corner of the world.

TO HER SON [SEPTEMBER-OCTOBER 1659]

My very dear and beloved son,
It was a great deprivation to see a ship arrive and not receive any letters from you. However, I was sure that you had written; I believed (and I was not mistaken) that your letters were in the first vessel, which brought us news that we would have a bishop this year, but this ship did not appear until long after the others.

This delay was such that we received the bishop before the news which promised him to us. But this was a happy surprise in every way. In addition to the happiness which comes to the whole country in having an ecclesiastical superior, it is a consolation to have a man whose personal qualities are so unusual and extraordinary. Aside from his birth, which is illustrious (he is of the house of Laval), he is a man of exalted merit and singular virtue. I understand clearly what you wanted to tell me about his election but one may say what one wishes, it is not men who have chosen him.[39] I do not say he is a saint; that would be saying too much. But I do say with conviction that he leads a holy life like an apostle. He does not know what human respect is. He is for telling the truth to everyone and he speaks frankly in his meetings. A man of this strength was needed here in order to wipe out the scandal-mongering which was flourishing and becoming deeply rooted. In a word, his life is so exemplary that the whole country is in admiration.

He is a close friend of M. de Bernières to whom he is devoted and with whom he lived for four years. Thus, one must not be astonished, if, after having gone to that school, he has reached the sublime degree of prayer in which we see him. A nephew of M. de Bernières wished to accompany him. He is a young gentleman who charms everyone by his modesty. He wishes to give himself completely to God in imitation of his uncle and to consecrate himself to the service of this new

---

39. The diplomatic squabble over ecclesiastical jurisdiction in Quebec had delayed the appointment of a bishop for Canada for several years, with the Holy See attempting to wrest authority from the bishop of Rouen and the Gallican Church. François de Laval, autocratic and deeply religious, seemed a perfect choice.

Church. In order to succeed the better, he is preparing himself to receive the order of priesthood from the hands of our new prelate.[40]

I told you that we did not expect a bishop this year, so there was nothing ready for him when he arrived. We have lent him our seminary, which is at the corner of our cloister and close to the parish church. There he will have the convenience and pleasure of a lovely garden. In order that both he and we be lodged according to Canon Law, he has had a cloister wall built. We will be inconvenienced because we will have to house our boarders in our apartments, but the occasion merits this and we will bear our inconvenience contentedly until such time as an episcopal house is erected.

As soon as he was consecrated bishop in Paris, he asked the Father General of the Jesuits for Father Lalemant who for the last three months has been rector at La Flèche to accompany him. This is very good for the whole country and especially for us, and for myself even more than for anyone else. For I will tell you in confidence that I was suffering from the deprivation of someone with whom I could communicate about my interior life.[41] All year I have had a feeling that Our Lord would send me help. He has done so now when it was time. May his name be blessed eternally. . . .

Our prelate will have jurisdiction over everything although he is here only under the title of bishop of Petraea and not of Quebec or Canada. This title, which is the result of some difference between the Court of Rome and that of France, has caused some talk here. The king wants the bishop of Canada dependent on him and ready to take the oath of loyalty like the other bishops of France. And the Holy Father claims to have some special right in foreign countries. This is why he has sent us a bishop, not as bishop of this country, but as apostolic delegate with the strange title of bishop of Petraea.

You are troubled about the affairs of this country. They are just the same as they were before the Iroquois made peace, for they have broken it and have already taken or killed nine Frenchmen in an encounter where they were not expected and where no one believed they had hostile plans against the French. They have already burned alive one of their prisoners, and it will be a wonder if the others are treated any better. . . .

You astonish me by saying that our mothers wish to recall us. God spare us from such a calamity! If we did not leave after our fire

---

40. Henri de Bernières, ordained in the spring of 1660, is the first priest of the regular clergy to be ordained in Canada.

41. Lalemant had been in France since 1650.

and with all our other losses, we will not leave for the Iroquois, unless the whole country leaves or a superior compels us to do so—for we are daughters of obedience and one must prefer it to everything. However, I would be astonished if this should ever happen. It is rightly said that an army of enemies is getting ready to come here but now that their plan is known it will not be easy for them. Nevertheless, if Our Lord had let them, they would have destroyed us a long time ago; but his goodness overturns their designs, warning us of them in order to put ourselves on guard. If our affairs were in danger, I would be the first to tell you so that you could provide for our security since our mothers have entrusted it to you. But thanks be to God we neither see nor believe that this will happen. If, however, it does happen, contrary to our feelings, should we not be happy to complete our life in the service of our Master, giving it to him who has given it to us? These are my feelings which you can make known to our mothers, if you consider it appropriate.

It is my personal feeling that if we suffer in Canada, it will rather be through poverty than by the sword of the Iroquois. And as for the country in general, its loss, in my opinion, will come not so much from the savages as from certain people who through envy or otherwise, write to the Gentlemen of the Company a quantity of lies against the holiest and most virtuous, and who by their calumnies tear apart those who maintain justice and who enable this country to survive through their prudence. As all these evil blows are dealt in secret, one cannot parry them; and since corrupt nature believes evil rather than good, one easily gives credence to them. From thence it comes that when one least expects it, one meets with most regrettable orders and obstacles. In all this God is very grievously offended and he would give us a great grace if he purged the country of these difficult and contradictory spirits.[42]

The last vessel was discovered at its arrival to be infected with purpural and pestilential fevers. It carried two hundred people, almost all of whom were sick. Eight died at sea and some others on land. Almost the whole country has been infected and the hospital is full. Our bishop is continually at the service of the sick, even making their

---

42. Marie is doubtless referring to the criticism levelled at their governor, Pierre d'Argenson. A young man, sensitive to his dignity, he had irritated the older residents by surrounding himself with inexperienced young men, ignoring the advice of those older and wiser. He engaged in a head-on battle with Laval over the question of precedence in public ceremonies. Marie, however, found much to admire and was strong in denouncing his calumniators.

beds. One does what one can to spare him and conserve his person, but there is no eloquence which can deflect him from these acts of humility. Father de Quen in his great charity caught the sickness and died.[43] It is an important loss for the mission. He was the oldest missionary to the Algonquins, where he worked for twenty-five years with unbelievable labors. Finally, leaving the duty of superior of the Missions, he lost his life in the exercise of charity.

The Hospital Sisters have been stricken by the disease. Thanks to God our community has not been attacked. We are in a very healthy place, exposed to strong winds which cleanse the air. My own health is very good. I do not stop longing for eternity, although I am ready to live as long as it pleases Our Lord.

TO MOTHER URSULE DE STE. CATHERINE, URSULINE OF TOURS[44] [OCTOBER 13, 1660]

Reverend and dear Mother,

This is just a little word that I consider my duty to write to you in confidence concerning Mother N.[45] Since she trusts me she lets me see some of her letters, and I noticed that she has written to you some things about the election of the mistress of novices which she has misjudged a little, not being entirely aware of how these things happened. You can rightly believe me concerning this since everything has come to my knowledge and even took place before my eyes since I have always accompanied our Reverend Mother[46] because of the office I hold or because of that which I held in the past.

Here, then, is how things happened. Our bishop, having come to see Reverend Mother in the parlor, after confirming her in her office, told her that he wanted the mistress of novices to be in charge of the young professed religious as well, and that this would be an elected office. This completely surprised us and we contested it sharply to

---

43. Jean de Quen was superior of the Mission during the absence of Lalemant and during that period when the authority of the Jesuits was being questioned by the bishop of Rouen. A quiet, peaceful man, he was unequal to the hostility with which he was confronted. When Lalemant returned in the summer of 1659, he replaced de Quen as superior.

44. Ursule de Ste. Catherine, now a member of the community council at Tours, will be elected superior the following year. During her period as novice mistress, Marie had been her assistant.

45. Anne de Notre Dame, who had come from Tours in 1644.

46. Marguerite de St. Athanase.

keep it from going into effect; but the reasons we were able to give, he did not want to hear. What we were able to obtain was that this election be for only three years, without sequel, and as an experiment which would enable us to see the success of this change. Reverend Mother could not help being displeased by this decision, for she was determined to let the Mother who had had this charge and who handled it so well continue in office. The election changed things completely for, as you know, in a matter of free choice one cannot arrange the votes as one would like. Certainly everything happened sincerely and according to God's will; you can believe me in this, for I was an eyewitness of everything that happened.

I can tell you in confidence that the reason why Mother N. was not considered in this election is that she is too free in expressing her thoughts and that she changes them a little too easily; this scandalizes those who do not know her thoroughly. She is, however, very virtuous and extremely exact in matters of regularity. There are certain foibles which remain with us till death no matter how holy we may be or what virtues we may have.

From these few words, dearest Mother, you can see what I mean; I was determined to give you my opinion in confidence in order that in the future you will not believe too lightly in what is told you. There are these little rebellions of heart, excited by a secret passion, that produce outbursts which one sometimes has time to regret, because once it is over one sees everything very differently from the way one saw it in the midst of emotion. Nevertheless, although Mother N. suffered a little mortification in this change, she never let it appear but in a spirit which seemed very detached showed herself content—and she assured me in particular of this. I believed her because I think she is sincere. It is very true that our Reverend Mother treats her with great love and trust and that she is one of those to whom she communicates all the important affairs of the house because she has good common sense when she is her ordinary virtuous self. And this makes me very happy. She is often angry with me—or better yet, pretends to be so—if I do not tell her everything I know. If I do not, it is not from lack of trust but because I must keep the secrets of those to whom I owe this. You see, dearest Mother, that I open my heart to you for the glory of God and the love I bear you and this dear mother whom I would sometimes like to hold close to my heart.

I also feel obliged to shed some light on what was written to you about having all our letters seen. It is true that they are seen but they are not opened or read. Since our bishop ordered Reverend Mother to open the letters that are sent from France, she is obliged to break the seal and this she does in order to obey. But I assure you that she does not read them at all. I am writing to you and you can write to me in complete confidence that this will be seen only by me. It is the same with regard to those letters our mothers and our friends write to us and those we write to them. Reverend Mother and I have always observed this faithfully when we were in charge in order to permit freedom to our Congregations to write to us whatever they wished. It must be that those who wrote these details to you have not understood the intention of Monseigneur which consists only, as I have just said, in the formality of breaking the seal. He has been right in exercising this, for the Rule says something of this sort which permits various interpretations. And, finally, one must keep some forms which show that the superior can always use her freedom.

Write to us, then, with your usual confidence; and if you love me, please believe that what I have told you is the truth. I will add to this that our Reverend Mother and I are in as perfect understanding as if we were only one heart. Nothing happens here nor does she undertake anything without telling me and asking me for my opinion, which cements our union very closely. You know how you are with Mother St. Bernard; it is the same with Reverend Mother and me. From whence it comes that in our house we make no distinctions between Congregations. There are, however, some whose feelings for their old home are not entirely dead and this makes me suffer sharply. Mother St. Joseph was pure gold in this regard. She is dead and she is now enjoying the reward of her great detachment. The ship which is going to take this is in such a hurry that I must end, telling you that I am entirely yours.

TO MOTHER URSULE DE STE. CATHERINE,
URSULINE SUPERIOR OF TOURS [SEPTEMBER 13, 1661]

My very reverend and honored Mother,
Please give me your blessing!

I was not astonished to learn the choice that Our Lord has made of you to govern our community at Tours. I expected it, dearest mother, and I have humbly thanked him who, in heaven, had already chosen you even before those who voted could follow his sacred inspirations.

I am grateful to Monseigneur the archbishop for having had your Customs Book printed and distributed. When I heard the news I was impatient to see it, and at the opening of our packages the book fell into my hands. I could not resist reading it. Everything I have read in it seems to me wonderful and judicious. I am not satisfied with this first reading; I will examine it more at leisure in order to tell you my feelings and to thank Monseigneur for the great present he has given you. This book will be very useful to us in our present affairs of which I am now going to give you an account.

Your long letter seems to infer that we lean toward changing our constitutions. No, my dearest mother, we have no inclination in that direction; but I will tell you that our bishop has a desire for this—or at least a desire to alter them considerably. Here is how this came about. Last year when he made his visitation, some of our sisters indicated to him—unknown to us—that it would be good if he would give us an abridgement of our constitutions. These words were not without effect, for he has done this following his own ideas. Although leaving what was of substance, he cut out what provides explication and what might facilitate its observance. He then added what pleased him so that this abridgement, more fitting for Carmelites or Religious of Calvary than for Ursulines, effectively destroys our constitution.

He has had this read to us by Father Lalemant, who has served God considerably in this matter since it was he who worked the most on our constitutions. He has given us eight months or a year to think it over. But, my dear mother, we have already thought it over and we have reached our conclusion: we will not accept this unless pushed to the extreme of obedience. Nevertheless, we are saying nothing in order that things not become more rancorous. We have to deal with a prelate of exalted piety, who, should he once be persuaded that this is for the glory of God, will never retract and we will have to go along with him, which will be very prejudicial to our observances.

Our singing has been very much curtailed. We are left with only Vespers and Tenebrae, which we sing as you used to when I was at Tours. For High Mass he wants us to sing *recto tono,* having no regard for what is done at Paris or Tours but only for what his spirit suggests to be best. He is afraid that we will become vain in our singing and that we will show a spirit of complaisance to outsiders. We no longer sing at Mass because, he says, this causes distraction to the celebrant and he has not seen it done in other places. Our consolation in all this is that he has had the kindness of giving us Father Lalemant as our director. He is our very best friend and we can deal with him in great confidence. He takes unbelievable care of us both spiritually and temporally and as he is very clever, he wards off many a blow which would be difficult for us to endure.

I attribute all this to the zeal of this most worthy bishop; but as you know, my dearest mother, in matter concerning the Rule experience should be put above mere speculation. When things are going well one should persevere in them because it is certain that they are going well. But in making changes one doesn't know if they will succeed or not. I have given you this little account, my dearest mother, in order that you can judge for yourself whether we really want to change our constitutions and to console myself with you in the pain I am enduring in this matter.

TO HER SON [AUGUST 10, 1662]

My very dear son,

I have spoken to you in another letter of a cross which I said was heavier for me to bear than all the Iroquois hostilities. This is what it is. There are in this country some Frenchmen so contemptible and so lacking in the fear of God that they ruin all our new Christians by giving them strong drink, such as wine and brandy, in order to get beaver furs from them. This drink ruins all these people—men, women, boys, and even girls—for each one is master in his cabin while he eats and drinks. They are immediately overcome and become like mad people. They run naked with swords and other weapons and force everyone to flee, be it day or night. They rampage throughout Quebec without anyone being able to stop them. As a consequence there are rapes, murders, horrible and unheard of brutalities. The Fathers have done their best to stop this evil both on the part of the French as well as on that of the savages, but all their efforts have been in vain.

When our Indian day pupils came to our classes we tried to get them to see the trouble they would be in if they followed the example of their relatives; since then they have not set foot in our place. This is the nature of the savages. They do everything they see the people of their nation doing where morals are concerned unless they have been solidly strengthened in Christian morality. An Algonquin captain—an excellent Christian and the first to be baptized in Canada—came to visit us complaining and saying, "Onontio (this is the governor) is killing us in letting them give us liquor." We said to him, "Tell him so that he will prohibit this." "I have told him twice already," he said, "but he does nothing. But if you yourself beg him to stop it, perhaps he will obey you."[47]

It is deplorable to see the tragic accidents which arise from this trade. Our bishop has done everything imaginable to halt this course as something leading to nothing less than the destruction of faith and religion in these regions. He has used all his ordinary persuasion to deflect the French from this trade, so opposed to the glory of God and the salvation of the savages. They have scorned his remonstrances because they receive support from a secular power which has a strong hand. They tell him that liquor is permitted everywhere. One answers them that in this new Church and among these uncivilized people it ought not to be since experience shows that it is contrary to the propagation of the faith and to the good morals one should expect from new converts.

Reason has done no more than persuasion did. There have been other very serious discussions on this subject. Finally, zeal for the glory of God triumphed, and our bishop has been obliged to excommunicate those who engage in this trade. This thunderbolt has shaken them no more than the rest. They have paid no attention to this, saying that the Church has no power over affairs of this nature.

Things having come to such a crisis, the bishop embarked for France in order to look for ways of providing against these disorders which bring such tragic accidents in their wake. He felt he would die of sadness because of this, and one sees him withering away on his feet. I think that if he cannot reach some conclusion he will not return, which will be an irreparable loss for this new Church and for all the poor French. He makes himself poor in order to help them. To sum up in a word everything I believe of his virtue, let me say: he bears the marks and the character of a saint. I beg you to commend to Our Lord—and to have others commend—this matter of grave importance, that it may please him to send our bishop back to us, who is our father and a true shepherd of the souls who have been entrusted to him.

You see that my letter speaks only of this matter that most dis-

---

47. Pierre d'Avaugour replaced d'Argenson as governor in August 1661. A soldier by profession, his energies were employed in building up Quebec's defenses. At first he and Laval had cordial relations but soon the inevitable question of authority divided them. Laval, unable to get d'Avaugour's support in the matter of alcohol, took the only means in his power to protest the abuse: excommunication. When this made no impression, Laval returned to France to win support for his cause in the summer of 1662.

turbs my heart because I see there the majesty of God dishonored, the Church scorned, and souls in manifest danger of being lost. My other letters will be in answer to yours.

TO MOTHER ANGELIQUE, URSULINE OF TOURS [AUGUST 19, 1664]

Reverend and very dear Mother,

I have received your letter in which your heart speaks more than your pen. It seemed to me in reading it that I was with you and that we were communicating heart to heart. . . .

You are right in believing that I want to die in this new Church, for I assure you that my heart is so deeply attached to it that unless God himself were to withdraw me, I would never leave it either in life or in death. Perhaps you think it is the savage children and women who keep us here, but I will tell you frankly my feelings on this subject. It is true that our cloister does not yet permit us to follow the preachers of the Gospel in those countries which they are constantly discovering. Nevertheless, inserted into this new Church as I am, Our Lord having done me the honor of calling me here, he has so linked me with them in spirit that it seems to me that I am completely one with them and that I labor with them in their precious and exalted conquests.

When we arrived in this country it was so teeming [with savages] that it seemed that the population would increase beyond number; but once they were baptized God called them to himself, either through sickness or by the hand of the Iroquois. Perhaps it was his plan to permit their death "from fear that evil would change their heart." Although there is still a large number, it is small in comparison with what it used to be, for out of twenty there now remains only a single person. It is not, then, on their behalf that we are kept the busiest, although we do our duty in their regard both inside the house and at the cloister grill and also on other occasions, for our monastery is the refuge of those who are in danger of being shipwrecked in their faith because of their husbands or their infidel relatives. But our work is mostly in behalf of the French girls, for it is certain that if God had not led the Ursulines into this country they would also be wild and perhaps even more so than the savages themselves. There is not one of them who has not passed through our hands and this reforms the entire colony and makes religion and piety triumph in all the families.

In addition to this there has been instituted in this country a Congregation of the Holy Family for the reformation of households in which the men are guided by the Fathers, the women by the Ladies of

Piety, and the children are cared for by the Ursulines until they are married.[48] They gather together every Sunday with us, where one of us has the task of giving an instruction in which one tries only to maintain in them the sentiments and practices which have already been taught them in the seminary. These, then, besides our work with the savages, are the bonds which link me to the holy will of God. Moreover, the country is being so heavily populated that it will give us still more work in a very short time, either here at Quebec or elsewhere. . . .

TO HER SON [SEPTEMBER 30, 1665]

My very dear son,

I have given myself the consolation of writing several letters to you. By this one, which is the fourth, I will tell you that this year Our Lord has sent us causes of both joy and consolation as well as sorrow. We have just learned that the Fort at Tadoussac was accidentally burned along with the church and the residence. This is a very great loss because it was a trading center and also a refuge for both French and Indians. Since there seems to be no thought of abandoning either of these to the invasions of the enemy, I think they will have to rebuild everything next spring.

Several days ago a very painful event occurred. Two of our domestics got into a brawl which resulted in the death of a man. As this happened in the house where our domestics are lodged, six of the nine who live there were immediately arrested and taken to the prison in the chateau. Since three of them were sick they let them remain there, but soldiers from the garrison were sent to guard them. With the influence of our friends we were able to get four of the men discharged, as well as the three who were sick. The judgment of the remaining two is deferred until the two guilty ones who fled immediately after the affair are captured. The men who remain in prison would already have been executed were it not for the influential people we have engaged so that nothing will be done without true and full knowledge of the evil deed. We cannot yet say what will happen.

If God strikes us with one hand, he consoles us with the other. All the vessels have finally arrived, bringing us the final portion of the

---

48. This devotion to the Holy Family, inaugurated by Madame d'Ailleboust, has played a strong role in French-Canadian piety.

army along with some very important personages whom the king has sent to help the country.[49] They thought they would all be lost because of the storms which caused the crossing to take four months. As they approached land, impatient with such a long voyage, they opened the hatches of the ship too soon so that air entered too quickly, bringing on sickness which caused a great deal of distress. Twenty died at once and one hundred and thirty had to be put in the hospital, among them several gentlemen who, out of a desire to give their lives for God, had volunteered for the voyage. Since the hall of the hospital was full, they had to be put in the church until that, too, was full to the doors so that one had to use the neighboring houses. This has exhausted all the religious but it has also profoundly increased their merit.

Although there were many vessels, they were filled with men and baggage so that most of our necessities and provisions are still in France. We are going to be seriously inconvenienced by this but we must suffer a little along with the others. I bless God for having put us in a country where, more than any place else, we must depend on his divine Providence. This is where my spirit finds its consolation, for among so many privations we have not yet lacked food or clothing but rather, it seems to me, we are always more than well provided.

As for the last portion of the army, it is firmly resolved to show its faith and courage. They have been made to understand that this is a holy war where one acts only for the glory of God and the salvation of souls; to encourage them to this, one tries to inspire them with real sentiments of piety and devotion. This is where the Fathers work wonders. There are some five hundred soldiers who are wearing the scapular of the Blessed Virgin. It is we who make these on which we work with delight. Every day they say the rosary of the Holy Family with such faith and devotion that God has shown, through a beautiful miracle, that their fervor pleases him.

This happened to a lieutenant who, unable to be at the assembly for the recitation of the rosary, withdrew into a thicket to say it by himself. The sentinel did not see him clearly and thinking it was an Iroquois hidden there, shot him point-blank and immediately threw

---

49. 1665 was a year of major change for Canada. That spring Governor de Mézy died after long and bitter conflict with his former friend, Laval. Louis XIV had begun, at last, to take a practical interest in the colony. The rights of the Company of One Hundred Associates had been rescinded and a new mode of government established. In the fall, Rémy de Courcelle arrived as governor, accompanied by Jean Talon as intendant. In addition came the King's lieutenant general, the Marquis de Tracy ("the biggest man I have ever seen," Marie wrote) and a regiment of French troops sent to deal with the Iroquois.

himself on top of him, thinking that the man would be dead. Actually, he should have been, for the bullet had struck him in the head, just above the temple. The sentinel was amazed to find on the ground not an Iroquois, but his own lieutenant all covered in blood. He was seized and put on trial, but the one who had been thought dead got up and asked pardon for his assailant saying that what had happened was nothing. He was examined and the embedded bullet was discovered, yet the man himself was not mortally hurt. This has been declared a miracle. The incident greatly increased devotion in the army, where the Fathers of the Company perform wonders.

We see other miracles, too, on behalf of those devoted to the Holy Family. Seven leagues from here there is a town called Le Petit Cap where there is a church in honor of St. Anne, in which Our Lord has performed wonderful miracles in favor of this holy mother of the most blessed Virgin.[50] There one sees paralytics walking, the blind regaining their sight, and the sick of whatever malady recovering their health. Several days ago someone who had lost his sight and who had special devotion to the Holy Family was brought to this chapel to ask God for his cure through the intercession of St. Anne. But this great saint did not wish to grant him this grace which she knew to be reserved to the invocation of the Holy Family. He was then led back to Quebec where, before an altar of the Holy Family, his sight was restored. This is how things are at the moment in these quarters. God is good and merciful every place in the world toward those who wish to love and serve him. Let us love him, then, with all our hearts; let us serve him with all our strength and he will shower us with his goodness and mercy.

TO MOTHER CHARLOTTE DES ANGES,
URSULINE OF TOURS [SEPTEMBER 3, 1666]

My very reverend and dearest Mother,

Our good God who has not yet wanted to take me to himself, does want me to reply to your letter—a letter full of that sweetness and cordiality which you have always kept for me.[51] It is only on account of my needs and wretchedness that I deserve your remembrance—

---

50. The beginnings of the Basilica of Ste. Anne de Beaupré.

51. The previous year Marie had been dangerously ill—a liver complaint, followed by severe pleurisy and a painful inflammation of the kidneys. The Last Sacraments were administered but she rallied and regained her health to some degree.

these needs for which God wants his best friends to implore him. It is for this that, after all his goodness, I owe him endless praise.

Father Richard has happily arrived with three other priests of the Company, having experienced terrible dangers from both the English and the Turks. To my great delight he has told us fully of your news and that of our community; for there is nothing so capable of touching my heart than hearing our dear mothers spoken of with whom I am always present in spirit. To think of them and speak of them is always a sweet and happy thing for me, dear mother.

We had hoped to have some religious from France this year, but the wars which have now extended to the seas have hindered them from coming. There are four at Bourges, as well as at St. Denis, along with some at Rouen and at Paris, all of whom have unparalleled desire to come to join us—I do not even mention the other monasteries. From all of these we have called only the two from Paris because their vocation, which they have had almost from their childhood, is clearly confirmed.[52]

There is a religious of our Congregation who has an ardent desire to come here. She is from the monastery from which someone wrote to Father Ragueneau that they had heard from Tours that our Constitutions here had been overturned in order to put in those of Paris. There was also a quantity of other details capable of offending the Fathers who have worked hard toward strengthening our Union. This good daughter, however, told the Father that all this talk did not cool her vocation. It is God who gives her these inspirations. Everything that is said concerning the overthrow of our constitutions in preference for those of our mothers of Paris is mere falsehood and conjecture. Only God and his glory have been sought to form a holy union, holily cemented, without regard for either Paris or Tours. If I had seen any distortion or preference in this important matter, I would have died rather than endure it. But in matters of this kind one must be reasonable, not wanting either all one side or all the other; otherwise it will not be union but an oppression.

These affairs, thank God, are in very good shape, and what we have done between us is approved by the Holy See through Monseigneur de Petraea, our apostolic delegate, who has given his approbation for our Union as well as for our constitutions, with the power of establishing us everywhere, presuming the permission of our superiors according to the regular forms.

---

52. No sisters arrived from France until 1671.

Things being thus, how can someone have the audacity to sow such discord which tends only to cast poison into hearts in order to alienate them from our mission? May God pardon them and bless them as he wishes. This has been talked about in the Congregation of Paris, but it has not lessened their charity toward us nor their zeal for Canada, although they would have more concern than we in this matter. I have poured this out to you, my dearest mother, in order to open my heart to you concerning the religious of whom you have written. We will not ask for any of them this year unless the vessels that are expected make us change our mind. We have novices who will help us while we await something better. I beg you to present my very humble greetings to those dear mothers who remember me. I embrace you with them in the loving heart of Jesus.

TO HER SON [AUGUST 9, 1668]

My very dear son,

Here is the answer to your third letter. . . .

You think that I am going to die. I don't know when that happy moment will come which will give me completely to our divine Savior. In a way my health is better than it has been in the last years. My strength, however, is severely diminished so that it would need only a little thing to carry me away, especially since I have never been completely rid of those bilious attacks which have lasted for such a long time, leaving me with that bitterness in my mouth which makes everything I eat taste like wormwood. I have grown used to this; otherwise I would die of weakness. My spirit, however, is content in this infirmity which constantly reminds me of the bitterness Our Lord endured on the cross.

Despite these discomforts, I keep the Rule. I fasted during Lent and for the other fasts of the Church and of the Rule. In a word, I do my duty, thanks to Our Lord. I sing so low that I can hardly be heard but I still have enough strength to recite the Office. It is difficult to keep kneeling during Mass. I am weak in this regard, and it is astonishing that I am not more so in view of the nature of my illness which lasted for such a long time and with such a high fever.

We were hoping to receive by this voyage Mother Cécile de Reuville of the Infant Jesus, a religious from Rouen, and I was getting ready to teach her the Algonquin language, convinced that this would be appropriate for her and that she would have the determination to learn it; for these savage languages are difficult and one must have great constancy to conquer them. My task during the winter mornings is to teach them to the young sisters. Some of them have succeeded in learning the rules and in analyzing the parts of speech, provided that I translate the savage language into French. But to learn by heart a number of words from the dictionary—this is difficult for them and very thorny. Only one among the young sisters pursues this energetically. Mother Assistant and Mother Ste. Croix know them quite thoroughly because in the beginning we learned them by heart.

These subjects are very hard, and I am determined before my death to leave as many writings as possible. From the beginning of Lent to the Ascension I wrote a big book in Algonquin on sacred history and other holy things, along with a dictionary and a catechism in Iroquois, which is a treasure. Last year I wrote a big Algonquin dictionary with a French alphabet and another with the alphabet used by the savages.[53] I am telling you this so that you will see that the divine goodness is giving me strength in my weakness to leave my sisters something to work with in his service for the salvation of souls. As for the instruction of the young French girls, we need no other study than that provided by our rules. And, finally, after we have done all that we could, we must consider ourselves as useless servants, little grains of sand at the base of the building of this new Church.

I am writing to you by all possible means, but since my letters can always be lost, I will repeat here what I have already told you concerning our work, since you want me to discuss it with you.

First, we have seven choir religious employed daily in teaching the French girls, as well as two lay sisters who take care of our business outside the cloister. The savage girls both live and eat with the French girls, but it is necessary to have a special mistress for their instruction, and sometimes more than one, depending on their number. To my great sorrow I have just refused seven Algonquin boarders because we lack food, the officers having taken it for the king's troops who were in need. Never since we have been in Canada have we refused anyone because of our poverty, and being obliged to refuse these now has caused me great pain. But I must submit and humble myself in our powerlessness which has just forced us to send some French girls home to their relatives. We are limited to sixteen French girls and three Indians, of whom two are Iroquois and one a captive to whom they want us to teach the French language. I say nothing of the poor who

---

53. All these have been lost.

are here in great numbers and with whom we must share whatever we have left.

But let us return to our boarders. People in this country take great care in the education of the French girls. And I can assure you that were it not for the Ursulines, their salvation would be in constant danger. The reason is that there is a large number of men here, and a mother and father who would not want to miss Mass on a feast or a Sunday, will leave their children at home with several men to watch over them. If they are girls, they would be in clear danger no matter what their age; and experience has shown that they must be put in a safe place. Finally, I can avow that the girls of this country are, for the most part, more knowledgeable in many dangerous ways than those of France. Thirty girls give us more work in our boarding school than sixty would do in France. The day pupils give us even more, but we do not supervise their morals as if they were in the cloister. They are docile, they have good sense, and they are faithful to the good when they know it. Since many are boarders for only a short time, the mistresses work hard on their education and they teach them, sometimes within a single year, to read, to write, to count, along with their prayers, Christian morality, and everything a young girl ought to know.

There are some parents who leave them with us until they are of age either for the world or for religious life. We have eight such professed sisters now, as well as novices who have not wished to return to the world and who are doing very well, having been raised in great innocence. We have still others who do not wish to return to their relatives, finding themselves very happy in the house of God. Two of these are the daughters of M. de Lauson who is well known in France. They are presently awaiting the return of M. de Lauson in order to enter the novitiate.[54] Some are entrusted to us to prepare them for their First Communion for which they spend two or three months in the boarding school.

As for the Indian girls, we take them at any age. It will happen that some savage—either Christian or pagan—will so forget his duty as to abduct some girl from his nation and keep her against the law of God. Then she is given to us and we teach her and take care of her until the Fathers come for her. Others are like birds on the wing, staying with us

---

54. Marie-Madeleine entered the monastery on September 8, 1668. The second daughter is not mentioned.

only until they become sad, a condition which the character of the savages cannot endure. As soon as they grow sad their parents will take them away, fearful they will die. On this score we leave them free, for we win more this way than by constraint. There are others who take off by whim or caprice. Like squirrels, they climb up our palisade (which is as high as a wall) and go running in the woods. There are also those who persevere and whom we raise in the French manner. Then marriages are arranged for them and they do very well. One of them has been given in marriage to M. Boucher, who has since been made governor of Three Rivers. Others return to their savage parents. They speak French well and are knowledgeable in both reading and writing.

These are the fruits of our little labors of which I wanted to give you some details in order to answer the gossip which you say is claiming that we are useless in this country and that the *Relations* do not mention that we are doing anything. The Fathers and our bishop are delighted with the education we are giving young people. They let our girls make their First Communion at the age of eight, finding them as well instructed as could be. If one says that we are useless because the *Relations* do not speak of us, then one must say that our bishop is useless, that his seminary is useless, that the seminary of the Fathers is useless, that the ecclesiastics of Montréal are useless, and that, finally, the Hospital Sisters are useless because the *Relations* do not say anything of all that. And yet it is these which provide the support, the strength, and even the honor of the whole country. If the *Relations* say nothing of us, nor of the companies and seminaries I have just mentioned, it is because it mentions only the progress of the Gospel and what is related to this. . . .

My very dear son, what we do in this new Church is seen by God and not by men. Our cloister hides everything and it is hard to speak about what one does not see. It is very different with the Hospital Sisters. The hospital, being entirely open and the good things done there seen by everybody, their exemplary charities can be rightly praised. But, ultimately, both they and we await the recompense of our services from him who penetrates even the most hidden places and who sees as clearly in darkness as in light. This is enough for us.

TO MOTHER CÉCILE DE ST. JOSEPH,
URSULINE SUPERIOR AT MONS [OCTOBER 1, 1669]

My reverend and most dear Mother,
May Jesus be our life and our love for all eternity!

I have received your letter with the love and respect due to your kind and charitable heart which keeps in mind the poor sisters in this corner of the world. . . .

Now, then, let me answer your wish to learn some details of our community. First, let me tell you that for over thirty years we have been established in Quebec, which is the port where all French ships arrive. When we came here there were only five or six little houses at the most. The whole country was a great forest full of thickets. Now Quebec is a town, and beyond it little hamlets and villages extend for more than a hundred leagues. In the beginning we were surrounded by savages—both men and women—naked to the waist, except in winter when they were covered with animal skins. Thanks to the modest example of the French, the natives, both men and women, are now very decently covered. We started with their daughters and wives, making them understand that each of them had an angel whom God had given them to protect them from demons and that he would flee from them if they were not modestly covered. The Jesuit Fathers gave long sermons on this subject.

We have learned their language from the start through rules and through study. All the people of this nation living in these places are presently good Christians, bringing up their children and their families like Frenchmen; but they have no permanent houses but only bark cabins held up by thick cedar branches which they demolish when they want to go hunting in the forest, where they usually spend the winters. In the spring they return to their places. This is the custom of the Algonquins; the other nations are sedentary. All of them live only by hunting and on Indian wheat from which they make a porridge. They clothe themselves in animal skins and they also trade these for blankets which they use like capes in the winter.

The day following our arrival there were brought to us both Indian girls and the daughters of the French who trade in this country, and this has continued up to the present. Since the country has grown, we now have ordinarily twenty to thirty boarders. The French give us one hundred and twenty pounds for board; the Indian girls we take free of charge. Even so, their parents, who love their children passionately, think they are doing us a favor. As soon as the girls arrive their parents take their children's rags, handing them over to us completely naked. We clean off their grease, for since they do not wear any underwear they grease themselves instead. We must look for something to clothe them, etc., which causes us quite some expense. Nevertheless, the goodness of God has assisted us so that, despite our meager income, we have never lacked help for our dear converts or for our own survival in this country where expenses are enormous.

As for our day pupils, I am not able to give you a number because some are forced to remain at home during the winter because of the extreme cold and snow. In a word, we have all those of the upper and lower city. The French bring us their daughters from more than sixty leagues away, although our bishop has provided school mistresses at Montreal while waiting for us to be established there.

We number twenty-two religious of whom three are still novices. Of that number, there are four lay sisters. We have six sisters who were professed in France; the others have made profession in this country. Seven of these are natives of this country as are two of the novices. The others are from France. Madame de la Peltrie is always with us; she is a saint.[55] We are not able to expand very much because everything is so exorbitantly expensive in this country. Only three of our religious have died since our establishment in Canada—that is, my dear Mother St. Joseph, a lay sister from France, and a choir sister, also from France. The latter was a sister of the governor of the country whom he had brought from France with his wife and who entered our community and made her novitiate and her profession here. We have sent away others who were not suitable for us. . . .

I must still say something concerning the present state of this new Church. You have formerly heard the Iroquois spoken of—a people who have exercised terrible cruelties on both the Fathers of the mission and the French, massacring them everywhere they encountered them. Now they have become docile to our holy faith. They are an important people and they occupy a large country; they have all their children baptized and give themselves assiduously to prayer and instruction.

Great nations have also been discovered more than three hundred leagues north of us; they are completely barbarous, having never heard God spoken of or seen any French. It so happens that God has prepared their hearts in such a way that they are the most open-minded in the world, docile to embrace our holy faith as soon as they have heard the grandeur of our holy mysteries spoken of. They have all their children baptized while they themselves are being instructed.

You must understand that it is no small matter to convert the savages. They are a very superstitious people who put belief in their dreams. If they dream that they want to kill a man, they will kill him,

---

55. Madeleine de la Peltrie died in her little house on November 18, 1671, after only a week of serious illness.

etc. They have many wives and they believe in sorcerers and diviners. These are not really sorcerers; they are jugglers like the buffoons in Europe. It is no small miracle when they are converted. Now the Divine is touching them and giving them belief in the workers of the Gospel. They fear the fire of hell, and one gives them vivid descriptions of hell as well as paradise. They admire this and believe in it.

Never stop, or have your community stop, my loving mother, praying for this new Church; and do not forget our little family who with me thanks you in love and respect. . . .

TO FATHER JOSEPH-ANTOINE PONCET, S.J. [SEPTEMBER 17, 1670]

Dear Reverend Father,

Your Reverence knows from experience that God's guidance of him is always to lead him where he does not wish to go and that he has always had to obey his orders with a blind submission. It is this obedience which manifests the kindness of his divine guidance, since it is from this he draws his glory. We are told that you are doing great good where you are. So, dearest father, think no more about the Islands or about Canada but die in the most loving will of God.[56]

Mother Catherine of Siena, superior of the Ursulines of St. Denis, tells me that neither she nor her sisters have yet lost hope of accomplishing their plan for Martinique. I beg God that it will succeed if it is for his glory. As for ourselves, we will be satisfied with our poor Canada, which is growing abundantly. Because of this we are asking for religious from France to help us although we are already twenty-two in number. Your Reverence will see by the *Relation* the wonderful progress of the faith through the extreme labors and incomparable zeal of your fathers. The Recollect Fathers are a new help to the country, but only for the French, not for the Missions to which the spirit of their Order does not seem to draw them so much. . . .

But now, my very dear father, I come to myself. What can I say of this poor sinner who is always just as you have known her? I can tell you that in my estimation I find myself full of unparalleled faults. I lack certain interior virtues which I feel necessary to bring me to the point where God wants me to be. I see myself powerless to achieve practices which are very obscure to me and which I scarcely understand. I feel myself in a poverty which crushes me with its weight at the feet of his

---

56. Father Poncet did, in fact, leave for Martinique in 1671 and died there in 1675.

Divine Majesty. Yet God makes all this compatible with a state of union which has kept me bound to his Divine Majesty for several years without deviating from it for a single moment. When business—either necessary or unimportant—encroaches on my imagination, these are only little clouds, like those which pass across the sun momentarily obscuring it, but then in an instant it becomes bright as day again.

Yet during this period God shines at the depth of the soul, which is, as it were, in waiting, like a person whom one interrupts while he is speaking to another and who, nevertheless, still maintains the sight of the person to whom he is talking. The soul, as it were, waits in silence before returning to its intimate union. Whether it is chanting the office or examining its faults and actions or whatever it is doing, all is done in the same spirit—that is to say, the soul never interrupts its actual love.

There you have a little sketch of the habitual dispositions of this soul—and which is its predominant grace. The effects of this state are peace of heart in temporal events and the desire to want only what God wants in all the effects of his divine providence as they occur from moment to moment. The soul experiences here true poverty of spirit. She has an understanding of all the mysteries but only by a single and simple sight, not through reflection which is impossible for her. The thought of the angels and saints can only be transitory, for in a moment and without giving it any thought she forgets everything in order to dwell in this center in which she is lost without any action of her interior senses. The exterior senses play no part in this inner activity; yet the soul is capable of all sorts of exterior occupations, for the interior working of God leaves her free to act. There are no visions or imaginings in this state. The one you know about happened to me formerly and was only in view of Canada. Everything else is in pure faith, where, however, one experiences God in a wonderful way.

There, that is what I can tell you and I tell it to you because you want me to. Please keep it secret and burn this paper, I beg of you. Pray for me who deserve to be forgotten by all holy souls.

SELECTED BIBLIOGRAPHY

WRITINGS OF MARIE DE L'INCARNATION GUYART

Écrits spirituels et historiques. Edited by Albert Jamet, O.S.B. 4 vols. Paris, 1929–39.
Catéchisme ou explication familière de la doctrine chrétienne. 3rd. ed. Tournai, 1878.
Correspondance de Marie de l'Incarnation. Edited by Guy Oury, O.S.B. Solesmes, 1971.
Lettres de la révérende Mère Marie de l'Incarnation. Edited by Pierre F.X. Richaudeau. 2 vols. Paris, 1876.
Martin, Claude, O.S.B. *La Vie de la Vénérable Mère Marie de l'Incarnation.* Facsimile edition. Solesmes, 1981.
The Autobiography of Venerable Marie of the Incarnation, O.S.U. Trans. by John J. Sullivan, S.J. Chicago, 1964.

STUDIES AND BACKGROUND WORKS

Actes de Profession. Archives of the Ursuline Monastery, Quebec.
Annales de l'Hôtel-Dieu de Québec. Edited by Albert Jamet, O.S.B. Garden City, 1939.
Annales du Monastère des Ursulines de Québec. Archives of the Ursuline Monastery, Quebec.
Beaumier, Joseph. *Marie Guyart de l'Incarnation.* Trois Rivières, Canada, 1959.
Bernard, Charles-André, S.J. "Le Message spirituel de Marie de l'Incarnation." Unpublished conference delivered at the Ursuline Monastery at Quebec, August 29, 1980.
Boucher, Ghislaine. *Du Centre à la Croix.* Québec, 1976.
Brébeuf, Jean. *The Travels and Sufferings of Father Jean de Brébeuf*

among the Hurons of Canada as described by himself. Trans. by Theodore Besterman. London, 1938.

Brémond, Henri. *Histoire littéraire du sentiment religieux en France.* 12 vols. Paris, 1930–39.

Chabot, Marie-Emmanuel. "Constitutions et règlements des premières Ursulines de Québec (1647–81)." *La Revue de l'Université Laval* XIX (Oct. 1964). 105–20.

———. "Demande-moi par le coeur de Jesus": Évolution de la dévotion au Sacré-Coeur chez Marie de l'Incarnation. Unpublished paper, n.d.

———. *Marie de l'Incarnation d'après ses lettres.* Ottawa, 1946.

Chalendard, Marie. *La Promotion de la femme à l'apostolat.* Paris, 1950.

Chapot, Louis. *Histoire de la Vénérable Mère Marie de l'Incarnation d'après Dom Claude Martin, son fils.* 2 vols. Paris, 1892.

Charlevoix, Pierre F.X., S.J. *La Vie de la Mère Marie de l'Incarnation.* Paris, 1724.

Chaumonot, Pierre. *La Vie du Révérend Père Pierre Joseph Marie Chaumonot.* New York, 1958.

Constitutions et règlements des premières Ursulines de Québec. Edited by Gabrielle Lapointe, O.S.U. Québec, 1974.

Cuzin, Henri. *Du Christ à la Trinité d'après l'expérience mystique de Marie de l'Incarnation.* Lyon, 1936.

Daniel-Rops, Henri. *Mystiques de France.* Paris, 1958.

Dodin, André. "Promotion de la femme à l'apostolat missionnaire." *Spiritus* XXVIII (Aug.–Sept. 1966): 266–79.

Dudon, Paul. "Lettre autographe et inédite de Fénelon à Bossuet sur le sacrifice absolu du salut." *Revue d'ascétique et de mystique* XVIII (1937), 65–88.

Faillon, Étienne. *La Vie de Mademoiselle Mance.* 2 vols. Montréal, 1854.

Glimpses of the Monastery 1639–1839. Quebec, 1897.

Gosselin, Amédée. *L'Instruction au Canada sous le régime français.* Québec, 1911.

Gosselin, Auguste. *Vie de Monseigneur de Laval.* 2 vols. Québec, 1890.

———. *La Mission du Canada avant Mgr. de Laval.* Evreux, 1909.

Grondin, François-Xavier. "Le Mystique itinéraire à Dieu." *Le Messager canadien du Sacré-Coeur* 48 (Sept. 1939): 467–73.

Gueudré, Marie de Chantal, O.S.U. *Histoire de l'ordre des Ursulines en France.* 3 vols. Paris, 1957–60.

Hubert, Marie de la Trinité, O.S.U. *Une Eminente Réalisation de la vocation apostolique, Marie de l'Incarnation, Ursuline de France et de Québec, 1599–1672.* Rome, 1957.

Huijben, J. "La Thérèse de la Nouvelle-France." *La Vie spirituelle, Supplément* XXII (1930): 97–128.

Jarry, Eugène. "Les Premières Missionnaires modernes." *Spiritus* XXVIII (Aug.–Sept. 1966), 280–304.

Jesuit Relations and Allied Documents. Edited by Reuben Gold Thwaites. 73 vols. Cleveland, 1896–1903.

Jetté, Fernand. "L'Itinéraire spirituel de Marie de l'Incarnation, Vocation apostolique et mariage mystique." *La Vie spirituelle* XCII (1955), 618–43.

———. "L'Oraison de Marie de l'Incarnation." *Spiritus* VI (1965): 55–66.

———. *La Voie de la sainteté d'après Marie de l'Incarnation.* Ottawa, 1954.

Kennedy, John Hopkins. *Jesuit and Savage in New France.* New Haven, 1950.

Klein, Joseph. *L'Itinéraire mystique de la Vénérable Mère Marie de l'Incarnation.* Rome, 1937.

Labelle, Suzanne. *L'Esprit apostolique d'après Marie de l'Incarnation.* Ottawa, 1968.

Lebreton, Jules. *Tu Solus Sanctus.* Paris, 1948.

Ledochowska, Teresa, O.S.U. *Angela Merici and the Company of St. Ursula.* Translated by Mary Teresa Neylan, O.S.U. 2 vols. Rome, 1969.

Lescarbot, Marc. *Histoire de la Nouvelle-France.* Paris, 1609.

Les Chroniques de l'ordre des Ursulines. 2 vols. Paris, 1673.

L'Heureux, Marie de Gonzague, O.S.U. *The Mystical Vocabulary of Vénérable Mère Marie de l'Incarnation and Its Problems.* Washington, 1956.

Lonsagne, Jacques, O.S.B. "Les Écrits spirituels de Marie de l'Incarnation. Le problème des textes." *Revue d'ascétique et de mystique* XLIV (1968): 161–82.

Mahoney, Denis, O.S.U. *Marie of the Incarnation: Mystic and Missionary.* New York, 1964.

Marie Léon-de-Venise, C.S.C. *L'Action à l'école d'une Mystique.* Montréal, 1964.

Marshall, Joyce, editor. *Word from New France: Selected Letters of Marie of the Incarnation.* Toronto, 1967.

Martène, Edmond, O.S.B. *La Vie de Dom Claude Martin.* Tours, 1696.

Michel, Robert. *Living in the Spirit with Mary of the Incarnation.* Translated by Veronica Moore, O.S.U. Montreal, 1986.

Oury, Guy, O.S.B. "Action et contemplation chez Marie de l'Incarnation." *Église et théologie* XV (1984): 203–16.

———. *Ce que croyait Marie de l'Incarnation.* Paris, 1972.

———. "La Correspondance de Marie de l'Incarnation d'après le registre des bienfaiteurs des Ursulines de Québec." *Église et théologie* III (1972): 5–44.

———. *Dom Claude Martin.* Solesmes, 1983.

———. "Jeanne Mance, Marie de l'Incarnation et Madame de la Peltrie." *Bulletin de la société historique et archéologique de Langres* XIV (1968), 322–37.

———. "Madame de la Peltrie et sa vocation canadienne." *Esprit et vie* XIX (May 1974), 153–60.

———. *Madame de la Peltrie et ses fondations canadiennes.* Solesmes, 1974.

———. *Marie de l'Incarnation.* 2 vols. Solesmes, 1973. This has also been translated by Miriam Thompson, O.S.U. under the title *Marie Guyart.* Cincinnati, 1978.

———. "Marie de l'Incarnation et la bibliothèque du noviciat des Ursulines de Québec." *Revue d'ascétique et de mystique* XLVI (1970): 397–410.

———. *Marie de l'Incarnation: Physionomie spirituelle.* Solesmes, 1980.

———. "Le Rayonnement de Marie de l'Incarnation et de Mgr. de Laval." Unpublished conference delivered at the Ursuline Monastery, Quebec, April 30, 1983.

———. "Marie de l'Incarnation: Son message dans le monde." *L'Église canadienne* XVI (Aug. 1983): 643–45.

Penido, M.T.L. *La Conscience religieuse: Essai systématique suivi d'illustrations.* Paris, 1935.

Poulain, Auguste. *Graces of Interior Prayer.* London, 1910.

Rayez, André. "Marie de l'Incarnation et le climat spirituel de la Nouvelle-France." *Revue d'histoire de l'Amérique française* XVI (1962): 3–36.

Registres des entrées des religieuses Ursulines de Québec. Archives of the Ursuline Monastery, Québec.

Renaudin, Paul. *Une Grande Mystique française au XVIIᵉ siècle: Marie de l'Incarnation.* Paris, 1935.

Rétif, André. *Marie de l'Incarnation et la mission.* Tours, 1964.

Richaudeau, Pierre F.X. *Vie de la Révérende Mère Marie de l'Incarnation.* Paris, 1874.

Robitaille, Georges. *Telle qu'elle fut: Études critiques sur Marie de l'Incarnation.* Montréal, 1939.

Rochemonteix, Camille. *Les Jésuites et la Nouvelle-France au XVIIe siècle.* 2 vols. Paris, 1896.

Roustang, François, S.J. *Jésuites de la Nouvelle-France.* Paris, 1960.

Schmidt, Josef. "Marie de l'Incarnation: Explaining the Inexplicable." Paper delivered at the Learned Societies Conference, German-Canadian Studies, June 5, 1985.

Thiry, André. *Marie de l'Incarnation: Itinéraire spirituel.* Paris, 1973.

Les Ursulines de Québec depuis leur établissement jusqu'à nos jours. 2 vols. Québec, 1863.

INDEX

Other Volumes in This Series

DATE DUE

BRODART

Cat. No. 23-221